Supply Chain Vector

Methods for Linking the Execution of Global
Business Models with Financial Performance

DANIEL L. GARDNER, CPIM, CHB

APICS.
THE EDUCATIONAL SOCIETY
FOR RESOURCE MANAGEMENT

Copyright ©2004 by J. Ross Publishing, Inc.

ISBN 1-932159-23 1

Printed and bound in the U.S.A. Printed on acid-free paper
10 9 8 7 6 5 4 3 2 1

Library of Congress Cataloging-in-Publication Data

Gardner, Daniel L., 1962–
  Supply chain vector : methods for linking the execution of global
business models with financial performance / Daniel L. Gardner.
       p. cm.
  ISBN 1-932159-23-1
1. Business logistics—Management. 2. International business
enterprises—Finance—Management. 3. Performance—Management. I. Title.
  HD38.5.G36   2004
  658.7—dc22   2003022393

Direct all inquiries to J. Ross Publishing, Inc., 6501 Park of Commerce Blvd., Suite 200, Boca Raton, Florida 33487.

Phone: (561) 869-3900
Fax: (561) 892-0700
Web: www.jrosspub.com

DEDICATION

This book is dedicated to
the two most influential people in my life,
Richard H. and Mary E. Gardner.

TABLE OF CONTENTS

PREFACE

Although firmly embedded in the lexicon of international trade, supply chain management cannot be considered a legitimate business discipline until quantitative links are created between operational execution and financial results. As much a business philosophy as a methodology, the globalization of supply chain management practices is perhaps the most relevant topic in business today. With increasing pressure on landed costs, lead times and inventory levels, the financial success of today's international companies relies on the ability to take strategies to a tactical level.

Supply Chain Vector analyzes the major components of supply chain activities and demonstrates the relationship between operational execution and financial results found on the income statement, balance sheet and cash flow statement. Founded on a philosophical understanding of the tenets of supply chain management, this book takes the reader through the early years of international trade and the commercial events that have shaped our business world. Globalization, outsourcing and governmental policy are all analyzed within the context of how modern business practices have evolved since the beginning of the last century.

The hypothesis that strong financial results are contingent upon landed cost control, lead time rationalization and inventory management is articulated throughout the text. Based on a contemporary case study of a global contract manufacturer and supported by dozens of examples, *Supply Chain Vector* establishes in a definitive fashion the causal relationship between execution and results. By presenting a fusion of time-tested business practices and modern business methodologies, this book enables academics, businesspeople and students to understand the true essence of supply chain management and its role in bringing products to global markets.

ABOUT THE AUTHOR

Daniel L. Gardner is President of Latin America for the Global Freight Management Division of Exel Global Logistics. With headquarters in the U.K., 70,000 employees and 1,600 locations, Exel provides logistics and related services to importers and exporters around the world.

A native of Lynn, Massachusetts, Mr. Gardner has spent 17 years in the third-party logistics business, a tenure that includes two overseas assignments. In addition to his professional experience, he has been an adjunct professor of logistics and supply chain management in the graduate business programs of Florida International University and the University of Miami, both located in Miami, Florida.

Mr. Gardner holds an MBA from the University of Miami, is Certified in Production and Inventory Management (APICS), is a licensed Customhouse Broker in the United States and holds a Green Belt in Six Sigma. He currently resides in Guadalajara, Jalisco, Mexico with his wife and two children.

ACKNOWLEDGMENTS

This book would not have been possible without the collective experience and wisdom of the hundreds of colleagues with whom I have had the opportunity to work over the years. To each of them, my sincere thanks. I would also like to extend my appreciation to Jorge Diaz, the most talented financial executive with whom I have had the good fortune of working. Additionally, I would like to recognize the professional support and good friendship of Ron Jordan and Joe Monaghan, two executives who showed their confidence in me from day one. Kudos also go out to David Guerra, Brooke Maguire and Dr. Humberto Serna for their input in this work. I value your attention to detail, patience and suggestions.

I would also like to express my appreciation to the people at J. Ross Publishing. Without the help of Drew Gierman, Sandy Pearlman and Lynn Cannon, this work would not have been possible.

Most importantly, I must thank my immediate family for their confidence in me over the years. To my brother, Richard, and sister, Kate, I cannot adequately express my appreciation. Finally, a special thank you to my wife, Patricia, and children, Nicolas and Isabella. There is a price to pay for every endeavor in life, and the time lost with them as I travel the world is testament to their commitment to family.

ABOUT APICS

APICS — The Educational Society for Resource Management is a not-for-profit international educational organization recognized as the global leader and premier provider of resource management education and information. APICS is respected throughout the world for its education and professional certification programs. With more than 60,000 individual and corporate members in 20,000 companies worldwide, APICS is dedicated to providing education to improve an organization's bottom line. No matter what your title or need, by tapping into the APICS community you will find the education necessary for success.

APICS is recognized globally as:

- The source of knowledge and expertise for manufacturing and service industries across the entire supply chain
- The leading provider of high-quality, cutting-edge educational programs that advance organizational success in a changing, competitive marketplace
- A successful developer of two internationally recognized certification programs, Certified in Production and Inventory Management (CPIM) and Certified in Integrated Resource Management (CIRM)
- A source of solutions, support, and networking for manufacturing and service professionals

For more information about APICS programs, services, or membership, visit www.apics.org or contact APICS Customer Support at (800) 444-2742 or (703) 354-8851.

Free value-added materials available from
the Download Resource Center at www.jrosspub.com

At J. Ross Publishing we are committed to providing today's professional with
practical, hands-on tools that enhance the learning experience and give readers
an opportunity to apply what they have learned. That is why we offer free
ancillary materials available for download on this book and all participating
Web Added Value™ publications. These online resources may include interactive versions of material that appears in the book or supplemental templates,
worksheets, models, plans, case studies, proposals, spreadsheets and assessment
tools, among other things. Whenever you see the WAV™ symbol in any of our
publications, it means bonus materials accompany the book and are available
from the Web Added Value Download Resource Center at www.jrosspub.com.

Downloads available for *Supply Chain Vector: Methods for Linking the
Execution of Global Business Models with Financial Performance* consist of
financial measurement and Six Sigma tools for global supply chains, Incoterms,
an international documentation checklist and a glossary of international trade
terms.

Understand the inner secrets and return to original simplicity.

—The Bushido Shoshinsu

INTRODUCTION

The most interesting aspect of the third-party logistics business is the exposure one has to commercial practices across a variety of international business models. Over 17 years I have had the good fortune to provide logistics- and transportation-related services to clients whose activities traverse the spectrum of industry, geography and culture. Whether in a cereal factory in Queretaro, Mexico or a cellular phone plant in Budapest, Hungary, the ability to simultaneously participate in and observe contemporary business can be a prodigious source of knowledge.

While the third-party logistics industry does serve as a window into the mechanics of import/export trade, true knowledge comes from an understanding of how business processes interact with and depend upon one another every day. Extending one's frame of reference beyond functional expertise allows for a more holistic approach to operations, thus providing businesspeople with a full view of the results of their tactical decisions.

This axiom is applicable to any business environment, but is particularly salient for a global production model. As products make the transition from raw materials to finished goods, comprehension of the dynamics between purchasing, manufacturing, logistics, sales and accounting is vital to the success of an organization. Of greatest importance, however, is the linking of operational execution with the bottom line financial performance of the enterprise.

In recognition of this point, it was in April of 2000 that work began on a pair of international trade seminars entitled "The Role of Logistics in Supply Chain Management" and "The Financial Measurement of Global Supply Chains." Shared with the import/export community in the United States and Latin America, these interactive venues focused on the primacy of lead time rationalization, landed cost control and inventory management in a global business operation. Since that time, thousands of executives from backgrounds as diverse as materials management, manufacturing, finance, information technology, sales and logistics have participated in the seminars. Industries represented include wearing apparel, health care, aerospace, footwear, telecommunications, automotive and high tech.

Whether in São Paulo, Silicon Valley, Santiago or New York, the willingness of colleagues to share their insights has been a source of both erudition and encouragement. The learning process was born of listening to people's opinions, experiences, tactics and best practices from markets around the world. The exposure to such diverse business experience made me realize that there is still a "higher supply chain truth" to be discovered, the quest for which is the inspiration for this book. Although influenced by the input of the international business community, the opinions expressed herein are exclusively my own. Any credit for advancing the discipline of supply chain management goes to the customers, colleagues, suppliers, government officials, competitors and strategic partners with whom I have had the good fortune to labor. Any flawed opinions or outright errors must accrue to the author.

If, however, the ideas and statements found here stimulate new thought on supply chain execution and bring businesspeople one step closer to that higher truth, the goal of the book will have been achieved. To that end, the following observations are offered.

THE VECTOR APPROACH

Decisions that affect international operations cannot be taken in a vacuum. Due mainly to organizational structure and corporate culture (the latter being a function of the former), managers tend to think in terms of how policies and procedures affect their departments. When marketing decides to add stockkeeping units to a product family, it probably is not thinking about what that does to setup times and utilization in the plants. If purchasing moves a critical part from a supplier in Hong Kong to another in Malta, it may be thinking about unit costs and volume discounts, not differences in customs duties or lead times.

To be successful, businesspeople have to make decisions with the lens wide open; otherwise, they will overlook details that foil what originally seemed like a good idea. To do that, businesspeople have to think "out of the cubicle" and consider the ramifications of decisions for other areas of the business, be they internal between departments or external with the business community. The best way to achieve this goal is to employ people with a multi-discipline and vast cultural background. Unfortunately, that type of talent doesn't grow on trees, and it takes years to cultivate an executive of this ilk. At the very least, people should stop and think about what they are doing, consulting with colleagues and soliciting advice in an effort to put forward the best plan of attack.

Open and honest communication is the preferred method to minimize the probability of bad decisions. As part of that process, businesspeople should also take a "vector approach" to dealing with opportunities, problems or competitive threats. Mathematically, a vector is defined as a quantity that has both magnitude and direction.[1] For example, the quantity 70 miles to the northeast is a vector because it has both size and direction. Graphically, a vector can be represented on a plane as two-dimensional using an ordered pair or can also be rendered in space as three-dimensional. It is this three-dimensional portrayal of vectors that is most analogous to the supply chain decision-making process.

An effective way of describing the vector approach is to envision the infrastructure that supports cellular phone communications and how authorities use this technology to pinpoint the location of suspected criminals. The backbone of any cellular system is the series of towers, antennas and dishes located in an area of coverage. If police can identify the cellular phone number used by a suspect, it's relatively easy to locate that person by placing him or her in a three-way vector amongst the towers. As illustrated in Figure 1, the phone's signal allows each tower to determine the distance and general direction from

Figure 1   The Vector Approach to Cellular Technology

its location. By using three towers, the distance and direction can be calculated to within a couple of meters.

The analogy for supply chain managers lies in the ability to view decisions from a multi-dimensional viewpoint. Policies about credit terms cannot be made without considering the impact on accounts receivable or future sales orders. Determination of plant sites or capacity sharing must not be executed without thinking about tax implications, currency conversion and repatriation laws. The list goes on and on, but managers who live in a one- or even two-dimensional world will eventually get themselves into trouble. For purposes of tactical supply chain management, a good starting point positions financial performance in the vector of lead times, landed costs and inventory levels. Figure 2 characterizes this point graphically.

One simple tool that I have come to use was developed during a stint as adjunct professor of logistics and supply chain management in the MBA programs at Florida International University and the University of Miami. Although some may consider it prosaic, the frame of reference management model

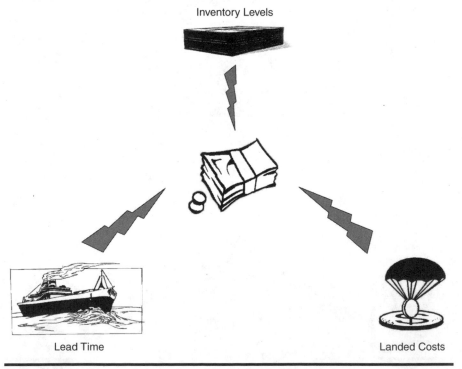

Figure 2 The Vector Approach to Supply Chain Management

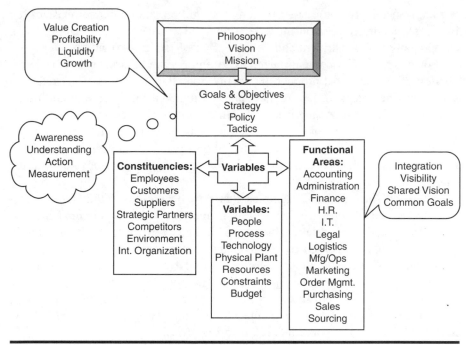

Figure 3   Frame of Reference Management Model

shown in Figure 3 is designed to condition people to keep a wide view of business activities. The power of the tool lies in its portrayal of business processes, functions and activities as both independent and dependent variables in an extremely complex operational equation.

As the speed of business accelerates, it is natural to develop tunnel vision. This model is intended to periodically remind people that they should be thinking about how their actions affect others, as well as how the decisions of colleagues affect them. Of course, this mentality extends beyond the walls of a company to consider relationships with vendors, government entities and strategic partners. If the overall process can be executed within the context of understanding an organization's vision, business model, financial goals and policies, the full purpose of the model will have been appreciated.

This tool is actually a simplified representation of what today has come to be known as the field of systems dynamics. In a much more comprehensive fashion, systems dynamics studies the nature of relationships in a commercial setting, using a variety of tools to isolate both planned and unanticipated results. Linked to the discussions in Chapters 3 and 8 on lean manufacturing and Six

Sigma, respectively, the frame of reference management model emphasizes the functional nature of relationships, decisions and actions, viewing supply chain components as both drivers and beneficiaries of tactical execution.

For example, if a company decides to enter a new market with the introduction of an additional product line, many potential cause-and-effect relationships must be analyzed. Do the new bills of material imply adding additional suppliers when the company is already attempting to rationalize its vendor list? Also, what are the manufacturing requirements in terms of both product and process engineering? How will capacity among plants be allocated? These and many other potential scenarios must be isolated and studied prior to pulling the trigger on a decision.

There are hundreds of examples that can be presented that require this systems dynamics approach to business management. In any circumstance, as many cause-and-effect relationships as is humanly possible must be identified, with decisions made based on an abundance of information.

Regardless of its simplicity, be assured that I keep a miniature version of the frame of reference management model in my PDA. When on a plane or waiting for a client, I pull it out and contemplate pending decisions using that slide. That same graphic has saved me a lot of money and headaches by helping me to fully grasp the consequences of my actions.

ORGANIZATIONAL STRUCTURE AND CORPORATE CULTURE

An organizational structure that is personified by departmental hierarchies does not possess the flexibility to either create or respond to rapid changes in its markets. Distance, time zones, language and culture all limit the effectiveness of a top-to-bottom hierarchal approach to international management, creating reporting lines that are out of touch with the needs of the people at an operating level. Also, while responsibility and ownership must be clear among the various business functions, strict departmentalization has a tendency to create a corporate personality that is self-centered and selfish by nature.

When people are organized by department, human nature dictates that they gravitate to and identify with the entity closest to them. Familiarity may breed contempt, but in business the contempt is often aimed at people least familiar to an individual, those who work outside one's area. A maxim of social psychology, this phenomenon occurs whether one is working at a plant, division office or corporate headquarters. When conflicting goals or budgets are thrown into the mix, the combination of human nature and disparate agendas can be damaging to an enterprise and its supply chains.

This partially explains why there are perennial conflicts between sales and accounts receivable, purchasing and manufacturing or two competing divisions in a company. In fact, if one breaks down the word "division," it is ironic to find that it is a derivative of the verb "to divide." Thus, the tendency to internalize not only is innate to the human condition but is built into our business vernacular.

The above dynamics are exacerbated by the way in which organizations compensate performance with bonuses. Managers, just like Pavlov's dog, respond to conditioning. When incentive plans are based solely on departmental performance and not on overall company results, myopia will set in. The response in this situation is most predictable, with managers reacting to the plan by achieving goals that may be "productive" for their department but are deleterious to the company as a whole.

None of the above is intended to suggest a structure characterized by a decentralized free-for-all. Unbridled liberty without policies and some semblance of coherency will do more damage than a centralized, hierarchal model. The question becomes how to create a structure that allows for adaptation to local requirements while fostering the desired corporate culture, adherence to strategic corporate fiat and the achievement of financial goals.

Sometimes the answer to difficult business questions can be found in the most unlikely of places. Benchmarking is a powerful tool, especially when companies can learn from unrelated industries and successfully apply practices to their own set of circumstances. When dealing with such ethereal issues as corporate culture or structure, seeking benchmarking opportunities from places alien to commerce may also be a wise practice and can have a direct impact on supply chain performance.

PAST AS TEACHER

Even a casual familiarity with world history would lead one to believe that one of the best sources for guidance on how to fashion an organization is found in the study of political science. Antiquity and the Common Era abound with examples, both good and bad, of how governments were constructed to accommodate the times (or, unfortunately, the ambitions of their leaders). Regardless of their original intent, the study of governments and the mechanisms that have either championed or thwarted the advance of mankind serve as a well of information for today's international businessperson.

One example that has commercial parallels is found in the similarities that exist between segregated departments in a company and the city-states of Italy both prior to and during the Renaissance. Compared to the enclaves of accounting, manufacturing or sales, the cities of Florence, Venice and Rome really were not that different. Because each operated autonomously with its own army and government, these cities took periodic beatings from Spain, France, the Swiss and even each other. Until such time as Italy was able to establish national solidarity with a common agenda, they were subject to the humiliation of their rulers. When departments in a company act as city-states, they too will be subject to the whims of the market and their competitors.

The Constitution of the United States, the culmination of 5,000 years of socio-political evolution, is the most definitive treatise ever written on the organization of a government, assuring what Jefferson called the inalienable right to "life, liberty and the pursuit of happiness." Commercially speaking, a company's constitution should foster "growth, liquidity and the pursuit of profitability." When viewed through commercial glasses, the Constitution provides the best mission statement and business plan for governmental success ever prepared. More than 200 years after it was written, countries of the world are still trying to achieve what was done by a collection of gentrified rebels in Philadelphia during the summer of 1787. Rife with compromise and recognition of the need for federally guided decentralization, all managers, be they American or otherwise, should study its content as they seek wisdom for their own organizational purposes.

The debate that took place at the Constitutional Convention is strikingly similar to the questions that businesspeople have contemplated for the last 100 years. Is a strong federal government the answer (centralization) or is a loose collection of states with their own sovereignty (decentralization) the best design for a nascent country? Also, how are the various government entities organized to assure a balance of power and still have the teeth to hold the nation together? For the global enterprise, this story sounds a lot like the need it has for a balanced relationship (albeit symbiotic) between a central entity that sets policy and the flexibility field operations requires to run their businesses.

The solution to the constitutional dilemma was strikingly similar to the one global entities will eventually arrive at — a compromise. Whereas the Articles of Confederation forged a structure in which there was no central authority, the Constitutional Convention drafted a plan that created a series of "checks and balances" between state and federal power. This same structure may be exactly what today's global companies require to be successful in their theaters of operation.

A major step in the commercial process of compromise and restructuring is observed in the formation of supply chain entities (not departments) in organizations. As recently as seven years ago one would never have received a business card from a colleague with the title director of supply chain operations or vice president of supply chain management. Today, it is quite common to see these positions crop up, as they are a manifestation of a commitment to create entities that transcend business units while removing obstacles at a local level.

While there are still many challenges to be met in designing the ideal global enterprise, the ability to compromise and subordinate departmental or divisional agendas to the benefit of the organization are two giant steps forward. Because corporate culture is a function of organizational structure, proper nurturing of the latter will promote an environment that allows people to see the forest through the trees, clearing the field for the disciplined execution of supply chain strategies.

THE INDIVIDUAL AND GLOBAL ORGANIZATIONS: A COMMERCIAL CONTRACT

There is no question that organizational structure influences individual, group and, ultimately, supply chain behavior. However, people are responsible for their own actions, all of which should be channeled toward the financial success of the organization that employs them. This being said, there are two characteristics that define the contribution that a person makes to the enterprise: preparation and attitude.

With regard to preparation, both the company and the employee must realize that training is a two-way street. A commitment to education and shared learning must be in the marrow of an organization's skeletal structure, manifesting itself in programs that build the skills people need to compete. The same can be said for the individual. In today's world, a college or business school degree is but a ticket into the big game. A diploma will get a player into the stadium, but what someone does on the field is left to how well the individual prepares himself or herself every day. If employees are not educating themselves independently, they are discounting their value to the company and will eventually be passed over or taken out.

Management's attitude toward investing in employees differs from company to company, with the only common ground being the lip service usually afforded the initiative. Recollection of a cartoon read in a long-forgotten business publication sizes up the situation pretty well. It went something like this.

While alone in an elevator, two managers are embroiled in a debate over the cost/benefit of employee training. The first manager says to his colleague, "What happens if we train all these people and then they leave?" The other, and obviously more enlightened, manager responds, "What happens if we don't train them and they stay?"

This little gem brings a vexing catch-22 to the forefront of any conversation on training, education and the ties to supply chain execution. On the one hand, organizations have come to be known as stoic beasts that will lay off people with 15 years of service at the earliest sign of a financial downturn. Conversely, many employees in business today are viewed as corporate mercenaries, changing jobs a half dozen times over the course of their careers. If people do not trust their employers and companies are hesitant to invest in people out of fear they will go to the competition, how can a culture be built upon a mutual interest in employee development?

There is no easy answer to this dilemma, but one could say that perhaps companies would not have problems if their people had been better trained. Similarly, if people had actively invested in their own careers like they expect companies to do for them, perhaps they would not have been among those who got whacked. While admittedly an oversimplification, there still may be some merit in these statements.

The fact is that in order for companies to be successful, they have to develop employees with a broad perspective on business. The first step in that process is to make a much-needed separation between training and education. Whereas some may consider any distinction a matter of semantics, forward thinkers will realize that there is an ocean of difference between training someone for a job and educating that person for a professional lifestyle.

Training is usually subject specific and only applicable to the position an employee occupies. Basically, people are instructed how to fulfill the technical aspects of their jobs. Training is also more event driven, short term in nature and lacks continuity or links with other initiatives in the organization. Education, on the other hand, is as much philosophical as it is practical, blending technical skills with the desire to develop responsible and proactive corporate citizens. More of a process than an event, education is wide in scope, long term by definition and all content is part of a comprehensive design.

Once management teams can separate training from education, initiatives can begin that establish technical skills *and* shape the corporate culture of the organization. From an educational standpoint, that process begins with an explanation of the company philosophy and what the characteristics are that personify its value system. When people do not understand the personality of their own organization, it is very difficult to adopt and display attitudes consistent with the corporate ethos.

Employees also need exposure to different cultures, languages, mores and methods of doing business. The simple opportunity to meet colleagues from foreign offices will do wonders for performance. In fact, the ability to meet and spend time with offshore colleagues is proof positive that team members are part of something larger than themselves and that subordination of personal agendas for the general good is to everybody's benefit. It is easy to disparage, criticize or be cynical with a stranger in an e-mail. It is not so easy when people know each other and have thrown back a beer or two.

In addition to job-specific preparation, training also means exposing people to functional disciplines that have seemingly nothing to do with their positions. A true supply chain mentality requires that purchasing professionals must be trained in capacity and production planning to fully comprehend the downstream results of their sourcing practices. It also means that salespeople need to spend time in logistics to understand the ramifications of their sometimes outlandish commitments to clients. There are many examples of relevant cross-training, but a good place to start is with the basics of accounting and financial reporting for every person in a company. Cultures differ from company to company; math does not (at least it never used to).

On the individual front, employees have to go the extra mile for themselves and the company. That means making an effort not only to perform well but to learn something new every day. Whether it is from a business journal, colleague, college course or water cooler conversation, at the end of a year the cumulative effect of this concerted effort will show its value.

Just as business leaders can find parallels for their organizational challenges in the field of political science, individuals should pursue sagacity in non-traditional places. Shakespeare, Mao Tse-tung, the Greek tragedies and Confucius all offer invaluable lessons for life and business that all professionals should embrace. Corporate hubris has been the downfall of more than one manager, a situation that may have been averted by visiting with the Athenians of ancient Greece.

The most famous rebuttal for continuous education, be it formal or otherwise, is that people do not have time. When employees convert an occasional activity into a way of life, there is always time. How people apply their intellectual bandwidth is a lot like the way in which production planning is carried out in a plant; everything is based on capacity and priority. If people have the native capacity, they should make learning a priority. At the very least, if they find themselves among the unlucky bunch that does get laid off in a downturn, they will be in a better position to bounce back.

Whether from the company or individual perspective, one must realize that learning is a process, not an event. Intellectual capital is the work-in-process inventory that never becomes finished goods. Unlike the company in the case study presented later in the book, this is the type of asset an international businessperson always wants on his or her personal balance sheet.

The second variable in the personal development equation is attitude. It is true that both organizational structure and a company's posture on employee development help to mold attitudes, but, once again, we are all responsible for our actions. Today's global enterprise must be populated with people who are willing to step outside their functional universe and give something of themselves for the good of the corporate physiology. This is the first step in creating a culture focused on supply chain performance. Without it, companies will never be able to maximize their potential.

A personal commitment and willingness to sacrifice are analogous to the series of compromises found in the U.S. Constitution. The individual states gave up their sovereignty to "form a more perfect union…promote the general welfare, and secure the blessings of liberty to ourselves and our posterity." An individual's behavior within an organization should not be much different than that of the states of the Union.

To illustrate this point further, consider the work of Jean-Jacques Rousseau in his publication *The Social Contract*. Written during the time of the Enlightenment, which so influenced the revolutionary generations of the mid to late 1700s, Rousseau wrote extensively on the relationship between the individual, his or her personal freedom and life in a country of laws. His hypothesis was that although a person is entitled to his or her individual freedoms, sacrifice of some of those freedoms to the "general will" would bring greater benefits to the whole of society and hence the individuals who make up that society. To leave matters to Rousseau himself:

> Each of us puts in common his person and his whole power under
> the supreme direction of the general will: and in return we receive
> every member as an indivisible part of the whole.[2]

For business purposes, the above must be tempered to allow for creativity and local decision making. However, the statement does not lose any of its force when taken from the standpoint of shelving individual or departmental initiatives that may not contribute to the overall (or general) well-being of the company. As such, each and every employee should tacitly create a "commercial contract" between himself or herself and the organization, committing to act in a manner that promotes the operational, cultural and financial health of the enterprise.

The state of the relationship between a corporate entity and the people who populate its environs is the crucible of the qualitative side of supply chain management. Products do not move themselves, and it is the desire to be part of something grander than any person could ever be individually that gets product into the hands of the consumer. People must also recognize that we live in an imperfect and conflictive world, shelter from which cannot be found in the confines of our offices, warehouses or factories. It is this same imperfection and innate sense of conflict that should lead people to seek compromise while always putting their best foot forward. Tesla, the metal band of the early 1990s, summed up the corporate tango most succinctly:

> It ain't what you got, it what's you give.
> It ain't what it's not, but what it is.

To the above end, all professionals involved with international trade have to operate out on the margin, constantly measuring the benefit of one additional unit of personal output against the cost of creating that output. Whether activities are related to improving customer relations, increasing revenues, better supplier management or cost reductions, people must push themselves and those around them to their physical, emotional and intellectual limits. If people are not operating out on the margin, they are probably just going through the motions. As Peter Drucker so aptly put it, "One should never confuse motion with progress."

EXECUTION

The not-so-invisible hand of global competition has seen to it that any early market lead established by a company is quickly erased.[3] Short product life cycles, competitive response, expired patents and generic substitutes all contribute to the erosion of margin and market dominance once enjoyed by domestic companies. Regardless of research and development, product development and multi-million-dollar marketing budgets, the competitive playing field gradually evens off, leaving companies to battle for supremacy in the trenches of operational execution.

It is the hypothesis of this book that while disciplines like research and development or global branding are vital to a company's success, it is the tactical follow-through in lead time rationalization, landed cost controls and inventory management that ultimately leads to financial success. While admittedly "Children of a Lesser God," these points are the life support of companies characterized by commodity-based models with little product differentiation beyond the creative license of their advertising agencies. As the visionary few labor toward what Jim Clark called "the new new thing," the rest of us are left to execute on the tactical models that will establish and prolong market dominance. This book hopefully contributes to that end.

NOTES

1. Douglas Downing, *Dictionary of Mathematics Terms,* Barron's Educational Series, 1987, p. 362.
2. Jean-Jacques Rousseau, *The Social Contract,* 1762, p. 15.
3. The term "visible hand of competition" was first used by Alfred Chandler of the Harvard Business School in his book *The Visible Hand: The Managerial Revolution in American Business,* Harvard University Press, 1977.

THE ORIGINS OF CONTEMPORARY SUPPLY CHAIN MANAGEMENT

The emergence of supply chain management (SCM) as the leading philosophy of companies committed to international trade has by no means been a mercurial event. More of an evolutionary process, the tenets of SCM were born in the markets of Europe, Asia and the United States and can be traced back to the first decades of the 20th century. Unlike some of its more faddish counterparts, SCM has a rich history that not only marks its place in the annals of commerce but also substantiates its relevance to business practitioners of all types.

For purposes of creating future value, it is the maturation of SCM and its ability to adapt to the demands of a global environment that will galvanize its claim as the driving force behind international business. That being said, certain conditions must exist within any enterprise in order for the SCM philosophy to generate tangible results:

1. The fundamental philosophy and its core beliefs, purpose and financial relevance must be clearly defined and communicated to an organization and its extended enterprise.
2. The strategic and tactical elements of SCM must be innate to the corporate culture and personality of an enterprise.

3. Quantifiable links between supply chain execution and financial performance must be identified and exploited throughout the organization.
4. Measurement tools must be applied that correspond to and are aligned with the SCM philosophy.

Each of these points will be dealt with in detail throughout the balance of this book. However, one cannot begin to discuss these issues without first establishing a baseline for SCM and its meaning in a contemporary framework. Because modern SCM is as all-encompassing as international trade itself, a definition that transcends industry, function, geography and culture is called for. Additionally, any definition must consider the timeless motives of capitalist enterprise, with a focus on the financial realities that drive business today: growth, profitability, liquidity and asset utilization. Using these points as a frame of reference, the following interpretation is offered:

> SCM is a business philosophy founded upon the shared understanding of an enterprise's vision, mission and strategy, both within the organization and among its key constituents. Successful SCM recognizes the interdependencies between functional areas, as well as the need to integrate processes throughout the enterprise.
>
> True SCM also links the dynamic of client, supplier and strategic partner activities to the value chain, continuously working to balance profitability with customer satisfaction. Fundamental to supply chain activities are landed cost improvements, stabilization of lead times and the need to match inventory investments with timely product availability. Ultimately, the entire supply chain is linked through information technology, creating ubiquitous visibility and access to information.

Upon isolating the core components of this definition and comparing them with the goals of businesspeople at the beginning of the last century, it seems that little has changed in commerce over the last 100 years. While recognizing the schism between Western and Japanese business models, it remains that the profit motive will never falter and the essence of balance sheet and income statement management has changed very little (excepting the recent financial alchemy used to arrive at reported results). In this context, why all the hype over SCM and its relevance to business today?

Since the first seedlings of the multi-national appeared in the early 1900s, many dynamics have played upon the evolution of those early business models. Although an argument could be made as to the impact of technology, product branding or changing demographics on business, to grasp why SCM is so important one need only look at two fairly recent commercial developments: globalization and outsourcing. Without an understanding of what each has meant to commerce in the latter part of the 20th century and, more importantly, their role in the first years of the new millennium, businesspeople will never fully be able to harness the power of the SCM philosophy.

However, in order to understand the part that SCM plays in the era of globalization and outsourcing, the enlightened manager must first look to the origins of the discipline and understand its history over the last hundred years. Whereas the term SCM came into vogue overnight, one can be assured that the benefits and tactics behind the hyperbole were born of the hard work of many talented people over a long period of time. Unfortunately, the emphasis of businesses on tag lines and platitudes as opposed to operational excellence has somewhat jaded the short-term significance of SCM. Notwithstanding any cynicism, it is the businessperson who has a historical appreciation of the discipline while placing its timeless principles in the context of international business who has the greatest probability of reaping its longer term benefits.

FOUR EVENTS THAT SHAPED SUPPLY CHAIN MANAGEMENT

The origins of contemporary SCM can be traced to four seminal events that took place in the first half of the 20th century. They are the perfection of mass production techniques, the introduction of product differentiation, the development of management techniques as science and the post–World War II arrival of Japan on the global stage. It should be pointed out that each of the four events to be discussed had its origins in the automotive industry and that the advent of both product differentiation and Japan's management approach was a direct descendent of the granddaddy of SCM, mass production. Given this pedigree, it is not an exaggeration to suggest that most industries have benchmarked and adopted tactics perfected in the automotive sector. For this reason, a detailed study of the automotive industry and its contributions to SCM is required reading for serious supply chain managers. While this volume touches on key aspects of the role of the auto sector in the evolution of SCM, it does not treat it in its entirety.

Mass Production

Allusions to the concept of mass production can be found in publications as early as 1776. In fact, it was Adam Smith in *The Wealth of Nations* who began the transition from cottage industry to factory life when he described his famous pin factory and how division of labor could increase output. Even with these early references, it was Henry Ford who perfected the concept of mass production when he melded market opportunity with machinery, manpower and methodology in the first decades of the 20th century.[1]

As any student of economics understands, mass production is driven by a variety of factors, but most notably by building standardized products that drive up the utilization of physical plant. Maximization of production capacity dominates the landscape, with all planning, resource allocation and enterprise-wide activities focused on getting the most out of the machinery in the factory. This mentality was certainly the case with Ford as he produced millions of Model Ts from the early 1900s well into the 1920s.

Of course, as utilization approaches 100%, costs go down due to economies of scale. As his costs plummeted, Ford was able to lower prices, thus creating more demand for his Model T. Viewed as a self-fulfilling prophecy of mass production, economies of scale and expanding markets were pursued by Ford in several ways. As the reader will note in subsequent passages, the supply chain ramifications of these practices were considerable and continue to have a telling impact on organizations 90 years later.

The most well-known achievement of Ford is, of course, the assembly line. Inspired by the need to maximize the utilization of assets and production output, the assembly line reduced cycle times in the plant to levels that were inconceivable prior to its introduction. This level of output was made possible not only by the speed of the line but also by the division of labor. Gone were the days of artisan production in which the same craftsman proudly perfected all phases of assembly. The new world order was characterized by thousands of employees executing specific tasks as cars moved down the production line.

Division of labor was a key component to Ford's vision of mass production, but it would not have been possible without the introduction of interchangeable parts and techniques that made assembly of a vehicle a relatively predictable process. Another innovation was that Ford engineers perfected the idea of measuring parts to specification, thus eliminating the variation innate to most craft-based business models. It was the combination of these practices that made it possible for Ford to produce 2.1 million Model T chassis in its apex year, 1923.

What should be clear to the reader is that the Ford model focused almost entirely on production output and left any customer-related issues in the hands of the dealer network. Ever-increasing output drove down costs, which allowed dealers to sell at cheaper prices, thus attracting more and more buyers. It was a model that worked extremely well in terms of its stated goals, but also left many supply chain questions unanswered. It was these fissures in the model that eventually opened the door for players more in tune with customer desires to capture market share.

Managing the Mass Production Supply Chain

It must be noted again that when Ford introduced the mass production system, manufacturing was driven not by demand planning but by plant capacity. In fact, during the early days of the auto industry, very little forecasting was carried out, with the manufacturer viewing its dealers as an outlet to move vehicles rather than a source of market information. Manufacturers pushed increasing amounts of finished good down dealer channels with little regard for the actual ups and downs of market demand. In this type of scenario, it is not hard to envision the potential buildup of raw materials, work in process and finished goods across the entire supply chain.

Beginning with raw materials, the steady-paced mass production environment of the 1900s required vast amounts of inventory to be held. Lead times, cost and quality controls were all tentative in the nescient auto industry, and for a factory not to have ample raw materials on hand was considered taboo. This buildup of inventories based on production rates created a slew of challenges for early auto executives.

The financial burden of acquiring raw materials before they are needed is obvious. While the rationale of the day deferred to the economies of scale gained through larger purchases, the netting out of carrying costs, storage, insurance, obsolescence and shrinkage has long since shot down that argument. In addition to these considerations, production-based inventories have much greater space and personnel requirements to receive, put away and deliver material to the production line. Both points imply more costs built into the supply chain and are a source of considerable waste.

Work in process is even more expensive to carry due to the value that has been added to the raw materials as they begin the transformation to finished goods. Bottlenecks, down lines and out-of-spec components all contributed to a buildup of work in process in the early days of the auto industry, with a glut of finished goods in cyclical markets only adding insult to injury.

Finished goods may have been the most visible of inventory issues for the auto manufacturers due to the fact that they had to look no further than the dealer's yard to see the results of their mass production efforts. With capacity driving production, it was common to see dealers with hundreds of cars on their lots waiting for buyers. Again, the carrying costs (for the dealers now), along with storage, insurance and obsolescence concerns, began to expose the softer underbelly of mass production.

Another issue that has plagued mass-production-based models over the years is the problem of product quality. Based on the very nature of mass production techniques, both component and finished goods quality carry serious supply chain consequences.

Because raw materials purchases are prioritized by cost and then quality, most mass producers tacitly recognized that a certain percentage of faulty materials would get onto the production floor. As long as defective merchandise was kept within a certain tolerance, manufacturers put up with the inconveniences. Even within acceptable limits, faulty raw materials can shut down production lines, inflate work in process and, more dangerously, spawn a corps of unhappy clients.

In addition to the raw materials quality issue, finished goods had their own challenges to deal with. Again due to the constant pace of the assembly line, quality issues only surfaced at the end of the production run. This meant that finished goods had to be reworked prior to final release, a scenario that required even more space and personnel. The combination of faulty raw materials along with production-related defects served to exacerbate an already challenged supply chain.

From a supply chain perspective, it is clear that the trade-off for maximized plant output was exorbitant amounts of waste. Supply chain waste comes in many forms, the least of which are defective products, rework, oversized work areas, additional personnel and extended wait times. The greatest legacy of waste from the mass production era, however, was excess inventories. As the auto industry began to mature, companies like Ford and General Motors labored vigorously to better manage their supply chains. The introduction of the new model year, product differentiation and the use of forecasts all contributed to modest improvements in this area.

Product Differentiation

Undoubtedly, it was Henry Ford who made the automobile affordable for the average consumer in the first decades of the 1900s. The only way he could have possibly achieved such a goal was to pursue a mass production model. It must also be noted that Ford was aware of at least some of the supply chain consequences of his business model and accepted the trade-off in waste for greater output. Finally, one must be cognizant of the fact that Ford was a pioneer in an industry that enhanced the human experience on a universal scale. Although he was always open to other companies benchmarking his operations, in the early years he had few opportunities to learn from others because he was the industry leader. In spite of the supply chain challenges Ford faced with the Model T, what he achieved was nothing short of remarkable.

While Ford continued to pursue the mass production model, other automotive companies perceived a shift in consumer attitudes, from viewing an auto as a means of transportation to an overall driving experience. In fact, Ford was so convinced of the future of his business that when asked about the possibility of offering different colors of the Model T, his response was that consumers could have any color they liked as long as it was black! This being said, market segmentation and, more important from a supply chain perspective, product differentiation became the domain of General Motors beginning in the early 1920s.[2]

When Alfred P. Sloan joined General Motors, it was well behind Ford in sales. However, instead of pursuing a game of volume catch-up, Sloan and the GM team devised a strategy based on market segmentation. It was at that time when brands like Chevy, Cadillac and Buick became household names in the United States. It was also during this period that GM introduced a market innovation of profound supply chain consequence: the new model year. Every year GM, and eventually all of its competitors, would offer a new model for the coming buying season. The confluence of the new model year with a wider variety of automobiles precipitated supply chain challenges not considered under the mass production model.

By no means did a strategy of product differentiation discourage GM from pursuing economies of scale; in fact, the pursuit of scale became even more intense. Because there were more models to produce and less time in which to produce them, management was fanatical in its pursuit of rapid engineering, improved tooling techniques, reduced setup times and use of common parts. As another function of the differentiation model, GM had to devise ways to reduce inventories across the board. Dealing with parts for an identical finished goods inventory was sufficiently risky, but having mountains of inventories laying about for a variety of models took risk to an entirely new level.

One notable advance by GM was the increased use of forecasts to aid production planning and inventory levels. While it was still reasonable to say that GM pursued economies of scale at every turn, it was also forced to be more in tune with market demands via its dealer network. Perhaps a first in large-scale production models, GM began to solicit historical and anticipated demand information from its dealers in order to better approximate their actual needs. Although far from optimal, this was a major step in the progression of early supply chain practices.

Management as a Science

Another important development for SCM occurred at GM, but this time far from the production floor. While GM can be credited with product innovations like the automatic transmission, it was also an innovator in organizational structure. Actually, Alfred P. Sloan is credited with "professionalizing" management as a science, taking traditional hierarchies to the frontier of organizational dynamics. Part of this organizational revamping involved the creation of entirely new departments, like marketing. Thus, while Ford sought to perfect the concept of division of labor on the production line, GM achieved what might be called division by function.

The GM of the 1920s was characterized by a department-oriented enterprise. Each division and business unit, as well as purchasing, sales, manufacturing and accounting, had its own domain, guided by corporate policy from headquarters. This was actually one of the first iterations of decentralization in a major corporation and it worked quite well, which is not to say, of course, that it did not have its share of unanticipated supply chain consequences.

First noted in the Introduction to this work, functional organization tends to push people into a mind-set that is constrained by both the real and imaginary walls of the department in which they work. As much a consequence of human nature as organizational design, functional orientation draws lines in the corporate sand, creating the famous silo approach so often alluded to in contemporary writings.

While the results of supply chain activities are more visible in a production environment (inventories, space requirements, rework, etc.), the ramifications of a functionally structured organization are much less tangible. This phenomenon revolves around the nature of communication and how it becomes more complicated as additional entities are added to the supply chain. Discussed in a quantitative fashion in Chapter 4, the need to communicate proliferates as organizations become more complex. The supply chain paradox lies in the fact that as entities become more and more fractionalized, they communicate less and less.

It is for the above reasons that many organizations in the first half of the 20th century had several forecasts instead of one. It may also be for this reason that purchasing departments still bought in quantities to achieve volume discounts regardless of what any forecast called for. Whatever the circumstance, while organization by function does offer certain benefits, the law of unintended circumstances always intervenes to create almost as many challenges as benefits.

The Japanese Get in the Game

Consistent with the comparison of governmental and commercial organization made in the Introduction to this book, it is not unreasonable to say that how companies operate is ultimately a reflection of the markets in which they find themselves. Ford saw a massive market for standardized transportation and developed a model that met that need. GM, on the other hand, anticipated the influence of human nature on automotive purchases and used product differentiation to its advantage. Each, as stated previously, implied its own set of supply chain challenges.

Following this line of reasoning, the sociopolitical circumstances in which Japan found itself after World War II had a profound effect on how industry was ultimately organized. Again borrowing from the automotive sector, the introduction of lean manufacturing techniques was very much related to the market realities the country confronted after 1945. While it is important to acknowledge that economic conditions in Japan helped to mold organizations and their supply chains, it must also be noted that the Japanese took advantage of the wartime devastation of their economy to develop a new philosophy on business.[3]

If necessity is the mother of invention, then the Japanese auto industry is the best 20th century example of this maxim. At the end of World War II, Japanese automakers found themselves under the political aegis of the U.S. government, custodian to an obliterated manufacturing base and with little foreign exchange to invest in technology. These conditions, coupled with a small domestic market and the government's explicit goal of rapid entry into global markets, forced industry heads to revamp the entire automotive supply chain. Clearly influenced by the circumstances in which they found themselves, Japanese automakers not only built their factories to suit their markets but also created a mental model that transcended the entire supply chain. The ensuing result has come to be known as *lean manufacturing*.

The fundamental tenets of lean manufacturing are as follows:[4]

1. A holistic view of supply chains, from product concept to final delivery to the customer
2. A team approach founded on a multi-skilled workforce and employee input
3. Commitment to continuous improvement of all processes
4. Elimination of waste throughout the supply chain

Even at this high level, the fissures between the mass production mentality and lean manufacturing come to the surface. Early Western models viewed manufacturing as the heart of the operation, while supporters of lean manufacturing view the manufacturing function within the context of the entire supply chain. Also, whereas Western models create division of labor at both a manufacturing and administrative level, lean broadens the skill sets of individual employees to enhance their contribution to the team's effort. Integral to this mentality is the requirement for employees to proactively build quality into processes and constantly seek ways to improve upon all aspects of the business.

Because the Japanese automakers had so much to do and so little time in which to do it, it is accurate to say that lean manufacturing is all about speed and the rationalization of resources. It is for these reasons that the elimination of waste mentioned in the fourth point above is the obsession of all practitioners of the discipline. For the lean manufacturer, waste includes excess inventory, wait time, rework, scrap and any non-value-adding activity included in the production process.

In the lean model, the quest for supply chain velocity begins with customer sensitivity; proceeds through product development; permeates all engineering aspects of product, process and manufacturing design; is fundamental to the management of suppliers and is incessantly pursued on the manufacturing floor. The proclaimed benefits of lean supply chains compared with more traditional models are:

1. Half the time for product development
2. Up to 50% less time required for engineering of products, processes and tools
3. Half the investment in physical plant
4. Half the space requirement in the factory
5. Gains in human productivity of up to 50%[4]

With such an emphasis on speed, quality and the elimination of waste, the importance of well-run supply chains cannot be overstated. Fewer inventories requires better understanding of market demand, interactive management of supplier relations, fanatical control of manufacturing processes and, more than anything, open communication. Beginning with the auto industry and later extending to other sectors, the Japanese have religiously developed, applied and enjoyed the financial rewards of lean manufacturing.

While acknowledging the recent malaise found in the Japanese economy, it would still be hard to dispute the success of Japan's industries since the end of World War II. Because the Japanese auto industry has been more in tune with consumer wants, it has been able to develop quality products faster and at a better price. As documented in business literature over the last 50 years, the commercial success of Japan has been attributed to everything from government intervention to protectionist policy, copycat engineering and cheap labor. There may be some truth to all of these points, but anyone who denies that the Japanese have progressed due to their ability to build better products at a cheaper price is living in denial.

U.S. and European automakers were certainly not in denial as they watched market share erode in favor of the Japanese producers beginning in the late 1950s and early 1960s. Although entrenched mentalities were still abundant, many managers from companies like Chrysler, VW, Ford, Renault and GM have adopted the lean mentality over the years and responded with many successes. Reductions in design lead time, team-based engineering processes and rationalized plants have all led to the raising of the collective automotive bar.

So, as companies respond to the new challenge of lean manufacturing, the chase continues. Incremental improvements will continue to be uncovered, particularly as the challenges inherent to global management proliferate. As illustrated in Chapter 3, Western companies still have an appreciation for the benefits of mass production while adopting techniques native to the lean environment.

An understanding of the modern history of Western techniques and how they have been melded with the demand for speed and flawless quality is essential to the study of SCM. This and other topics are the subject of Chapter 2. Upon completion of the analysis of Western supply chain thought, the story returns to a more detailed analysis of lean manufacturing and its impact on the post–World War II globalization of domestic economies.

NOTES

1. For a more detailed discussion of mass production in the United States, see Robert H. Hayes, Steven C. Wheelright and Kim B. Clark, *Dynamic Manufacturing,* The Free Press, 1988, pp. 31–60.
2. A comprehensive treatment of the history of General Motors from the early 1920s through the end of World War II can be found in Alfred P. Sloan, Jr., *My Years with General Motors,* Doubleday, 1963.
3. An excellent reference on the evolution of post–World War II Japanese industry is James P. Womack, Daniel T. Jones, and Daniel Roos, *The Machine That Changed the World: The Story of Lean Production,* Harper Perennial, 1990.
4. James P. Womack, Daniel T. Jones, and Daniel Roos, *The Machine That Changed the World: The Story of Lean Production,* Harper Perennial, 1990.

2

TWO ROADS EQUALLY TRAVELED

The post–World War II development of tactical supply chain management (SCM) in the United States and Europe can be traced to a handful of changes in business practices that date back to the 1970s. Of interest is the fact that although these projects shared the goals of process integration and enhanced performance, they were undertaken completely independent of one another. Whether this is a phenomenon best attributed to the idea that "great minds think alike" or because organizations of the period were completely devoid of internal communication is best left to debate. The final result is a confluence of best practices that form the Western component of the genesis of global SCM.

The first efforts to integrate what were then domestic supply chains involved the linking of forecasts with the purchase of raw materials and finished goods production. Although far from science, a combination of closer contact with end users and better forecasting techniques had advanced the discipline since its inception in the early part of the century. Even today, there is room for improvement in any methodology that unites real market demand with production planning. However, by the 1970s, advances in forecasting had brought tangible benefits to the plant floor and the integration of business functions.

These ties were actually part of a comprehensive approach to manufacturing that was known as *manufacturing planning and control* (MPC). A methodology that is still in use today, MPC is an integrated process that helps organizations to determine raw materials requirements, develop production plans, allocate capacity and establish delivery schedules to customers.[1] Whereas the system itself was intended to connect the sales function (in the form of a finished goods forecast) to purchasing, manufacturing and distribution, the first true signs of

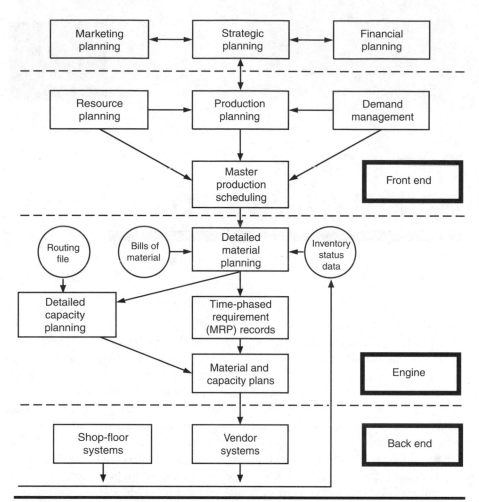

Figure 2.1   Manufacturing Planning and Control System (From Thomas E. Vollman, William L. Berry, and D. Clay Whybark, *Manufacturing Planning & Control Systems,* Irwin McGraw-Hill, 1997, p. 15. With permission.)

integration at a tactical level were found in the area of *materials requirements planning* (MRP). Illustrated in Figure 2.1, MRP is that part of MPC that involves the quantification and time phasing of the purchase of raw materials for consumption in a manufacturing process.

As part of the attempt to integrate purchasing and production via MRP, two pivotal activities were developed: gross to net exploding and lead time offsetting. Driven by the raw materials requirements detailed in a product-specific bill of material, gross to net exploding first takes the original or *gross* amount of raw materials needed to meet weekly production levels and subtracts from that figure what is currently in inventory. After accounting for raw materials that are already in inventory, the second step is to subtract amounts that are on order from suppliers. The deduction of current inventories and scheduled receipts from the original gross amount permits the calculation of a new or *net* requirement.

Whereas gross to net exploding determines what quantities of raw materials will be required in weekly periods, lead time offsetting synchronizes the placement of purchase orders with the cumulative lead time required to bring components to the production floor. In other words, offsetting matches the date when raw materials are needed with the time required to get the goods to a production site. This practice creates raw material order dates that are intended to precisely offset the lead times into a plant.

Even though companies in Europe and the United States were still doing much of their sourcing and manufacturing domestically in the early 1970s, the advent of MRP and its impact on the future of SCM should not be discounted. Within the context of the overall MPC system, MRP can be credited with the tactical integration of the purchasing and manufacturing functions and can also be considered a forerunner to what today is called international materials management. As business became a bit more global in scope in the mid-1970s, the tactical importance of MRP was more pronounced and made an even greater contribution to the evolution of SCM.

Using the U.S. domestic market of the early 1970s as a reference, it can be said that the execution of MRP models was less stringent than today's international models for three reasons. First, because U.S. manufacturers were still sourcing a substantial percentage of their raw materials domestically, there was less variation in transportation lead times. Understanding that lead time stability is the first pillar of MRP, the process showed immediate value. Second, most manufacturing was still done in the United States, a situation that contributed to the ability to manage raw materials inventories on a local or at least domestic level.

With the accuracy of raw materials inventories as the second component of the MRP success formula, the combination of fairly predictable lead times and easy access to inventories qualified the discipline as the best that domestic business had to offer at the time. Finally, while noting some exceptions, most U.S. production in the early 1970s was dedicated to domestic consumption, a scenario that favored not only MRP but also the entire MPC model.

The real benefit of the MPC system is that it begins with a forecast for finished goods and *cascades* requirements through the entire process, linking discrete functions all the way to the delivery of finished goods. Contemplating variables that include demand management, MRP, production scheduling, capacity planning, inventory management and available to promise (ATP), the MPC model is quite comprehensive when considering the need to prioritize activities and allocate limited resources accordingly.

When discussing the importance of MRP to SCM, one must also consider the contribution that the MPC model has made in the area of distribution management. The ATP component of master planning, which deals with the delivery of finished goods, has come to serve as another building block of SCM. Defined as that part of unallocated finished goods inventory and future production capacity, the ATP process allows companies to commit to both order quantities and delivery schedules in upcoming weekly periods. Conceptually similar to the MRP concepts of gross to net exploding and lead time offsetting, ATP uses unallocated inventories and available future production capacity to determine the quantities of product that can be committed to clients in approaching periods, as well as the timing of delivery of each order.

Much like the value of MRP to U.S. producers in the 1970s, the ATP component of the MPC system had considerable appeal. Again driven by relatively predictable lead times and access to inventories (now in the form of finished goods), ATP was a powerful tool that served as the final link in the entire production process. Taken as a whole or individually, both the MRP and ATP components of the MPC system should be considered a major contributor to what today is known as SCM.

Needless to say, MPC had a considerable impact on how business was done in the 1970s and continues to influence business practices well into the 21st century. Not unlike most systems, however, it was not without its weaknesses. Perhaps the biggest flaw associated with MPC is its dependence on forecasts and their requisite accuracy. Because the forecast drives the entire cascading process, any variance between actual and anticipated numbers has a negative effect on overall execution. Even with improvements in forecasting, variance has been the bane of MPC since its introduction, with the result being an excess of inventories in the pipeline or, conversely, acute shortages of much-needed goods. In a global business model, either scenario can translate to disaster for an organization.

Another weakness associated with MPC is actually related more to organizational structure than any issue inherent to the system itself. As noted earlier, a key benefit of an MPC system is its integration of functional processes (sales, purchasing, production, distribution, etc.). In spite of these advantages, MPC can be compromised due to the way in which companies have traditionally been organized and measured. Based mainly on a functional reporting structure, organizations have made discrete entities of purchasing, sales, finance and other departments, each with its own organizational chart, budgets and methods of measurement.

This scenario has created conflict amongst departments, a situation that discourages cooperation and inhibits communication. Taken to the extreme, it is important to note that not only are companies organized by department, but that the materials management side of the business oftentimes has no relationship or formal reporting ties to the distribution management function.

The next step in moving the functional organization, a legacy of the early company structures studied in Chapter 1, to a supply chain mentality is the synthesis of materials management with the activities of demand fulfillment. The development of organizational matrices that reflect this market requirement is a major challenge for management teams around the world and offers fertile ground for the continued advance of the SCM discipline.

Viewed in its proper historical perspective, MPC has soldiered along since its introduction in the 1970s, weathering the advent of important business developments like just in time, Quick Response and Efficient Consumer Response. Undaunted by the onslaught of acronyms and myriad management techniques du jour, MPC has endured because it works. By no means perfect, the system does offer some fundamental benefits to SCM, including the integration of functional disciplines, cascading of information throughout the organization and the intended linking of materials management with distribution management. As organizations structure themselves in ways that encourage not only the systemic but also the physical and cultural integration of activities, the benefits of MPC will continue to impact business well into the future.

Predictably, the MRP and ATP elements of the MPC system increased in value as companies began to engage wholeheartedly in international trade. Whether in Europe or the United States, companies in the early 1980s found themselves sourcing more raw materials from offshore suppliers, as well as seeking foreign sales opportunities through their newly formed export departments.

Almost overnight, the significance of inbound flow of raw materials, lead time reliability, inventory accuracy and finished goods movement graduated from mundane status to an operational priority. Finally, as more companies expanded abroad with sourcing, production and sales activities across multiple geographies, the magnitude of functional integration grew as well, solidifying the importance of the fundamentals of MPC. It is these activities that continue to serve as the building blocks of the structure that is global business operations.

A final note on MPC and its influence on SCM involves the development of software to support the above-mentioned processes. The design work that was done in the 1970s and 1980s in the area of task automation and process integration not only has had a long-lasting impact on performance and productivity but, of equal significance, set the stage for what today is known as enterprise resource planning software.

It is historical fact that the discrete software packages that automated the MPC system inspired the next generation of software designers to modularize systems development. This event not only integrated the entire MPC process but also promoted interoperability between suppliers, buyers, strategic partners and government entities. Coupled with the 24/7 appeal of the World Wide Web, genuine software integration will be a driving force in related process improvements, supply chain visibility and enhanced financial returns for the foreseeable future.

LOGISTICS AND THE EVOLUTION OF SUPPLY CHAIN MANAGEMENT

As business became more international in scope and the MPC system was adjusting to the demands of global trade, a quiet revolution was brewing in a perennially underappreciated area, logistics. In fact, long before the addition of the term "logistics" to the business lexicon, this function was viewed as no more than a necessary evil that bore the domestic label of "transportation" or "traffic." Based on the significance of lead time dependability, landed cost control and inventory accuracy to a global model, logistics was gradually recognized as a legitimate business discipline.

Not long after this discovery, boardrooms around the world were evangelizing the importance of solid logistics to the success of their international endeavors. Prior to that movement in the mid-1980s, the transportation function was viewed as a non-value-adding activity that only served to detract from the bottom line. International business has changed that viewpoint and the very nature of logistics forever.

The reason why logistics has assumed such a vital role in SCM can be summed up in two words: *process variation*. In statistical terms, variation in any process is defined as the quantifiable difference between a desired outcome and the actual outcome of a given event. Quite simply, an international operation, be it in sourcing, manufacturing, sales or logistics, offers a greater probability of process variation or, stated differently, opportunity for defects than a domestic model. Whereas domestic operations afford a greater margin for error, global operations are much less predictable and the stakes considerably higher.

With worldwide operations and the movement of raw materials, work in process and finished goods in several directions, the possibility for errors in landed costs, lead times and inventory accuracy is overwhelming. The smallest variance from plan can send operations into a tailspin, closing down production lines and vaporizing revenue opportunities. For the exact same reasons why MRP and ATP are so relevant to SCM, logistics joined the pantheon of globally relevant business disciplines.

INTEGRATED LOGISTICS

Although MPC and logistics were converging on one another in many organizations, it was actually the third-party logistics industry that forced companies to recognize the real value of what came to be known in the late 1980s as *integrated logistics*. Described as providers of transportation, distribution and related services (international air/ocean/overland transportation, customs brokerage, warehousing, etc.), the third-party logistics community was able to bring value to client relationships by synthesizing what had formerly been highly fragmented, transportation-focused processes.

Whereas at that time organizations had used several unrelated entities to carry out logistics activities, the "integrated logistics" approach espoused the use of one entity to manage the entire process. Examples of this include the use of one company for international transportation and customs clearance services in the country of importation. Another more evolved example is to use the same company for international transportation, customs clearance and subsequent distribution in domestic markets. In either case, the instant appeal of lead time reduction, enhanced visibility and cost improvements catapulted the third-party logistics industry to the forefront of global business, setting the stage for even more progress in SCM.

It is undisputable that the pioneers of integrated logistics have had a profound and long-lasting effect on how international business is conducted. However, the impact of these companies on trade hardly stopped with the marriage of functional activities. Once the potential to integrate the logistics function was identified, third-party logistics companies, in concert with the logistics and purchasing departments of their clients, recognized that the next step was to integrate processes not only vertically in a single area but *horizontally* across departments. It was from this moment forward that the concept was extended to include external service providers.

Essentially, these visionaries took a new slant on the importance of lead time reliability and inventory accuracy to the offsetting and gross to net exploding components of the old MRP models. What made this exercise different was the proactive involvement of the third-party logistics community in planning and carrying out the flow of raw materials. While recognizing the work done in formalizing traditional supplier relationships, it must be stated that it was the combination of functional integration and involvement of third parties that established the foundation upon which modern SCM is constructed.

The best example to illustrate this point is the geometric, if not exponential, growth of imports into Europe and the United States from Asia in the late 1970s and early 1980s. This period witnessed a huge influx of raw materials and finished goods from industries as diverse as wearing apparel, automotive, high tech and footwear, each with a common need to stabilize lead times, level the flow of goods to match demand and maintain target margins. Because purchasing had become the logical domain of offshore sourcing, the need to share information with the logistics department should have been intuitively obvious from the outset. As difficult to believe as it may be, the early days of importing into the United States displayed little or no communication between purchasing and logistics, a disconnect that created stark contrasts between inventory overload and a total absence of much-needed materials.

It was at this point that two critical processes unfolded. First, purchasing departments began to share MRP data with their logistics counterparts in order to coordinate the timely arrival of merchandise. Based mainly on access to supplier-specific purchase order information, logistics personnel were then able to make important tactical decisions that included mode of transport, estimated time of arrival calculations and logistics cost models. Taken further, when a company's logistics and purchasing teams began to share upstream information with third-party logistics providers, a host of benefits were derived.

Using the same supplier-specific purchase order information, the third-party logistics firms could actively monitor the status of shipments in far-off origins like Jakarta, Hong Kong or Taipei, confirming shipment dates, quantities and condition of the merchandise. This extended visibility allowed logistics professionals to not only streamline operations and reduce costs but to also make decisions based on real information as opposed to optimistic speculation.

This information sharing was essential on a tactical level, but it also enhanced the precision of an all-important exercise, determination of landed costs. As offshore labor costs became a smaller component in determining cost of goods sold, transportation and related expenses (duties, taxes, etc.) became a larger element of the overall cost of goods sold structure. Real-time access to this information augmented cost of goods sold calculations, helping companies to determine their margins more accurately. By mining its own operating information, the external third-party logistics companies contributed to these margin initiatives with mission-critical information on the per-unit costs of local and international transportation, customs clearance costs, as well as all duties and taxes.

SUMMARY

An understanding of the origins and subsequent evolution of Western management techniques is necessary to put new supply chain developments in their proper perspective. While the development of the MPC system and integrated logistics has helped to forge modern SCM thinking, it is important to note that they were both born of the mass production mentality of the early 20th century. In order to take the discussion on the history of SCM full circle, it is of equal importance to understand advances in Japanese management science in the post–World War II world.

NOTE

1. Thomas E. Vollman, William L. Berry, and D. Clay Whybark, *Manufacturing Planning & Control Systems,* Irwin McGraw-Hill, 1997.

3

LEAN MANUFACTURING

A quick return to the definition of supply chain management provided in Chapter 1 will remind the reader that it is a business discipline built upon a core philosophy. The development of most philosophical schools of thought is usually a continuation of or variation on an existing theme, and nearly all are a reflection of the times in which they were conceived. Most shifts in thought are based on experience, not theory, and are a phenomenon that can be observed in any area of human endeavor.

The supply chain management school is no exception to this belief, as it was influenced by several political, demographic, technological and commercial events during the course of the last century. Most definitely a product of globalization, the development of new supply chain tactics has been motivated by the market's demand for innovation, quality, availability and price. A familiar refrain is that the combination of sophisticated customers and brutal competition has engendered a sort of "commercial Darwinism" where supply chain velocity determines what species of company will advance.

There is no disputing the fact that mass production dominated the development of supply chain management in the first half of the 1900s. Of equal historical merit, it has been the principles of lean manufacturing that have most influenced global supply chain management since the 1950s. While this is a true statement, it is important to mention that lean itself was born of the work done by men like W. Edwards Deming in the areas of total quality management and statistical process control. This is but one example of how disciplines borrow the best that each has to offer in an effort to continually improve supply chain performance. Many Six Sigma tools (to be discussed in Chapter 8) have been borrowed from its predecessors, including lean manufacturing and statistical process control.

While recognizing the contributions of its predecessors, the original principles of lean manufacturing, along with further developments in lean thinking, have afforded a commanding view of the supply chain panorama. However, for any business philosophy to defy conventional wisdom, it has to stack up against the vigor of the marketplace. In order for this to happen, said philosophy has to be based on a value system that can be translated into action in the real world. In essence, if a company wants to create value, it must first be able to articulate what its own values are.

THE LEAN MANUFACTURING VALUE SYSTEM

The principles, goals and desired outcomes of the lean system were briefly presented earlier in this volume. While important, a more basic understanding of the discipline should be sought by asking what the values are that drive this philosophy.

If one were to look for a single thread that weaves its way through the lean tapestry, one would find that it is an emphasis on proactive participation by all parties engaged in the supply chain. Starting with client involvement, the same pursuit of communication, input and collaboration can be found in supplier relationships, across functional disciplines and embedded in employee development.

Similar to the case of supply chain management, tired clichés like "our most important asset is our people" have the potential to blunt lean's appeal. However, the more pensive manager will realize that this sincere, humanistic approach to business is what drives the entire system. Manufacturing techniques do not bring products to market; people develop the techniques that make production possible. Processes do not put merchandise in customers' hands; human beings design the processes that facilitate the purchases of goods and services. If both management and labor buy in can be achieved on this most fundamental aspect of the lean value system, its potential for building market dominance will know no limits.

How does the lean value system translate into competitive advantage? Given its comprehensive and integrated application across business activities, a study of the major components of lean is called for. The best way to conduct that analysis is to categorize them as mentality, manpower, machinery and methodology. Using the doctrine of lean manufacturing first mentioned in Chapter 2 as a guide, this breakdown is easier to follow:

1. A holistic view of supply chains, beginning with product concept through final delivery to the customer
2. A team approach based on a multi-skilled workforce and employee input
3. Commitment to continuous improvement of all processes
4. Elimination of waste throughout the supply chain

Mentality

The lean mentality can be succinctly characterized as the relentless quest for the removal of waste in all operations. For the lean manufacturer, waste appears in the form of excessive inventories, long cycle times, rework, underutilized floor space and the presence of personnel on the production floor who add no real value to the process. Elimination of this type of waste is achieved through the utilization of multi-skilled work teams bent on continuously improving all aspects of the manufacturing function.

It should be emphasized, however, that lean thinkers do not initiate their continuous improvement efforts on the production floor. The lean mentality is much broader in the sense that practitioners seek to build quality into all upstream processes that feed into the production environment. Starting with a customer-focused plan for product design, this practice revolves around the idea that it is better to feed quality into the process upstream as opposed to constantly fixing the same problems downstream. Basically, lean thinkers believe that the cost of quality is much less than the expense of fixing mistakes, especially after consumers already have made their purchases.

Because of all the challenges and potential for waste associated with a production environment, it made perfect sense for lean thinkers to focus their initial efforts there. Of major significance to the development of global supply chain management, however, is the fact that zealous lean companies have not stopped their initiatives with manufacturing. Now known as lean thinking,[1] the crusade to eliminate waste via continuous improvements has been applied to the entire supply chain.

If one considers the potential application of the lean mentality to other areas of business, the opportunities for improvement are endless. Most businesspeople agree that 20 to 30% of every sales dollar is consumed by non-value-adding activities or fixing mistakes. One can only envision the potential for applying the lean mentality in areas as diverse as bid responses, order management, billing and accounts receivable. The important point at this juncture is to adopt the lean mentality. Without it, analysis and applications in the areas of manpower, machine and methodology will never reach their full potential.

MUDA AND MAJOR LEAGUE BASEBALL

Ask Major League Baseball players Hideki Matsui and Ichiro Suzuki the meaning of the Japanese word "muda" and they will tell you it means "waste." Ask Major League Baseball Commissioner Bud Selig the meaning of the word and he will tell you it translates into lower attendance, smaller television audiences and big chunks of lost revenue.

Disciples of lean manufacturing know that the primary goal of any process improvement is to eliminate waste from all activities, including cycle times. Major League Baseball has discovered that its audiences are dwindling in part due to the length of the games and the minutes wasted during a cycle time of nine innings. Pitching changes, between-inning warm-ups and just plain stalling have all contributed to games going into the late hours of an evening. As such, fans are less likely to attend or watch entire games on television.

Major League Baseball is a business that has taken the time to bring operational definition to its critical-to-quality characteristic of game length. From an all-time slow in 2000 of three hours per game in the American League, the figure has improved each year. Major League Baseball set a goal in 2003 of 2 hours and 46 minutes, and as cycle times come down, many more fans will come back.

Manpower

The original intent of lean manufacturing with regard to manpower was to develop individuals with multiple skill sets. Employees who could multi-task would eliminate the need for so many people on the production floor. It is for this reason that manufacturing personnel have been trained not only in machine operation but also in basic problem solving, changeovers and machine maintenance. With newly acquired skills, employees can join multi-discipline work teams to pursue the continuous improvement initiatives so important to productivity.

Lean thinkers are convinced that the greatest amount of knowledge about a job, function or process lies closest to where the action takes place. The ability to harness the knowledge that production employees possess is integral to the lean thinking process. More implicit in this activity, however, is the need for employees to *want* to share their knowledge. The transformation of employees from corporate subjects to proactive citizens is perhaps the greatest challenge for lean thinking (or any other management discipline, for that matter). When employees believe that the company is truly interested in their opinions, ideas and general welfare, that transformation can begin.

The idea of the "commercial contract" presented in the Introduction to this book has strong ties to this component of lean management. However, in order for any contract to work, there must be an element of quid pro quo between the contracting parties. If employees are expected to make the extra effort and not just do the minimum required, there has to be reciprocity on the part of management. The early Japanese practitioners of lean manufacturing offered workers employment for life and advancement based on seniority. Cleary untenable in the new millennium, management and labor must work together to find new ways to create mutual interest in the well-being of the organization.

As also mentioned in the Introduction, training and education are integral to the development of proactive and concerned employees. Beginning with an education on the philosophy, value system and strategy of the organization, employees can begin the journey to a different professional lifestyle. The lean approach certainly emphasizes long-term investments in employee development, but also takes the concept a step further.

The lean mentality involves training for employees outside their field of expertise, often asking new, non-production employees to spend their first weeks in manufacturing. This mentality also extends beyond the walls of the company in the form of sponsoring employee exchange programs between suppliers and customers. In the global arena, it is now common to see promising young executives spend time in operations overseas, gaining invaluable experience in market tastes, cultures, business practices and languages.

Just as the lean mentality can extend beyond the manufacturing floor, so can the specific practices associated with the application of manpower. Quality circles, for example, can be developed in an office environment and include functions like purchasing, human resources, information technology or sales. Office staff who are oftentimes far removed from the "front line" should have frequent opportunities to visit plant sites, suppliers or even customers.

There is perhaps no more fertile ground for cross-training than the administrative or functional areas of a company. Cross-training not only shifts an employee's frame of reference from a functional to a process-based orientation but also contributes to productivity. If people are trained to do more than one job, they are intellectually stimulated, have greater self-esteem and are more valuable to the organization. A multi-functional background also makes it easier for employees to move about the company, gain more experience and make more money.

The application of these elements of lean management to all aspects of an enterprise can create a virtuous circle where continuous improvement becomes second nature. Whether in manufacturing, logistics or some far-removed back-office function, the harnessing of manpower to eliminate waste is a prerequisite for success in global markets. Without it, the sheer scope of international operations will create an organization with too many people engaged in activities that bring no value to the customer experience.

Machinery

It could be said that the entire lean movement began with the need to better utilize machinery. For the Japanese, this was born more of necessity than anything else. Right after World War II, Japanese companies had very little funds to invest in mass production technology. They needed equipment that was multi-purpose and that could be utilized in small production runs. It was this reality that compelled Japanese engineers to design innovative ways to change over machines quickly, as well as use the same machines for multiple production purposes.

Quick changeovers and multi-purpose machines allowed engineers to use less space and better utilize the scarce assets they possessed. Also, the combination of operator problem solving and small production runs caused any defects to show up almost immediately, instead of at the end of the production run. Early defect detection practically eliminated the need for rework areas, thus saving space due to the versatility of the machines employed. This effect was probably the first step in the virtuous circle of lean manufacturing, promoting and perpetuating the benefits of lean thinking through the entire manufacturing process.

By now, it should be clear that the lean mentality can be applied to any facet of a business. But if machinery is only found in the factory, how can the principles of lean thinking for plant and equipment be used in an office environment? While this may seem like a perplexing question at first, some examples will illustrate its transcendental effectiveness.

There are certainly no production machines in an office, but there are plenty of desktop computers, fax machines, scanners, printers and telephones. Any lean-inspired factory layout is designed to minimize the amount of walk time for employees. The same can be done in an office by organizing copiers, faxes, etc. to allow quick and easy access. Three people waiting in line to send a fax is no less wasteful than a bottleneck on a production line.

Too many people sharing a network printer is but another example of waste and lost productivity. Perhaps the greatest of offenders is an overloaded system, which can cause wait times between screen changes that add up to hours of lost time every day. Most people can recall an instance when they waited far too long at their laptop for a critical e-mail attachment to finally download.

If you are still not convinced about the application of lean principles to office equipment, think for a moment about the nature of the latest innovations in this area. The Japanese have led the charge in eliminating discrete copiers, scanners and fax machines. Cutting-edge equipment incorporates all features into one unit, eliminating not only walk time between pieces of equipment but the machines themselves. Also, because the units are integrated and increasingly smaller, they take up less office space. It is clear that the need for space can easily be cut down in a well-designed office layout. It is no coincidence that the Japanese brought this innovation to world markets based on the principles of lean product design.

Methodology

It is relatively easy to articulate the principles of a business discipline when it is broken down by mentality, manpower and machinery. Things become a bit dicier, however, when it comes to describing the specific methods used to achieve better productivity and profitability. The history of lean manufacturing abounds with examples of how work teams, multi-purpose machines and small lot sizes achieve monumental gains in product variety, quality and reliability. In a world characterized by globalization and outsourcing, it is best to shift the conversation on methodology to the two most pressing aspects of the lean school: inventory management and supplier relationship management.

INVENTORY MANAGEMENT

Discussion of just-in-time (JIT) inventory practices as well as a comparison with other inventory management techniques is provided in Chapter 7. While that analysis is relevant to a broader study of inventory management, JIT is actually an offshoot of the overall lean manufacturing body of work and should first be studied in that context.

With a focus on zero defects, small production runs and a demand-driven pull environment, JIT embodies all of the lean principles. For the lean manufacturer, the greatest manifestation of waste can be found in unneeded quantities of raw materials, work in process and finished goods. It was this desire to eradicate inventories that brought about new thinking in the areas of quality at the source, quick changeovers and small lot sizes. As a manifestation of the virtuous circle that embodies the lean enterprise, inventory management starts the process in motion.

At the heart of JIT is the idea that raw materials should be pulled down a production line as a function of demand. As already mentioned, this is a complete reversal of the mass production mentality of pushing goods down the line to maximize output. Because production is demand based, investments in raw materials are synchronized with the exact moment of need on the production line. As a natural by-product of this practice, both work in process and finished goods stocks are also minimized or, ideally, taken out of the equation entirely.

The primary way in which this is achieved is by a practice known as *kanban.* A Japanese term, kanban was first developed and practiced at Toyota. The process took more than a decade to perfect. Kanban is based on providing more parts for a production step only after the first allocation of parts in that step has been consumed. Also known as a two-bin system, the signal for the parts provider to send more raw materials to the consumption point is an empty bin sent back to the point of supply. In exchange for the empty return, a second, full bin is provided to the machine operator.

One does not need to be a production engineer to recognize the high level of risk associated with running a kanban system. If one step in the entire production process falters, the entire line goes down. While some perceive this likelihood as a huge risk, the Japanese see it as the most appealing aspect of the entire process. Without any inventory backup, operators and other production employees know that there is nowhere to turn if things go wrong. With such a high level of risk, it is DEFCON 5 at all times in the plant, with everybody on the lookout for potential problems long before they shut down a line.

The obvious question for global supply chain managers is how to run such a tight operation with suppliers and production lines spread across multiple continents. Running a JIT system within the confines of a purely domestic operation has been proven to be more than feasible. But what happens when a critical parts supplier is 5,000 kilometers and three time zones away? Development of domestic suppliers in the form of industrial campuses is one way around this dilemma, but it is not a foolproof solution. Also, vendor-managed inventories offer an alternate approach to assuring the reliable flow of goods. At this juncture in the evolution of international JIT practices, it may be prudent to focus on the principles of zero defects and no inventories while utilizing the time-tested element of manufacturing planning and control outlined in several sections of this book.

If JIT practitioners have any hope of achieving the full benefits of the discipline, it is going to have to come from better visibility into supply chains. Only when planners have a real-time and accurate view into the whereabouts of inbound shipments will they remove the safety net of buffer stocks. The World Wide Web has created the window into global supply chains, but a great deal of work remains to be done in the areas of system compatibility, open architecture and the adoption of standards. Perhaps the application of supplier-related principles of lean manufacturing will expedite this inevitable move forward.

SUPPLIER RELATIONS

The principles of lean manufacturing have been in use since the early 1950s. Since that time, many Western companies have improved their operations using its tools, but there are still those that lag behind. Companies at the forefront of lean thinking realize that as markets become increasingly global, the tactics associated with the discipline are even more relevant. Impatient customers with no tolerance for defects are but two reasons why organizations must continue to pursue excellence via lean manufacturing. Of equal relevance for the supply chain management movement, the rapid globalization of markets and the trend toward outsourcing are two more compelling reasons to get on board.

The lean attitude toward product defects centers around the idea that all upstream processes impact the quality of the finished products coming off the line. In the lean factory, poor quality is not compensated for at the end of a production run via rework; quality is built into every step of the process, beginning with product design. Lean enterprises understand that quality begins well outside the confines of their factories with suppliers, strategic partners and, most importantly, customers. If an organization is unable to share lean practices with its business partners, it will never approximate the real potential of lean manufacturing. In a manufacturing environment, the journey to lean excellence centers on supplier relations.

As is the case in all lean-related endeavors, the drivers behind supplier relationship management focus on the elimination of waste and continuous improvement. Within that framework, the basic principles of the approach are as follows:

1. Strategic collaboration with raw materials suppliers on all facets of procurement, from component design to final delivery
2. Rationalization of supplier networks and the creation of open-book partnerships
3. Long-term relationships as opposed to short-term contracts
4. Recognition of the profit motive, with an emphasis on cost reductions over time

In order for international organizations to increase velocity in their supply chains, the above principles must be applied consistently across all theaters of operation. While this is indeed true for partnerships with raw materials suppliers, the same principles and goals can be applied to all types of vendor endeavors. Beginning with raw materials suppliers, lean companies must find ways to increase velocity in product design and time to market. Given the capricious and fast-changing tastes of today's consumer, speed is a requirement for any company to create sustainable competitive advantage.

TIME TO MARKET AND SUPPLIER RELATIONS

Whereas inventory is the foremost manifestation of waste on the production floor, a major culprit in supplier relations is time. In the mass production model, the greatest consumer of man-hours has been the progression of product concepts through design engineering and production. There are many reasons why it has historically taken so long to get products off the drawing board and into customers' hands, including the engineering of complex dies, problems with production process layouts and delays in building production equipment. While each represents a potential bottleneck, lean thinkers analyze ways in which early involvement of raw materials suppliers can eliminate time wasted on these and other important components of the overall process.

The traditional buyer/supplier relationship has always been adversarial by nature. Neither party wants to share information about its internal operations so as not to tip its hand on cost structure, forcing one of the parties to leave margin on the negotiating table. Without providing any visibility into their design or production processes, manufacturers show up at a supplier's door with a component schematic, much like the proverbial stork shows up at a house with a newborn. Without insight as to how the component works with other raw materials or how its design (or lack thereof) will impact the production process, the vicious circle of redesign and engineering changes begins. By the time this exercise is completed with the hundreds of suppliers involved in a product launch, months and years can pass.

Lean supply chain managers, on the other hand, involve raw materials suppliers in the design process from the very beginning. From the outset, suppliers have a line of sight toward the final product. They understand not only the role their component(s) plays in making the product work but also how design of their raw materials contributes to the manufacturability of the good in question. An element of the lean school that has yet to be mentioned in this work is component design for ease of assembly, which figures prominently in the early stages of supplier relationships. A throwback to the days of interchangeable parts, it is for this reason that suppliers play such a prominent role in the collective design of components.

One way that manufacturers and suppliers work together is by sharing employees. It is quite common for lean supply chain members to engage in employee exchange programs or be members of quality circles at each other's facilities. This open exchange of information and insight into each other's processes allows for the analysis of the entire materials management process instead of just fragments of isolated activities.

Once vendors actually begin moving raw materials into a factory, all parties involved adhere to the principles of JIT. Moving from the page to the stage, open communication and shared learning are equally critical as lines are fed based on product demand.

One result of lean thinking is the need to invest considerable time and resources in supplier relationships. With finite manpower, time and travel budgets, this aspect of lean manufacturing forces producers to rationalize their supplier network and pare down the number of vendors by an order of magnitude. While sole sourcing is the extreme of lean supplier management, the philosophy still calls for a major philosophical shift in vendor relations. Gone are the days of inviting 30 companies to bid on a one-year contract and awarding the job to the cheapest bid. Lean managers develop strategic relationships with a much smaller supplier base and work with them to continually reduce costs across the supply chain.

The downsizing of supplier bases has considerable implications for managing global operations. With so many demands on people's time, the lean mentality is quite simple: the fewer players there are, the more time that is freed up to develop legitimate long-term relationships. The amount of time wasted in "managing" multiple vendor relationships and processes is difficult to measure but very easy to illustrate. Consider for a moment the typical bid process for goods and services in most companies.

The process starts with the manufacturer sending out 20 or more Requests for Information to potential suppliers. Based on the quality of the replies from the vendors, the list is shortened to 10 companies that will be invited to actually bid. By the time that takes place, three months has passed. During the interim, potential suppliers use woefully inadequate bid specifications to determine what their costs will be. When suppliers are not panicking about covering phantom costs, they are sucking up to the customer, jockeying for position based on past performance or connections.

After receiving the bids, the manufacturer will take another three months to create a short list of finalists that will be invited back for more thorough presentations, as well as the opportunity to "sharpen their pencils." At this point, rather than vendors and customer working together to take costs out of the supply chain, they are dreaming up ways to get over on each other. Oftentimes, the slant of vendors is to submit lowball pricing just to get in the game, with the implicit intent of raising prices later on. They are betting that they can raise prices once they are in the door and hope that the customer will quietly take the increase as opposed to the high-profile and professionally embarrassing exercise of reopening the bid process. By the time somebody starts moving product, the relationship is tainted, perpetuating the already antagonistic nature of supplier relations.

If this is the drill during a bid process, one may be compelled to ask what the rest of the relationship is going to be like. Lean thinkers usurp this vexing question, as well as the whole drawn-out exercise, by working strategically with suppliers to remove both cost and waste from the supply chain. Lean manufacturers understand that vendors have to make a fair profit, but also realize that the highest price they will pay is probably the original price submitted. From the inception of a long-term program, vendor and manufacturer work together to remove waste from the process. As costs go down, so do prices to the manufacturer. This is the exact opposite of the first example, where the lowest price a manufacturer will pay is more than likely the original bid price. The combination of incremental costs and time wasted on bid processes is one area that the lean mentality attempts to eradicate.

With so much information sharing between supplier and manufacturer, an open-book policy on costs has to be present in the relationship. This is important in keeping all parties honest, but it also brings supply chain managers to an important catchphrase in the modern supply chain management lexicon: supply chain transparency. Elaborated upon further in Chapter 5 on outsourcing, it is transparency that brings velocity to supply chains. With the proliferation of outsourcing in global business models, the application of this same approach will enhance time to market, productivity and profitability for participating parties.

SUPPLIER TIERS

Whether in a lean environment or not, the quickest way to rationalize supplier relationships is to work with fewer of them. The lean mentality toward vendors is not, however, based solely on taking companies out of the game. In fact, if a manufacturer reduces its supplier list but continues with the same approach toward its relationships, the result will be even worse than the original version. The rationalized list represents a smaller universe of adversaries, oftentimes forcing the manufacturer to invite other companies back to bid in order to "level the playing field." Supplier creep sets in, with the companies that were originally shut out of the bid sensing desperation and therefore bidding higher. The possible ramifications of such an attitude toward working with fewer suppliers are endless, and none brings any value to the manufacturing process.

While supplier rationalization is a powerful agent for increasing velocity, the lean methodology also employs a concept known as supplier tiers to exact additional supply chain benefits.[2] Supplier tiering involves the categorization of suppliers by their level of component integration and direct contact with the manufacturer. For example, a traditional manufacturer of cellular phones may use ten different suppliers to source the parts that go into the phone's keypad. The lean manufacturer, on the other hand, will create an arrangement with one supplier (tier I) that is responsible for delivering the entire keypad to the manufacturer's plant. The suppliers that provide parts to the tier I supplier are known as tier II vendors, suppliers that work with tier II are then tier III suppliers, and so on.

Use of the tier methodology reduces the level of daily contact with multiple suppliers, but by no means reduces the transparency of the entire supply chain. Quite the contrary, more advanced lean manufacturers organize suppliers into associations that are in constant contact with the manufacturer. This methodology once again brings the importance of supply chain transparency to the forefront of modern thinking. With this type of organization, a manufacturer has full visibility into supply chain activities but does not have to manage relationships on a daily basis. In the case of the cellular phone manufacturer, for example, vendor associations could be organized by component type, with electronic, electromechanical and plastics vendors represented.

As more companies engage in outsourcing part or all of their manufacturing, is it possible to consider the contract manufacturer a "super tier I" supplier? If the contract manufacturer indeed takes over the manufacturing planning and control functions alluded to in Chapter 5, it would behoove both the contract manufacturer and the contracting party to take a lean approach to managing relationships across all tiers. What is important is that all parties are actively engaged in nurturing these relationships from product concept to final delivery. Although this practice is not fully evolved to date, continuation of traditional supplier management tactics in a globally outsourced model would be the death knell for supply chain velocity.

EXTENDING LEAN SUPPLIER MANAGEMENT

At this point, it should be clear that the application of lean tactics extends well beyond factory environs. Whether one analyzes the discipline from a manpower, machine or methodology perspective, the potential for applying tactics developed on the production floor to other areas of a business is huge. The combination of inherently complex supply chains with the trend toward outsourcing makes this point even more salient and offers boundless opportunity for the continued elimination of supply chain waste. Because most of the participants in a manufacturing-based supply chain provide a product or service to the manufacturer, the search for increased supply chain velocity should focus on those relationships. While this discussion has articulated many of the finer points of managing raw materials suppliers, it now turns to the quest for velocity via the refinement of other supply chain alliances.

A major postulate of this book is that logistics plays a transcendental role in global supply chain management. Given its pervasive involvement in both materials and distribution management, logistics can be viewed as the glue that holds the entire supply chain mosaic together. With offices and expertise in markets around the world, the inclusion of third-party logistics (3PL) companies in supply chain design is essential. From a tactical perspective, potential improvements in areas such as order management and documentation flow are plentiful and can be facilitated by the 3PL firm.

THE LEAN LOGISTICS CHAIN

Much like the exercise associated with raw materials suppliers, the first step in bringing lean practices to logistics is to reduce the number of service providers. It is quite common for large global players to employ dozens of freight forwarders, customhouse brokers, distribution outfits and trucking companies in support of their global supply chains. This type of structure creates the need for armies of administrative personnel to engage in areas like rate negotiations, cargo tracking and the auditing of freight bills.

While each of these areas is important to an organization, the back-office administration of *multiple* relationships is wasteful and adds no value to the customer experience.[3] Given the depth and breadth of today's global 3PL companies, a multi-national manufacturer should be able to manage all major theaters of operation (Asia, the Americas, Europe, the Middle East and Africa) by using no more than four service providers. In many cases, progressive users of logistics services have reduced their number of suppliers to as few as two or even one.

The administrative relief associated with rationalizing 3PL relationships allows organizations to focus on the real business of supply chain management: the control of landed costs, stabilization of lead times and the pursuit of reduced inventory levels. When 3PL companies are brought into existing supplier associations or quality circles to offer their logistics perspectives on supply chain management, the benefits that accrue to the enterprise begin to multiply.

The nature of logistics chains and their myriad participants also lends itself to the lean concept of supplier tiering. During the course of the last 15 years, many organizations have seen the benefit of designating lead logistics providers (LLPs) or "4PLs" to coordinate the entire logistics chain. Conceptually identical to the idea of a tier I supplier, LLPs are responsible for organizing all service providers into a cohesive whole, delivering logistics solutions much the way that tier I suppliers deliver assemblies to a manufacturer.

Not only does the LLP model bring direct cost savings to a supply chain, it also affords the transparency so critical to global operations. Now in a logistics environment, organizations have full visibility into the process without the burden of daily administration. Under this model, supply chain executives are expected to manage relationships and processes, not tasks. In that sense, the systemic integration of lean supplier management across all vendor relationships makes the whole much greater than the sum of the parts taken individually.

Once the work of rationalizing logistics chains is complete, the task of removing waste can begin. Many examples of non-value-adding activities can be found in a logistics operation, including overspending on services, administrative overload, extended transportation lead times and redundant processes. For purposes of tactical illustration, a focus on the role of documentation and the waste associated with its journey across the supply chain provides a harvest of low-hanging fruit ripe for the picking.

Every time cargo or information changes hands in the supply chain, a document is generated. Whether an invoice, warehouse receipt, customs entry or pre-alert, the number of documents that accumulate during a transaction is staggering. If the logistics function is as far-reaching as claimed (and it is), why not utilize its omnipresence to work on taking documentation waste out of supply chains? Since 3PL companies already provide a variety of documentation services, why not extend the concept further and remove unnecessary steps from the process?

A simple example of removing waste from the logistics chain is to use the same 3PL provider at origin for cargo forwarding and at destination for customs clearance. Originally presented in the section on integrated logistics, use of the same service provider at origin and destination removes several steps from the process. Because waste is interpreted as time unnecessarily spent, the two-day saving in documentation exchange is of immediate appeal to lean supply chain managers.

It is also suggested that 3PL firms provide a quasi audit of commercial documentation when they receive shipments from exporters. The 3PL firm matches the accuracy of documentation from shippers with the transportation documents generated by its own personnel, thus assuring the avoidance of customs-related bottlenecks at the destination. If this practice is already in place, why not have the 3PL firm issue commercial documents on the exporter's behalf? Since the 3PL firm already spends a considerable amount of time fixing mistakes, this process improvement makes a lot of sense. That fact that many companies have employed 3PL firms to take over their entire order management function is proof positive that lean thinking works in a logistics environment.

SUMMARY

Examples of how supply chains can be enhanced through continuous improvements in logistics supplier management are not hard to find. The same can be said of managing vendor relationships in areas as diverse as legal advice, payroll outsourcing and external training. The point is that all members of an organization have to embrace the lean mentality and share it with each of their constituents. If the philosophy is understood, methods can be developed that cut across functional lines and bring value to the harnessing of manpower and machines.

For all of the reasons discussed in this chapter, supply chain velocity is one of the most important variables in an organization's competitive equation. To that end, an understanding of the history, philosophy and methodology behind lean manufacturing is necessary to apply its value to contemporary supply chains. While this has been the goal of Chapter 3, the next chapter prepares supply chain managers for the application of the lean discipline in a much different, global setting.

NOTES

1. James P. Womack and Daniel T. Jones, *Lean Thinking,* Simon & Schuster, 1996.
2. James P. Womack, Daniel T. Jones, and Daniel Roos, *The Machine That Changed the World: The Story of Lean Production,* Harper Perennial, 1990, p. 146.
3. An interesting benchmarking case for lean logistics can be found in Audie G. Lewis, *Streamlining Healthcare Operations: How Lean Logistics Can Transform Health Care Organizations,* Jossey-Bass, 2001.

4

THE IMPACT OF GLOBALIZATION ON SUPPLY CHAIN MANAGEMENT

The globalization of business is the best thing to happen to supply chain management (SCM) in the last 30 years. This seemingly bold statement is made not because globalization has made SCM any easier — quite the contrary. Driven by overwhelming market forces, globalization has forced countries and companies to become more efficient, creating the infrastructure and competitive advantage necessary to survive the early rounds of a brawl that will undoubtedly go beyond the last bell. Unfortunately, whether one is in favor of or against globalization is irrelevant for purposes of this discussion.

Although both sides of the globalization debate have valid points, the fact is that it will continue. Reality dictates that if companies intend to not just survive but prosper in a hyper-competitive environment, they would be well advised to acknowledge the complex nature of the terrain in which they find themselves deployed. What *is* relevant to this discussion, however, is a basic understanding of what globalization is and its significance to the field of SCM

GLOBALIZATION, THE WORLD TRADE ORGANIZATION AND TRADE AGREEMENTS

Globalization assumes many faces, but in the realm of economic development it revolves around the nurturing of commerce through the removal of both tariff and non-tariff barriers to trade. Driven mainly by the World Trade Organization (WTO) and its predecessor, the General Agreement on Tariffs and Trade (GATT),[1] countries that embrace globalization allow access to their markets through lower tariffs while seeking reciprocal business opportunities in member countries around the world.

On one side, reduction or removal of high tariffs allows for broader access to target markets, a scenario that purportedly promotes a more even distribution of quality products across demographic strata. Of equal importance, removal of non-tariff barriers to trade (import licenses, inspections, quotas, etc.) facilitates and accelerates the movement of goods around the world, an element of globalization that is not lost on enterprises interested in optimizing their lead times.

FREE TRADE AND THE U.S. CONSTITUTION

The perceived and real benefits of globalization have not come without acrimonious debate. On the one hand, big business boasts of a better world through ubiquitous access to market-priced goods and services. Opponents of globalization point out salient negatives, including environmental abuses, human rights issues and child labor exploitation. The high-profile protests of the World Trade Organization in Genoa and Seattle are but the vanguard of a movement that is as relentless as the very pace of international trade.

The United States has had no shortage of exchanges between these opposing groups, both of which have valid points to make. It is instructive to note, however, that regardless of one's opinion, the stage was set for free trade in the United States when the Constitution was written in Philadelphia in 1787. While recognizing administration-specific trade agendas over the years (Abraham Lincoln was a staunch protectionist, for example), the genesis of free trade can still be traced to the tenets of Article 1, Sections 8 and 9 of the Constitution.

The commercial success of the United States over the last 200 years can be attributed to many factors. The good fortune of being born on the cusp of the Industrial Revolution created an environment of invention and innovation unprecedented in the history of mankind. Also, investment in infrastructure for the development of roads, rail, ports and then airports has accelerated the pace of growth considerably. It is no coincidence, however, that just as the aforementioned articles of the Constitution set the stage for international growth, it is feasible to argue that they also established a structure that was highly conducive to domestic trade.

From a national perspective, Section 8 of Article 1 establishes a common currency for the entire country. A seemingly innocuous occurrence, one need only look to Europe prior to the introduction of the euro to understand the ramifications of a multi-currency structure and how it complicates business.

Another important cornerstone for the growth of domestic trade in the

Organizations like the WTO have also promoted globalization through the development of policies in the areas of trademark, patent and copyright protection. Member countries are pledged to adhere to WTO rules regarding these points, particularly as they relate to the enforcement of infringement of said rights. These are important issues to companies that have historically invested quite aggressively in the pursuit of patents, only to have them pirated by rogue entities that have never been prosecuted by their own governments. The knowledge that trademarks, copyrights and patents of WTO members are protected is critically important to companies in industries like pharmaceuticals, music and wearing apparel, encouraging them not only to export products but to establish a presence in international markets.

United States can be found in Article 1, Section 9, a point that clearly prohibits internal tariffs. This means that no customs duties can be affixed to goods traded between the states, nor can any customs formalities be executed at each state's border. Needless to say, this point had a clear effect on landed costs and transit times from the earliest days of interstate commerce, making quick and cost-effective access to products commonplace for the American consumer.

In a more contemporary sense, the Constitution has also had a profound effect on international trade. Article 8 made three important contributions to the growth of commerce via its establishment of foreign exchange policy, a common external tariff and trademark/patent protection. With regard to the first point, the ability of a merchant to know exactly the value of both domestic and foreign currency at any given moment is vital to running a profitable business. Second, the common external tariff meant that the same customs duties would be applied to all products in a uniform fashion on a national level, regardless of the port/state of entry. Once again, consistency and predictability of landed costs are essential to even the most nescient of business models. Finally, patent and trademark protection encouraged investment in R&D, activities that accelerated and perpetuated the innovation of the Industrial Revolution well into the present day.

Article 9 also made a tangible contribution to the proliferation of international business in that it prohibits export taxes. Any tax makes a product more expensive, and although prosaic in a modern context, the elimination of export duties in the late 1700s was considered ultra-modern economic policy.

So, as the debate rages between those in favor of or against globalization, one point is certain. As it relates to U.S. citizens exercising their right to free speech under Article 1 of the Bill of Rights, those citizens should realize that the same Constitution is what paved the way for international trade. In that context, all involved in the debate on globalization would be well advised to read a bit further in the Constitution to understand exactly with what they are dealing.

Without question, today's supply chain executive must be armed with the knowledge of what globalization is and how entities like the WTO and its various trade initiatives impact SCM. Once this knowledge is acquired, a more tactical, micro-level understanding of how these policies and decisions trickle down to an operational level is required for companies to respond intelligently. In the case of the WTO, the reduction of tariff and non-tariff barriers to trade has encouraged investment by foreign companies in both existing and emerging markets, changing the business model from arm's-length business agreements to much more integrated, ownership-oriented arrangements.

Whereas companies once exported and imported through agents or commercial representatives, now many have set up shop in foreign markets, creating buying and/or selling entities of their own. As these changes occur, the differences in supply chain dynamics become much more pronounced, creating the need to contract local expertise, language skills, knowledge of logistics infrastructures and financial savvy. It is the ability to quickly adapt to these and other changes wrought by globalization that will determine who the most successful supply chain players will be. Without an understanding of the cause-and-effect relationship between macro-economic policy and the corresponding requirements of tactical supply chain execution, companies will be left to speculate as to their hopes for success.

THE TRADE AGREEMENT

Independent of the WTO, another driver of changing supply chain dynamics is the trade agreement. The countries of the world are picking sides, and the more astute organizations will not only react to change but either directly or through industry associations put themselves in a position to influence the content of these trade agreements. Whether one focuses on the ramifications of the European Common Market, the North American Free Trade Agreement (NAFTA), the Association of Southeast Asian Nations (ASEAN) or Mercosur, the implications for supply chains are apparent. Depending on the level of cooperation among participating countries, membership may imply important responsibilities like the free movement of goods, services and people amongst member states, a common external tariff or tariff-free trade between countries. At a minimum, countries are interested in building trade with each other but, more precisely, stimulating commerce within the confines of their own borders. Table 4.1 provides a sample of major trade pacts around the world and the magnitude of each.

Because trade agreements are preferential by nature, it is important to understand two supply-chain-related considerations that encourage a local market

Table 4.1   Major Trade Agreements and Unions

Name	Member Countries	Population (approx.)
Association of Southeast Asian Nations (ASEAN)	Brunei Darussalam, Cambodia, Indonesia, Laos, Malaysia, Myanmar, Philippines, Singapore, Thailand, Vietnam	500 million
Mercosur	Argentina, Brazil, Paraguay, Uruguay	230 million
North American Free Trade Agreement (NAFTA)	Canada, Mexico, United States	420 million
European Union	Austria, Belgium, Denmark, Finland, France, Germany, Greece, Ireland, Italy, Luxembourg, Netherlands, Portugal, Spain, Sweden, United Kingdom	370 million

presence: substantial transformation and local content. Originally a customs-related term, *substantial transformation* addresses the importation of raw materials that are manufactured or assembled into a new, or "substantially transformed," product. *Local content* rules, on the other hand, dictate that a certain percentage (35% in many cases) of the value of component parts and labor be of domestic origin. Needless to say, although beneficial for participating countries and companies, the supply chain ramifications can be intimidating.

Substantial Transformation

A good example of substantial transformation is the importation of plastic casing, circuitry and wiring from Asia into Mexico for manufacture into desktop computers. Taken individually, the ad valorem duty amount associated with each product and its country of origin normally would have to be paid. Under export-oriented programs designed by the Mexican government (Maquiladora or Pitex, for example), the raw materials can be temporarily imported free of duty and assembled into a computer, an entirely "transformed" product that qualifies as Mexican country of origin. From there, the Mexican company qualifies for NAFTA origin, reducing or entirely eliminating the amount of duty paid upon export to the United States or Canada.

Although the above arrangement is appealing at a macro level, the amount of expertise required to execute on the operational model is an entirely different story. For example, the documentation aspect of managing an export program requires error-free compliance. A company operating under this type of regimen in any country has to substantiate not only the value and origin of all its raw material imports but also the value, destination and proof of export of all of its finished goods. As is the case in most government-sponsored export programs, the inability to produce this documentation can result in exclusion from the program, assessment of duties or punitive fines and, in the worst of cases, potential loss of operating rights.

Additionally, the logistics of importing raw materials into Mexico from Asia are different than for direct Asian imports into the United States. The routings are different, flight and sailing availability varies and transportation costs can be higher. This means that lead times will be longer and cost of goods sold models will change accordingly. Apart from inbound logistics considerations, the nature of the customs infrastructure with its demanding procedures puts extra pressure on an already challenged supply chain.

The point is that Mexico is an ideal example of a country that is committed to participating in world trade. However, in order to enjoy the intended benefits of any export program or trade agreement, companies have to abide by the rules, with supply chain execution as close to 100% accurate as possible. If not, processes will be suboptimized and, as a direct result, margins depleted or consumed entirely.

Local Content

Local content rules are similar to substantial transformation in that they encourage a local presence, or at least domestic participation, in the production process. Designed to stimulate domestic activity in the form of job creation, local content rules apply to a combination of the amount of domestically sourced materials and local labor. Although many organizations still operate via agreements with external suppliers or representatives, local content rules have pushed the larger players into markets as commercial entities.

This rule changes the nature of supply chains due to the fact that companies must seek domestic suppliers for key components as well as have assembly/manufacturing operations to qualify for local labor input. Much like substantial transformation, this must fit into a company's strategy as it not only wants to qualify for country of origin status where it is operating but also seeks to gain the benefits of selling competitively within the trade block(s) to which the host country is party.

A brief return to the auto industry provides a relevant example of this phenomenon. As auto suppliers began to understand what local content rules meant to their operations, they quickly figured out that the presence of an assembly operation in foreign countries would not permit them to reach the content threshold. For this reason, many manufacturers established engine plants along with aggressive local supplier campaigns to quality for the coveted country of origin status.[2]

Local content changes the supply side of the equation as well. Whereas companies may have accumulated experience in exporting from their home countries, they probably lack the experience necessary to comply with the export laws of their host governments. Many countries, for example, still require customs clearance for exports. While an archaic practice, non-compliance with local regulations will freeze exports for weeks at a time. As countries expand over seas to benefit from trade agreements or country of origin rules, they should staff their operations with locals who possess the requisite level of knowledge to expedite the movement of goods.

THE INDUSTRIAL CAMPUS

Another interesting supply chain phenomenon that is a result of trade agreements, substantial transformation and local content rules is the advent of the "industrial campus." An offshoot of the preceding automotive example, these campuses are analogous to a shopping mall with its "anchor store" and supporting cast of smaller specialty stores. Basically, the anchor store serves as the big draw, with the other retail outlets rounding out the appeal of the shopping center. Industrial campuses are similar in that one or two major manufacturers will set up operations in a country and require (or, depending on their leverage, demand) that suppliers establish operations on the same campus. Needless to say, the resulting matrix of possible combinations of sourcing, manufacturing and selling is almost infinite.

One example of this is the development of industrial campuses by large high-tech manufacturers. It is common to see campuses of over 5,000 people that are a massive combination of company employees, suppliers and logistics service providers, all contributing to the production process.

These campuses can be found from Spain to the free zone of Manaus in northern Brazil, and the supply chain complexities that they foster are truly amazing. Whether dealing with lead time issues, production schedules or delivery commitments to distant customers, if countries and companies cannot develop the infrastructure, customs laws and internal processes to execute efficiently, the model will once again be compromised.

The bottom line is that companies engaged as commercial entities in trade agreements around the world are *chasing margin,* forever trying to optimize their models to the benefit of the organization and its shareholders. As our planet continues to be partitioned into competing factions, the ability to design supply chains around the realities of operating in these environments is paramount to financial success.

ACQUISITIONS AND INDUSTRY CONSOLIDATION

Another result of globalization is the consolidation of industries, through either attrition or acquisition. Whereas most companies can only hope to influence the content of trade agreements via industry associations or lobbying, the players themselves directly influence the structure that their particular industry assumes. One need look no further than the U.S. auto business for proof. When the industry began in the early 1900s, there were dozens of car manufacturers. In a very short period of time, a combination of competition, lack of financing, bad decisions and acquisitions drove the industry down to three major players. In contemporary times, consolidation has hit industries that include health care, telecommunications, pharmaceuticals, consumer electronics and high tech, all of which carry supply chain considerations of mammoth proportions.

Globalization has forced industries to consolidate for a variety of reasons. Issues that include market share, distribution networks, brand power, patents, economies of scale, time to market and access to key supplier/customer bases have all compelled organizations to systematically remove players from the field. Even though less congested, these new structures still offer considerable supply chain challenges. For example, as companies acquire competitors, the issue of how to best rationalize production facilities around the world is a daunting task.

Also, acquisitions and mergers force former competitors to share logistics routes and capacity in the form of available flights or sailings. Again, the challenge of rationalizing and allocating finite logistics capacity, in either a material management or distribution environment, is much more complicated than most organizations anticipate. Finally, competitors that once jockeyed for production capacity with raw materials suppliers or contract manufacturers must now determine how to balance the capabilities of these entities in the various markets where they operate. When viewed from any variety of perspectives, industry consolidation has made many supply chains at least as complex as their stand-alone predecessors.

GLOBAL SUPPLY CHAIN PLAYERS

Whether a company is responding to macro-economic events over which it has little control or pushing the global envelope via strategic maneuvers, globalization has forced SCM into the primary role of making or breaking a company's sales, gross profit and net income. At its most fundamental level, SCM is about the movement of goods, information and funds around the world.

There is no doubt that strategic decisions about target markets, product portfolios and pricing schemes determine to a great extent the success of any company. This being recognized, as competitive playing fields continuously even out over the medium term, it is the company that can *execute* on the tactical components of strategic SCM that will maximize its return on investment.

A look at the components of a basic international transaction illustrates the complexities that globalization has wrought on supply chains. At the risk of oversimplification, consider an international purchase made between a supplier in Hong Kong and a manufacturer in Warsaw, Poland.

This two-entity buyer/seller relationship does not include all of the departments from each organization engaged in the transaction. Also, this stripped-down exchange does not consider the input of banks, insurance firms, inspection agencies or other non-delivery-related entities. Finally, the example considers only the potential lines of communication that exist across the supply chain but not combinations involved in the handoff of goods, documentation or funds. The use of mathematical combinations will illustrate the complicated nature of global commerce, substantiating once and for all the importance of communication and execution to successful SCM.

In order to make the above point, one must first identify the nine entities involved in the Hong Kong to Warsaw exchange. The players in this simplified transaction are listed below and shown graphically in Figure 4.1.

- Hong Kong supplier
- Origin trucker
- Origin third-party logistics firm
- Origin customs
- Airline
- Destination customs
- Destination third-party logistics firm (customs broker)
- Local trucker
- Warsaw buyer

The essence of combinatorial math revolves around the use of factorials, an exercise designed to count the number of ways that a set of distinct objects can be arranged (or, in this case, communicate with each other). In the above example, those objects are the participants in the international transaction. If the order in which the objects are arranged is important, that arrangement is called a permutation. If order is not important, the arrangement is called a combina-

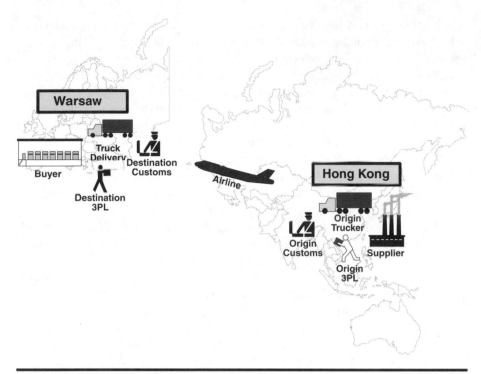

Figure 4.1   Supply Chain Players in a Basic International Transaction

tion. Because communication on a given supply chain issue can be initiated by any entity in the process and in any order, this example will be considered a combination.

Finally, it is important to observe that both permutations and combinations operate under the assumption of non-replacement, which means that any object can appear only once in a given ordering scheme. This is an important point for supply chain communications, as it implies that once a communication chain is initiated, an object cannot be counted again (when objects are used more than once, that is called an arrangement). In the real world, supply chain communications, and the people who initiate them, do reappear often in the form of callbacks, follow-up e-mails, etc. Even with this point in mind, the use of combinations remains a compelling method to illustrate just how challenging SCM really is.

The simplest use of factorials is to consider the total number of combinations of all objects in a group. For example, the number of ways to arrange ten people in a line is ten factorial, stated in mathematical terms as 10!. Expressed in longhand, the total number of possible combinations is the product of:

$$10 \times 9 \times 8 \times 7 \times 6 \times 5 \times 4 \times 3 \times 2 \times 1 = 3,628,800$$

In this case, there are 3,628,000 possible ways to arrange ten people in a line. Needless to say, application of this math to the referenced international transaction creates a scenario where the possible lines of contact seem endless. With nine entities in the most basic international transaction, the possible combinations are 9!, or 362,880. No wonder mathematicians use an exclamation point to express factorials!

The first observation one should make regarding the above calculation is that the number of times every player in the supply chain communicates with every other member is infinitesimally small. That statement is 100% correct under normal conditions, but in the case of disaster recovery or contingency plan execution, all parties would have to communicate with each other. What is not unusual is for several supply chain entities to be talking to each other at any given moment about dozens of different issues. Fortunately, combinatorial math recognizes this type of situation and offers a formula to measure a more reality-based scenario.

Consider for a moment a situation that is played out in supply chains around the world every day. The buyer's factory in Warsaw is about to go down for lack of a critical component sourced from the supplier in Hong Kong. Because the shipment is super hot, the normal ocean mode of transportation is upgraded to airfreight, which makes the exercise more expensive and puts unneeded pressure on gross margins.

Of the nine players in this supply chain, four will engage in direct communication to move the goods from Hong Kong to Warsaw, clear the shipment through Polish customs and deliver the components to the factory floor. They are the buyer, seller, origin freight forwarder and destination third-party logistics firm (forwarder and broker are unrelated). The number of ways in which these four entities can communicate is 4!, or 24 different combinations.

This may seem like a manageable number, but keep in mind that it applies to an isolated circumstance. This situation, when extrapolated to the hundreds if not thousands of communication lines established every day in a company's global supply chain, adds quantitative support to the prose surrounding the multi-dimensional nature of SCM.

As a final point, it is reasonable to state that at any given moment at least four out of the nine supply chain entities will be engaged in some form of communication with each other. This common situation creates the mathematical need to quantify a much more robust set of circumstances. The combinations formula used to quantify the possible number of combinations (C) that (r) objects can take from a set of (n) objects is

$$C,n,r = n!/r! \times (n - r)!$$

In the case of the Hong Kong to Warsaw supply chain, this means:

$$C = 9!/4! \times (9 - 4)!$$

For purposes of a nine-entity supply chain, there are 126 possible sequences in which any four entities can communicate amongst themselves.

As previously pointed out, the above examples do not include other players in the supply chain, nor do they include the various departments within each company. The reality of global supply chains from both a communications and operational perspective is that an organization would be hard-pressed to find a more troublesome operating environment.

If the number of supply chain players is a driver of the complexity of a business model, it would be prudent for management teams to identify all participants in their model and support that study with a definition of each player's role in the supply chain. Activities that are vital to minimizing the inevitable variances between planned and actual results include process design, task ownership, communication paths, documentation flows, technology links, escalation mechanisms and output measurement. As variances are identified, measures can be taken to continuously improve upon current structures and processes, hopefully leading all participants to supply chain excellence.

One such example of how companies have endeavored to improve upon supply chain structure while maximizing tactical performance is through the outsourcing of manufacturing and service activities. The study of outsourcing and its potential for improving supply chain performance must form an integral component of any SWOT (strengths, weaknesses, opportunities and threats) analysis or cost/benefit exercise undertaken by companies seeking innovative ways to improve their operating and financial performance.

NOTES

1. An in-depth understanding of the WTO and its structure and methodology for administering international trade is available at www.wto.org.
2. An example of local content rules can be found in the Japanese auto industry in the United Kingdom during the Thatcher administration. James P. Womack, Daniel T. Jones, and Daniel Roos, *The Machine That Changed the World: The Story of Lean Production,* Harper Perennial, 1990, p. 254.

OUTSOURCING AND GLOBAL SUPPLY CHAIN MANAGEMENT: CONTRACT MANUFACTURING

It is feasible to state that the growth in several branches of the outsourcing field has been precipitated by the onslaught of globalization. As operating environments become more complex, companies are compelled to seek outside expertise that complements their own arsenals of human, physical and digital capital.

By definition, outsourcing implies the use of third parties to carry out functions that are not native to the "core competencies" of an organization. In today's market, outsourcing has come to incorporate the subcontracting of services and/or manufacturing activities and extends to payroll, information technology, logistics, light assembly and full-blown manufacturing, among other areas.

Theoretically, a company outsources non-core competencies so that limited resources can be focused on activities indigenous to its business model. In reality, outsourcing creates the potential to reduce costs at an operating level (less in direct payroll, for example), as well as improve the balance sheet by reducing the value of assets that are shown there (less in raw materials inventory through outsourced manufacturing, as another example). In each case, supply chain managers must analyze the true value of outsourcing within the confines of strategic and tactical initiatives, determining both the operational and financial consequences of any such undertaking.

Regardless of the motivation behind outsourcing and the varying opinions on its long-term future with supply chain management (SCM), its effect on global processes and communications in undeniable. Entire outsourcing industries have been born under the guise of strategic focus and functional expertise, with thousands of jobs and billions in revenue generated in the process.

When focusing on the specific strategic and operational impact of outsourcing on SCM, the two most important industries to consider are contract manufacturing and third-party logistics. It is in these two businesses where the greatest potential for optimization of supply chain efforts can be found, with an in-depth understanding of how both industries play on operations a prerequisite to supply chain superiority. Taken in hand with globalization, the outsourcing component of global SCM and its bottom line significance to profitability and asset utilization is a field rich in potential for future productivity gains.

CONTRACT MANUFACTURING

By all indications, the contract manufacturing industry came to life in the 1970s. Whereas the original contract manufacturers (CMs) were engaged strictly in assembly and manufacturing operations, today's industry has broadened its scope to include product design, prototyping, manufacturing and distribution. In fact, in an effort to offer a complete package to their clients, several CMs have established sophisticated logistics entities that wrap inbound/outbound transportation and related services around manufacturing expertise.

It is precisely this broadening of scope that makes contract manufacturing such a key player in modern supply chains, creating myriad opportunities and challenges along the way. In perhaps one of the greatest paradoxes of contemporary SCM, the positioning of strategic third parties in the supply chain (be they CMs or otherwise) suggests that adding more players will create greater productivity gains. Obviously, this hypothesis contradicts the recent discussion on combinations and the complexity inherent to adding more objects to a group. If the math passes muster, how is it possible that adding an additional player to a supply chain will optimize performance?

The answer to this question lies in the concept of supply chain transparency introduced earlier in the book. Without a proper understanding of the term, transparency runs the risk of being relegated to the ranks of inane buzzwords that discount legitimate supply chain endeavors. Companies that embrace the lean mentality and have a solid grasp of international markets will, however, see immediate value in its application. Perhaps the best way to bring meaning to the practice of supply chain transparency is to first determine what it is not intended to do.

In the early days of outsourcing, many companies were under the erroneous impression that once a service or function was turned over to a third party, their involvement in operations ceased. Companies that assumed this approach quickly learned that outsourcing relationships actually require more management time, especially in the first months of a launch. The transition of an internal function to a third party requires extensive planning and the use of proven project management techniques. Value propositions, cost models, process designs and internal communication are but four of the many points that must be covered to assure the success of a cutover. As the transition nears completion, the management team can move away from dealing with daily operations to focusing on managing relationships, continuous improvements and taking waste out of all processes.

In the above context, transparency means that a company has a line of sight into daily activities but is not necessarily involved in them. Transparency also means that there is two-way visibility between the vendor and contracting party. This reciprocal visibility allows for continuous evolution of strategic planning between parties, as well as adjustments in their daily operations to accommodate market demand. This mentality is consistent with lean thinking and is a basic requirement in any supply chain relationship and in particular with CMs.

If the benefit of working with a third party is to allow the contracting company to focus on core competencies, this would imply that the need for daily management of certain players in the supply chain would be reduced. In the contract manufacturing model, for example, the entire manufacturing planning and control (MPC) process comes under the auspices of the CM, reducing the need for reams of internal and external communication at the contracting company. In essence, all of the operational activities once controlled by the internal purchasing, production planning and manufacturing departments are now the domain of the CM.

Based on the contracting party's forecast, the CM is responsible for master production scheduling, materials requirements planning (MRP), capacity planning and many other functions that require communication internally and across the external support structure. When executed properly, all of these activities become *transparent* to the contracting company. It is irrefutable that these activities still exist in the supply chain, creating a series of communication and tactical combinations that are complicated by their very nature. The point is that to the extent that the CM can manage its portion of the operation, the contracting party will be able to truly focus on core competencies. If the policies, procedures and communication links are in place, the value of using a CM can be most compelling.

Another example of supply chain transparency that exists in a contract-manufacturing-centric model is supplier relationship management. With most global players sourcing from over 300 suppliers at any given time, the investment in managing individual relationships is significant. Operationally, the role of MPC figures prominently in supplier relationship management, driven, of course, by the MRP process. Because MRP "explodes" raw materials requirements based on the forecast provided by the contracting company, all product-specific requirements must be shared with companies in the supplier base in order for them to begin their own planning and production activities.

As was the circumstance with an internally executed MRP module, the accuracy of gross to net exploding and lead time offsetting (now executed by the CM) is perhaps the most important aspect of the supply side of a contract-manufacturing-based operation. Returning to the nucleus of MPC, the entire exercise relies on how accurate the forecast is. In the case of a contract manufacturing relationship, it also depends on how well the parties communicate with one another, how flexible they are and, finally, how quickly they can adjust to the inevitable changes in the forecast. It should be obvious that the application of lean thinking to the management of these relationships will show benefits farther down the supply chain in time to market, product quality and profit margin.

The finished goods side of a contract manufacturing relationship offers the same amount of supply-chain-related opportunities and challenges. In fact, the demand component of the contract-manufacturing-centric business model may be even more exacting given that it implies delivery of finished goods to the end user. Recognizing that the operational importance of SCM revolves around the movement of goods, information and funds, special care must be taken in designing exactly how those processes will work.

For example, if the contracting party is shipping directly from CM manufacturing facilities to customers around the world, how will the documentation process be handled? Implicit in this model is a dual role for documentation, one between the CM and the customer (internal sales price) and the other the invoicing between the contracting party and its customer. Specifically, a process must be designed that allows the CM to invoice the contracting party for production and related services, while another set of commercial documents must be generated that shows the "transaction value" of the goods (price actually paid or payable).

While the CM and the contracting party use the former for billing purposes between themselves, the second set of commercial documents must be prepared and made available to the consignee in the country of import for customs clearance. Additionally, the contracting party will use these same documents to track its accounts receivable with the end user. It should be clear that the slightest mistake in documentation can create supply chain issues as varied as customs delays, additional duties, increased costs and the inability to collect receivables.

When analyzed at the proper level of detail, it is easy to see just how important management of a contract manufacturing relationship is. Implicit in a contract-manufacturing-based model is the wholesale shift of core manufacturing and related activities to an outside company, a move that has substantial operational issues associated with it. In this instance, it should be clear that the application of lean techniques, especially in the area of supplier integration, must be innate to the model. If not, the financial benefits of working with a CM will not reach their full potential.

CONTRACT MANUFACTURING, OPERATIONS AND FINANCIAL RESULTS

There are several variables that impact the quality of a supply chain, many of which have been discussed briefly in this chapter and will be covered in greater detail throughout the remainder of the book. One transcendent axiom of SCM, however, is the need to balance income statement performance (net income) with the balance sheet investments (both current and fixed assets). In fact, the two primary reasons why branded companies utilize CMs are to drive down costs and to reduce the investment in assets on their balance sheets.

Undoubtedly, the equilibrium between profitability and investment is the Holy Grail of SCM, and any outsourcing initiative must be evaluated with both sides of the equation in mind. For purposes of measuring the financial value of subcontracting manufacturing services, one of the best financial tools available to decision makers has been in use for over 80 years: the DuPont formula.

Mentioned briefly in the Introduction and discussed in detail as part of the case analysis in Chapter 11, the DuPont formula (return on investment) multiplies the result of a net margin percentage by the total asset turnover calculation. By using this tool and, more importantly, understanding the operational drivers of each ratio, executives can delve deeper into the cause-and-effect relationships that are the kernel of all supply chain activities. For reference purposes, the DuPont formula is

$$\text{Net income/Sales} \times \text{Sales/Total assets}$$

Even a superficial analysis of these two ratios and their product distills SCM down to an exercise designed to maximize profits while decreasing asset investment. Both ratios present interesting supply chain opportunities to the contract manufacturing industry, with the final results being a question of tactical execution. By breaking down the equation into net margin and asset utilization, some important supply chain considerations are exposed, each of which can be categorized by issues related to cost of goods sold, asset investment and overall supply chain velocity.

The most obvious question regarding the use of CMs is the cost. Cutting to the chase, can a CM produce the same quality of product as a branded company for less money? As it relates to expenses that represent cost of goods sold, working with a CM can offer many advantages. Bearing in mind that the major CMs have yearly revenues in the range of $10 to $20 billion, their leverage relative to raw materials purchases and supplier management cannot be overlooked. Also, expertise in production engineering, process design and manufacturing techniques can enhance productivity and time to market, both critical elements in today's fast-paced environment.

Another key advantage is the reduction in manufacturing-related payroll for the contracting party, as well as access to the less expensive labor that CMs enjoy from facilities in regions like Eastern Europe, Asia and Latin America. Also, because CMs operate in several geographic areas, their flexibility in shifting production to countries that benefit from the trade agreements alluded to earlier offers a breadth of operations that most branded companies can only dream of (or, conversely, may not even want).

Finally, a CM's ability to quickly change production sites can offer mid- to long-term benefits when dealing with fluctuating currencies. As currencies depreciate, production can be shifted to target countries where exports prices are more attractive as a result of the weaker currency. Based on these points, and many more that will be discussed in future chapters, the potential for CMs to take costs out of the supply chain is substantial. At the risk of becoming redundant, how well-branded companies structure their strategic and tactical links with CMs will figure prominently in the success of their business model.

From an asset perspective, the biggest attraction for branded companies to work with a CM is the appeal of reducing the amount of cash tied up in inventories and physical plant. By nature of the relationship between a CM and its clients, many take ownership of all raw materials inventories that go into the production process. Because raw materials oftentimes represents upwards of 35% of the total investment in inventories, financial relief in this form is very appealing. The potential benefit is equally attractive with finished goods, but a bit more complicated.

What happens, for example, when finished goods come off the line of the CM? Do they appear on the books of the contracting party or are they the property of the CM? If the good are shipped directly to a client, the issue is moot as a sale is recorded and inventories are depleted accordingly. However, if merchandise is going into finished goods inventory, it is a very important consideration. This is an interesting point because if the CM has ownership of raw materials at the front end of the process, it would somewhat defeat the purpose of the asset management exercise only to have them reappear as finished goods on the contracting party's books.

This scenario also begets the question of transfer of title during the supply chain processes. This is an important consideration from not only a balance sheet perspective but also invoicing, collection and product liability. These are all key supply chain questions that must be answered as part of the negotiation process, the result of which leaves important operational issues for all involved.

On a more long-term basis, the customer also decreases (or even eliminates) the need for investment in machinery and factories. This arrangement not only reduces the amount of money invested in fixed assets but also has implications for the income statement in the form of depreciation, a line item that detracts from net income. The combination of reducing investments in both current and fixed assets along with the added enticement of lessening the impact of depreciation on the income statement are benefits that have made contract manufacturing so alluring to branded companies. From this viewpoint, the potential upside of working with a CM goes to the heart of what SCM is all about and is a model that cannot be overlooked by organizations intent on thriving in global markets.

MAKE OR BUY?

Unfortunately, taking costs out of the supply chain and maximizing asset utilization arc much harder to do than they are to talk about. Apart from the many operational challenges associated with both exercises, there are several strategic, organizational, cultural and historical issues that must be dealt with when maximizing a contract manufacturing relationship. One logical place to begin a cost/benefit analysis of this nature is to determine whether or not the organization in question has a history of manufacturing or if it is a new player in either an existing or new industry. Needless to say, the supply-chain-related consequences of moving to a contract manufacturing relationship from an established manufacturing base are considerable.

Plant closings, asset liquidation and severance costs are but a few of the issues that must be considered when contemplating a "bet the business" decision of this magnitude. Conversely, it is much easier for a new entrant or an existing company introducing a new product line to establish a successful contract manufacturing relationship. There is no existing physical plant to deal with, no employees to lay off and no new organizational structure to contemplate, just the management of the contract manufacturing component of the overall business model. While by no means a guarantee of success, the latter scenario certainly carries a lot less baggage with it, eliminating (or at least reducing) the transitional issues that are such a major consideration for entrenched manufacturers.

There are many contemporary examples of the preceding scenarios, but two that best bring the point to light are Microsoft's venture with the Xbox and the birth of the hand-held computer or personal digital assistant (PDA) business. From the outside, it appears that Microsoft's decision to get into hardware hinged upon its ability to successfully undertake a relationship with a global contract manufacturer.

With no manufacturing expertise to speak of (other than burning CDs and packaging manuals), it would seem untenable for Microsoft to invest in manufacturing sites around the world for a product whose future would be determined by a notoriously fickle gaming community. Instead, Microsoft decided to focus on what it does best, software development, and leave the heavy lifting associated with sourcing, manufacturing and distribution to a well-established CM. With this model, Microsoft has a great deal of flexibility, access to world-class manufacturing capabilities and well-established supplier relationships and can piggyback on the existing logistics infrastructure of the CM. To date, it appears that the strategy has been successful.

Another business that has attracted the services of CMs is PDAs. This is an interesting situation, because it involves not only new entrants to the market but also traditional tech manufacturers that are broadening their product families. In the case of the former, the companies that are new entrants to the field are in essence marketing organizations. The business models of these organizations are characterized entirely by third-party relationships, from both a hardware and software perspective. Driven by a focus on product features and big-time marketing budgets, the new players contract for the manufacturing of the product while licensing the operating systems from outside companies.

So, apart from slick marketing and product features that are easily duplicated, what determines the winning recipe in the PDA arena? Not surprisingly, the answer is supply chain execution. To the extent that companies can keep up with product enhancements, maintain investments in marketing *and* manage global contract manufacturing relationships, their probability of success is favorable. Otherwise, they, like many other start-ups, will be crushed by the established players that have created hybrid relationships between internal and third-party manufacturing models.

When an established manufacturer introduces a new line of products to its portfolio, the ripple effect on the company's supply chain cannot be underestimated. Because it may be less cumbersome to launch a new product with a

CM as opposed to the transition of existing product lines, decisions as to what product(s) and in what quantity to outsource are important questions that must be answered prior to any launch.

A good example of this type of scenario involves globally branded manufacturers of personal computers and peripherals and how their endeavors with PDAs have impacted overall supply chain execution. It is no secret that many branded tech companies utilize a combination of in-house and third-party manufacturing in their supply chains, with results in the majority of cases favorable for all involved.

However, how a new product will be plugged into this model is a very interesting exercise that must consider factors such as allocation of production capacity (both internally and externally), use of common parts, leveraged buying power, similar production processes and shared target markets among products. In the case of PDAs, it seems that the outsourcing methodology has not only brought benefits related to product costs but has also allowed companies to acquire valuable experience in working with CMs in general.

Whether dealing with the transition of established manufacturers to a contract manufacturing model or new entrants in a virgin industry, the future of third-party manufacturing and SCM is at a crossroads. In both cases, the nexus of success lies in the ability to translate the high-level financial goals of profitability and asset utilization to an operating environment that emphasizes comprehensive planning and flawless execution. The contract manufacturing arena offers benefits from both an asset and bottom line perspective. How well those initiatives pan out in a company's annual report is a question of supply chain follow-through.

6

OUTSOURCING AND GLOBAL SUPPLY CHAIN MANAGEMENT: THIRD-PARTY LOGISTICS

Another supply chain entity that exemplifies the virtues of the outsourcing philosophy is third-party logistics (3PL). Originally designed to provide transportation and related services to regional importers and exporters, 3PL has evolved into a worldwide industry that complements customer initiatives through a host of primary and value-added services. Whether operating a vendor-managed inventory facility, aiding in product postponement projects or executing a precision merge in transit services, the modern 3PL firm operates in a truly global environment, with major players tallying sales north of $7 billion per year.

Interestingly enough, the same financial appeal that has spurred the growth of the contract manufacturing business is also innate to the 3PL business model. There are considerable gains to be achieved from both an income and asset utilization perspective when properly utilizing the services of a world-class 3PL firm, many of which actually complement the contract manufacturing model. Not unlike its kindred spirit in the contract manufacturing arena, use of a 3PL provider offers several opportunities and challenges, all of which are a function, once again, of process design, accountability and tactical execution. Whereas the logistics business was put in its proper historical frame in Chapter 2, the focus of the remainder of this chapter is the operational and financial implications of working with 3PL firms as part of an outsourcing initiative.

As the 3PL business became more global in scope, the attraction for organizations to engage such services grew in kind. Growth in the 3PL business implies having operations in major commercial areas around the world, a setup that can be very beneficial to importers and exporters. Depending on their own scope of operations, these organizations see considerable value in working with a company with a global network that features local expertise, key government or business contacts, knowledge of customs procedures, logistics infrastructure and a slew of other capabilities.

Also, 3PL activities transcend industries, creating a base of knowledge that will not be found in any other business. It is not unusual for 3PL employees to be working with Asian footwear imports one minute, medical equipment exports to Europe in another instant and Brazilian warehousing operations the next. The value of this accumulated expertise and access to non-proprietary best practices cannot be measured, and the application of lessons learned to other models has advanced the general state of the supply chain management (SCM) discipline. Perhaps it is for this reason that more and more supply chain players continue to recruit talent away from the 3PL industry to work for them.

In addition to the high-level appeal of having "another set of eyes" around the world, 3PL providers offer several benefits at an operating level. First and foremost, transportation costs can be reduced by contracting with a 3PL firm. Because a mainstay of the 3PL model is the consolidation of cargo between shipping points around the world, contracting with such an entity can reduce transportation costs. As a non-asset-based operator, the 3PL firm contracts for space allotments with steamship lines, airlines and trucking firms and gets a volume discount in exchange for its guarantee to pay for any unused space. The 3PL firm in turn sells the allocations to individual importers and exporters at a price lower than what most companies could negotiate independently. This creates a win/win situation whereby market prices are maintained at a competitive level, a valuable service is provided and the 3PL firm is compensated for its efforts. As mentioned previously, the 3PL community has built several value-added activities into its service portfolio, but freight consolidation and distribution still remain at its core.

THE PAPERLESS SOCIETY

A very important but often overlooked element of successful SCM revolves around the proper handling of paperwork. A false assumption that has been precipitated by the "digital age" is that hard-copy documents no longer play a role in international trade. There is no statement more erroneous in global business; the improper handling of both commercial (invoice, packing list, etc.)

Table 6.1   3 Cs Approach to Documentation Flows

Complete	Commercial invoice, packing list, bill of lading, certificate of origin, import license, certificate of inspection, letter of credit
Consistent	All information is the same on all documents: consignee/shipper name and address, product description, pieces, weight, country of origin, marks and numbers
Correct	All information on documents is accurate and matches cargo: labels, piece count, purchase order number, sales order number, import license number

and transport (bill of lading or airway bill) documents is the fastest route to paralyzing an entire supply chain. As first mentioned in the context of lean thinking in Chapter 3, a 3PL firm can play a value-adding role in the proper handling of documentation.

The key to successful management of document flows depends on adherence to what can be called the "3 Cs," or correct, complete and consistent, as summarized in Table 6.1. "Correct" means that all information is consistent with the physical merchandise (weight, product description, number of pieces, etc.) and characteristics of the transaction (shipper and consignee information, unit price, currency, etc.). "Complete" means that no individual document is missing from the packet.

Requirements vary from country to country, but a complete document package might consist of the commercial invoice, packing list, certificate of origin and ocean bill of lading. If any one of these documents is missing, the shipment will be delayed at some point in the chain, most likely in customs. "Consistent" is meant to convey the need for all documents to match in terms of their content. Shipper addresses, notify parties, country of origin and marks and numbers are but a few of the items that must be exactly the same on each document. If, for example, the consignee address on the commercial invoice does not match the address on a certificate of origin, delays are inevitable, with the possibility of fines or product confiscation very real, depending on the country with which one is dealing.

With a realistic understanding of the importance of proper documentation, the value that 3PL firms can bring to this element of SCM is unimpeachable. In an export transaction, the 3PL firm at origin receives not only the merchandise but also the commercial documentation that is intended to accompany the cargo. It is at this point that the 3PL firm generates its own transport documentation, using the 3 Cs methodology to match it to the commercial set provided by the seller. Finally, the 3PL firm checks the documentation against the labels, marks and numbers on the merchandise itself, in order to minimize at origin the probability of problems farther down the supply chain. Given that the majority of all logistics-related problems are generated upstream in the process yet only manifest themselves downstream (when it is too late), this procedure enhances supply chain execution with a minimum of additional investment or expense.

When dealing with export transactions, the 3PL firm can offer similar benefits through its knowledge of requirements from both the country of export and the destination country. Using its global network and access to local expertise, the 3PL firm can again take an upstream approach to avoiding downstream difficulties. Whether working with documentation or physical cargo, imports or exports, the operating expertise offered by the 3PL firm is indispensable to the proper management of any supply chain.

From only a pair of examples, it should be obvious that the value proposition of a 3PL firm is very consistent with the lean mentality. First, the idea of building quality into upstream processes is native to the 3PL operation. The presence of 3PL firms in major operating centers around the world also offers the opportunity for local participation in quality circles, supplier associations and general continuous improvement initiatives. Given the task-intense nature of moving goods around the world, it also is a prime area for continuous improvement initiatives. The examples of documentation flows are but one manifestation of this potential and should be viewed as the tip of the iceberg. If the objective of lean thinking is to eliminate waste by removing redundancy, unnecessary handoffs and rework, the logistics field is a good place to seek improvements.

CUSTOMS BROKERAGE

A service offered by most 3PL firms that not only complements but also begins to integrate logistics activities is customhouse brokerage. This process is vital to supply chain execution and requires that the customhouse broker (the 3PL firm) engage in the "classification and valuation" of merchandise for entry into the importing country. At best, this is a complex process that, when handled incorrectly, can inflate landed costs and create unnecessary lead time troubles.

In the parlance of customs clearance processes, classification involves the proper identification of products based on the product description provided for in the supplier's commercial invoice. Echoing the importance of the 3 Cs, the information taken from the invoice allows the customs broker to "classify" the product(s) according to the nomenclature of the customs entity in the country of importation. Made up of thousands and thousands of possible classifications, every conceivable product iteration has a corresponding tariff number that identifies to customs in a numerical format exactly what the product is.

GOVERNMENT AND THE FACILITATION OF TRADE

Business process improvement is not the only way in which international trade can be facilitated. Governments play a vital role in the proliferation of commercial activities and, not unlike large corporations, must seek ways to enhance their global competitiveness.

In recent years, governments have made a great deal of progress in their efforts to remove both tariff and non-tariff barriers to trade. With a tangible link to landed costs, lead times and inventory levels, trade policy must continue to eliminate processes and procedures that impede the international movement of goods. One such entity that endeavors to facilitate international trade is the World Customs Organization (WCO). Originally founded in 1952 as the Customs Co-operation Council, the WCO is an intergovernmental body committed to the facilitation of trade amongst nations. Today, the WCO works with 159 member governments to better manage their customs entities and expedite the flow of goods, documents and information. The primary way in which the WCO facilitates customs processes is via its adoption of the Harmonized System.

The Harmonized System is an internationally recognized, standard nomenclature for the classification of merchandise, collection of internal taxes and compilation of trade statistics. Prior to the introduction of the Harmonized System, countries around the world used discrete nomenclatures for the classification of products. This, of course, generated a great deal of confusion not only between buyers and sellers but also among the customs entities of trading nations. Today, the Harmonized System covers 5,000 commodity groups, is used by 190 countries and accounts for 98% of the worldwide classification of goods.

Based on a six-digit common nomenclature, the impact of the Harmonized System on day-to-day business cannot be underestimated. Because trading partners are capable of classifying products and determining any customs duties in advance, landed costs can be calculated with extreme accuracy. Also, because there is no question about product classification, there is no time lost in preparing customs documentation. Finally, as governments link their customs databases to accelerate commerce even further, the entire system will be built upon the Harmonized System. Already in place in many countries today, this facility will allow the clearance of merchandise prior to arrival, reducing cycle times even further.

If individual governments need an example of how their activities either facilitate or impede international trade, they need not look much farther than the WCO and the Harmonized System. Whereas the WCO has been a boon to commerce, many countries still adhere to archaic customs laws and procedures that only stand to make them less competitive in global markets. It will be the continued elimination of waste-ridden customs laws that makes developing nations more attractive to do business with and increases trade volumes.

Source: World Customs Organization Web site (www.wcoomd.org)

Additionally, each tariff number has a duty rate assigned to it, which allows the customs broker to determine exactly what duty, if any, is applied to the import under consideration. Not surprisingly, duty rates vary by country of origin depending on the nature of trade relations between nations, whether they belong to the World Trade Organization and if they are party to any trade agreements.

Valuation forms the second and equally critical portion of the customs clearance process. Whereas classification determines the duty rate assigned to a product based on its description and country of origin, valuation specifies how much the product is worth, or what is known in customs terminology as the price "actually paid or payable." Although beyond the scope of this discussion, suffice it to say that issues such as ex works price, transfer pricing, assists and underinvoicing are quite familiar to customs entities. For purposes of this analysis, valuation is an important component of the import process because it determines the monetary amount upon which duties will be assessed. To summarize, classification determines the duty rate, whereas valuation ascertains the dollar amount upon which that duty rate will be applied.

Whether viewed from an operational or financial perspective, it should be very clear just how important the customs clearance process is to SCM. Given this understanding, the importance of the 3PL firm to the entire process should be equally apparent. The slightest variation between planned and actual execution can create customs delays, fines and, ultimately, loss of market opportunities. On the other hand, a misclassification of products can have a negative impact on landed costs and eventually cost of goods sold.

The difference in duty between one tariff classification and another can be several points, and it is common to see duty rates vary 5 to 10% between similar line items. If a product is classified incorrectly due to poor product description on the invoice, inaccurate country of origin information or simple human error, the landed cost will also increase by that same percentage difference. It is said in business that "the devil is in the details." In this and many other supply chain instances, so are the euros, dollars and pesos.

Operationally speaking, it would be difficult to dispute the value of 3PL companies to SCM. Whether or not an organization is a disciple of the outsourcing philosophy, it is undeniable that certain supply chain functions are best carried out by a 3PL company. Not surprisingly, it is precisely these functions that collectively drive supply chain performance, creating the opportunity for financial enhancements on both the income statement and balance sheet. Similar to the benefits described in the section on contract manufacturing, when negotiated and managed correctly, an outsourced 3PL model offers advantages that a company could never achieve on its own.

LOGISTICS COSTS

At a landed cost level, the first and most obvious benefit derived from working with a 3PL provider is in direct transportation expense. As mentioned earlier, the ability of the 3PL firm to offer discounted prices to the market is reflected in a company's cost of goods sold line on the income statement. While transportation and customs-related costs continue to play a prominent role in landed costs and cost of goods sold calculations, analysis of the logistics function will remain a major consideration for international companies.

There are also several benefits to working with a 3PL firm when trying to control expenses below the cost of goods sold line. The greatest potential is found in payroll. When an organization operates its own logistics department, the model implies a fairly substantial investment in manpower. Whether discussing the executives and office personnel who monitor import/export logistics or the labor-intensive warehousing and trucking operations that must be operated, the cost is high and oftentimes fixed.

The 3PL model, conversely, is inherently variable, driven by the volume of cargo moved with the designated service provider. Because the 3PL firm's costs are built into the rate structure offered to the customer, in practice payroll and other operating expenses shift to the 3PL firm. In more evolved relationships, clients have enlisted the services of "in-house" personnel from the 3PL firm. In such cases, the 3PL firm provides employees to work at the customer's location, facilitating and oftentimes running the entire logistics operation. This practice is not meant to suggest, however, that an organization divest itself of its own human capital. As is more consistent with lean thinking, smarter companies will retain an element of their international talent pool to work with suppliers on managing relationships and continuous improvement initiatives. If a company does not have a commensurate amount of global experience on staff, it may compromise internal communication channels, miss shared learning opportunities or simply become too dependent on a service provider.

Next to payroll, the most prominent operating expense for international players is communication. Even with e-mail and instant messaging, there is a colossal number of telephone calls and faxes moving across supply chains to the point where communication can consume up to 15 cents of every gross margin dollar. This is not small change to companies, and the ability to use 3PL firms to communicate on their behalf is a feature of the relationship with which customers are quite happy. That "extra set of eyes" quickly becomes a vehicle for international communication, saving customers the time and expense of addressing logistics-related issues with clients, suppliers and strategic partners around the world.

The more one delves into the operating model of a 3PL firm, the more one should recognize the potential to remove waste, improve operations and enhance visibility in all of his or her operations. The 3PL relationship does require an investment in time and resources to maximize performance. However, the benefits that accrue to the customer in operational effectiveness and, hopefully, financial performance far outweigh any short-term expenditures.

THIRD-PARTY LOGISTICS AND ASSET MANAGEMENT

The discussion of how a 3PL provider can reduce a customer's cost of goods sold is more straightforward than the rationale behind using a 3PL firm for improvements in asset utilization. For this reason, the analysis is best presented in two parts. First, a plausible argument can be made as to how a 3PL firm can help to actually decrease a client's investment in raw materials, work in process and finished goods. Second, and perhaps more obvious, is the ability of a 3PL firm to reduce the need for clients to tie up cash in warehouses, trucks and other distribution-related assets.

Each area offers special benefits to the customer, and the merits of any 3PL relationship are based on the ability to drive down expenses *and* positively influence asset investment. Prior to determining the role of a 3PL firm in improving asset utilization, however, a more fundamental question must be asked: Where in the relationship between buyer and seller does title to the goods change hands? Whether an importer, exporter or purchaser of raw materials or finished goods, clarification of this contractual clause is paramount to designing effective supply chains and is a driver of how well a 3PL firm can really influence asset utilization.

Transfer of title holds a high position in the SCM hierarchy due to the fact that as ownership transfers, the assets are assumed on the balance sheet of the buyer. From both a cash flow and return on investment perspective, inventories that hit the balance sheet sooner than they need to have an adverse effect on multiple financial ratios; this scenario will be analyzed in the case study presented later in this book. When taken in conjunction with logistics operations, modes of transport and 3PL provider performance, transfer of title becomes even more important to supply chain managers.

Consider, for example, the purchase of raw materials from a supplier in the Philippines for shipment to a production facility in Campinas, Brazil. The mode of transport is ocean freight, and the transfer of title takes place at the point of loading the container (the supplier's facility in Manila). In this instance, transportation lead time, which includes customs clearance at destination and delivery to the Campinas facility, can be upwards of 45 days. From an asset perspective, this means that goods are on the buyer's books for 45 days before the buyer even has the opportunity to put them into a production process and get the finished goods out for sale. Obviously, this puts the buyer at a financial disadvantage long before the shipment ever leaves the Philippines.

For supply chain purposes, the point is that transfer of title is negotiable between buyer and seller and should be carried out based on leverage with the supplier, mode of transport and cumulative lead times. In the preceding example, title transfer could take place as of the date of the bill of lading, date of first port of arrival in Brazil, or delivery date to the plant, each of which would improve the buyer's balance sheet and cash flow statement. Once the point of title transfer is established, the 3PL firm can be engaged to work on reducing transportation lead times to the operational and financial benefit of the client.

LOGISTICS AND INTERNATIONAL MATERIALS MANAGEMENT

As was illustrated in the section on the operational role of a 3PL firm in global supply chains, many of the tasks exclusive to the logistics arena have far-reaching consequences for an organization. Based on the quality of 3PL execution, the strategic question becomes: What is the broader effect on supply chains as these activities resonate across the operating model? Returning once again to the heart of manufacturing planning and control, the answer can be found in lead times and inventory accuracy. Digging a bit further into the lexicon of manufacturing planning and control, the role of logistics and its enterprise-wide value can be linked to a trio of terms that have yet to be discussed: order points, safety stock and min/max systems.

Even with the advent of just-in-time (JIT) systems and their emphasis on zero inventory levels, many organizations use either a hybrid of materials requirements planning (MRP)/JIT or have stuck with their battle-tested MRP systems. The reality of working globally is that most organizations, especially manufacturers that deal with suppliers and customers in several countries, still carry a sufficient amount of inventory to cover both forecast and supply chain variances. For this reason, those same companies utilize software that designates order points as well as order quantities. The former is referred to as an *order point system,* and an example of the latter is the *min/max system. Safety stock,* on the other hand, is defined as additional inventory that is kept to offset errors in a forecast. If these terms sound familiar, it is because they are the tactical handmaidens to the frequently mentioned and all-important practices of lead time offsetting and gross to net exploding. Based on these discussions, the relevance of logistics and the role of a 3PL provider in this exercise should at this juncture be predictable.

Order points are very important in global operations due to the expansive nature of an international model. With suppliers oftentimes in dozens of countries, each component in a bill of material must be accounted for and its corresponding order point designated in the individual component's software file. Needless to say, order points can vary depending on production volumes, supplier location and mode of transport. Although these factors are important, the technical definition of order points singles out the logistics function as a critical factor to success. The order point formula is

Demand during lead time + Safety stock

As a part of the MRP process, cumulative lead times are estimated for each component that goes into a product; the planning horizon for any end product is as long as the longest cumulative lead time for a specific component. The accuracy of cumulative lead times, defined as the total amount of time that transpires from the moment a need is recognized until that need is fulfilled,[1] is essential to seamless supply chain movements. Because transportation lead time can represent a significant percentage of cumulative lead time, the accuracy and consistency of this variable are equally important to operational success. If lead times are not accurate, variation is introduced to the process, which creates repercussions that invariably result in growing levels of inventory.

Although the logistician's perspective is important to this discussion, to understand the supply chain role of the 3PL firm one must take the position of a production planner or buyer. Based on the information found in the component files of a bill of material, planners or buyers theoretically know exactly when they have to place an order so that it will arrive at the moment needed in production. However, when a product or component does not arrive as scheduled, two very human occurrences take place. In order to avoid the future possibility of lost production time or lost sales, buyers will place their orders sooner and typically buy more than is called for in the gross to net exploding calculation.

Whereas this creates a sense of security for the buyer or planner, the downside is that inventories increase disproportionately to what was designated in the forecast. From this vantage point, the reliability of lead times has a tangible effect on inventory levels and the amount of money committed to them. As lead times become reliable and the trust of planners and buyers is earned, orders can be placed in the quantities and at the times originally set up by the MRP module and in some cases reduced. Ideally, an organization can look to its 3PL provider to assure the reliability and consistency of lead times.

Achieving lead time reliability is the first step in eliminating "nervousness" from supply chain processes. Once this is achieved, efforts can be made to reduce lead times, an exercise that also has an effect on inventory levels. Recall that the order point calculation is the sum of demand during lead time + safety stock and that the planning horizon for a product is equal to the longest cumulative lead time for a given component; therefore, any reduction in lead time will lead to a corresponding reduction in inventory investment. From the 3PL viewpoint, the transportation component of cumulative lead time can be improved in a variety of ways.

One area in which to focus involves the use of ocean transportation for international shipments. It is common knowledge that ocean transportation is less expensive than airfreight, so organizations that plan well are willing to forego lead times for costs savings. Although an argument could be made that the carrying costs of goods on the ocean may offset the savings in transportation, under normal circumstances and depending on the product, ocean transportation is a reliable and cost-effective way to move goods. Within this mode of transport, however, there are tactics that can be used to enhance the slower lead times inherent to it.

For example, some organizations focus on the cost of ocean freight without considering the service levels (i.e., transit times) available for specific routes. Based on the steamship line employed, lead times may vary for the same route (Asia to Europe, for example), based on the number of ports called upon during the journey. Thus, whereas a company may "save" $500 on a 20-foot container with one steamship line, its lead time may increase by as much as 12 days due to multiple ports of call along the way. Other options, although $500 more expensive, will have fewer ports of call and arrive at the destination port sooner.

Depending on the value of the goods, the carrying costs for 12 days in this instance may far outweigh the $500 savings. The company that takes this advanced approach to logistics and SCM would more than likely opt for the shorter lead time with nominal increased costs. The 3PL firm, with its vast knowledge of ocean carriers, ports of call and transit times, takes a lead role in determining the best options available to the client.

In two separate instances, the discussion on logistics has alluded to the benefits of using the same 3PL firm on either end of an international transaction. For reasons already discussed, there are many benefits to using the same service provider at origin and destination, including greater control over the flow of goods and better supply chain visibility. With regard to asset management and cumulative lead times, there are also benefits.

When the customs broker at the destination is related to the forwarder at the origin, documentation and information necessary for customs clearance go directly to the broker. Depending on the country of importation, a pre-clearance can be effected or, at the very least, the customs entry can be prepared for submission in advance of the arrival of the merchandise. When the parties are not related, documents are first sent to the destination office of the forwarder and then transferred to the unrelated customs broker. There are costs inherent to the latter exercise (currency adjustment and/or documentation transfer fees), but perhaps more important is the time lost in completing the additional steps in the process. Under the best of circumstances, at least two business days are lost in the destination port while the transfer of documentation is completed to the assigned customs broker.

Two days may not sound like a lot, but when an organization deals with millions of dollars in merchandise during the course of a year, two days in carrying costs adds up to serious money. Operationally, two days of lost production time or sales opportunities also represents considerable unnecessary inventory investment and revenues that cannot be recovered. Also, if a company is paying a premium for airfreight services, two or three days lost at the destination airport defeats the purpose of moving the goods by air. For all of these reasons and many more, use of a 3PL company that seeks ways to reduce costs while improving lead times is invaluable to any global organization.

Recall that the order point formula is demand during lead time + safety stock; therefore, anything a 3PL firm can do to reduce lead times will result in placement of smaller orders and, hence, less cash committed to inventories. Focus on the demand during lead time component of the formula makes this point abundantly clear. Specifically, if the lead time is reduced, the quantity needed for the shorter period is also reduced. Table 6.2 offers an example. For a component with a cumulative lead time of six weeks, a forecasted weekly consumption of 10,000 units and safety stock of 15,000 units, the order point is at 75,000 units. If cumulative lead time were improved by one week vis-à-vis 3PL initiatives, the new order point would be hit at 65,000 units.

The improvement wrought by the 3PL firm has allowed the inventory of this component to be depleted by an additional 10,000 units prior to having to place

Table 6.2 Order Points and Lead Time Reduction

Cumulative lead time	6 weeks
Weekly consumption	10,000 units
Safety stock	15,000 units
(6 weeks × 10,000 units) + 15,000 units = 75,000 unit order point	
Cumulative lead time	5 weeks
Weekly consumption	10,000 units
Safety stock	15,000 units
(5 weeks × 10,000 units) + 15,000 units = 65,000 unit order point	

another order, thus delaying the implications for inventory and accounts payable on the balance sheet by one week. If the component costs $5, that delays $50,000 worth of inventory hitting the books by seven days. For a product that has a hundred different components, the overall effect of 3PL activities on inventory levels adds up to a significant amount of cash.

The preceding discussion considers the effect of 3PL on inventory levels as it relates only to *reducing* lead times. However, the impact that 3PL can have on safety stock must also be considered. In a domestic model, the definition of safety stock is additional inventory that is carried to cover for errors (variation) in the forecast.

In a global model, many companies carry safety stock to cover not only forecast error but also supply chain unknowns such as transit time variance, customs clearance delays and supplier problems. Although a 3PL firm cannot do a lot about supplier problems (except maybe inform its client about past-due purchase orders), it certainly has an effect when it comes to *stabilizing* transportation lead times. As was the case with order points, if the 3PL firm can bring predictability to international lead times, organizations are more inclined to reduce or even eliminate safety stocks, with the desired effect of reducing overall inventory levels.

In addition to the impact that 3PL can have on order points and safety stock, it also can figure in the determination of min/max quantities. Basically, min/max systems are used to set a range of quantities that can be ordered for a given component or product. They are designed to minimize the amount of money dedicated to inventories while assuring product availability, and the accuracy of min/max systems weighs heavily on SCM. Specifically, as raw materials are consumed in a production process (or sold as finished goods), the amount kept in inventory cannot fall below the minimum amount specified in the component/product file. Conversely, the maximum figure represents the amount up to which a new order can be placed.

For example, if a given component has a min/max of 1,000 and 6,000, this means that the minimum quantity of inventory cannot fall below 1,000 units and the replenishment amount cannot exceed 6,000. Not unlike the rationale behind the relationship between lead times and safety stock, the reliable lead times managed by 3PL firms can also compel an organization to reduce the minimum amount required in inventory for products and/or components.

FIXED ASSETS

By now, the performance of a 3PL provider and its effect on current assets should be apparent. However, use of a 3PL firm should also be contingent upon its ability to help a company drive down fixed assets. Financially speaking, the deployment of fixed assets across supply chains must be done with caution due to the fact that they appear not only on the balance sheet but also on the income statement in the form of depreciation. Taking the financial ramifications of fixed assets a step further, they can also have period-specific impact on the cash flow statement. Given the transcendental effect of fixed assets on supply chains, the use of a 3PL firm and *its* assets can bring considerable benefits to global organizations.

The most significant investment that 3PL companies make in their own infrastructure is in the form of warehouses, equipment (forklifts and materials handling apparatus), systems hardware/software and trucks. When a 3PL firm has the sufficient depth and breadth of geographic coverage, asset substitution moves the customer from a fixed cost structure to one that is based on the volume of weight, cases or pallets moved through the 3PL network.

The upside for the 3PL firm is that it can build critical mass into its models by utilizing facilities, equipment and manpower in a multi-user structure. Thus, whereas an individual company may use dedicated facilities rife with fixed costs, the 3PL model espouses the idea of multiple customers in a facility. This arrangement spreads fixed costs across a greater volume of transactions, with the financial benefit accruing to all of the clients of a facility. As such, the ideal situation for a client is one where variable costs are reduced due to the critical mass achieved by the 3PL firm and its fixed costs are eliminated completely.

The use of 3PL firms has grown considerably in the last 15 years, a trend that has been fueled by companies that either "rationalize" their distribution networks or move 100% to an outsourced model. There are many instances where companies have divested themselves of truck fleets or sold off company-owned distribution centers, choosing to sign contracts with global 3PL firms instead. Again, this model offers income statement, balance sheet and cash flow statement benefits to the contracting party. Variable costs are reduced on the income statement due to greater efficiencies achieved by the 3PL firm, with additional savings in depreciation coming from fewer fixed assets. Second, balance sheets gain relief when huge investments in land, physical plant, handling equipment and trucks are no longer part of the model. Finally, cash flow statements can be affected as assets are sold off (a source of cash) and investments in additional assets are no longer required (a use of cash).

FIXED ASSETS AND TIME TO MARKET

Two additional components of fixed asset management are flexibility and re-action time. Short product life cycles, changes in market tastes, variations in cost structures, currency fluctuations and favorable duty rates all require that a company be extraordinarily nimble. In this type of market environment, fixed assets can be viewed as a ball and chain, hampering a company's ability to move quickly and adeptly across markets. As in the case of contract manufacturing, the 3PL model allows companies to respond quickly to market shifts or distribution requirements without having to worry about leaving a trail of unused fixed assets in their wake.

The above is true not only for markets where companies already operate but also in new markets where they want to reduce long-term risk. In existing markets, the benefit of outsourcing logistics services lies in the points already discussed, reduced costs and less investment in distribution-related assets. In markets where companies are planning a launch, the benefit lies not only in these areas but also in time to market. In a company-centric model, it would take several months, if not years, to acquire land, build distribution centers, implement systems, install equipment and train personnel. By the time a company went through that exercise, it would either be too discouraged to continue or find its market window closed shut.

In a 3PL model, the contracted service provider already has the infrastructure in place and, when well executed, could have a company up and running in 180 days or less. To bring this point to life, consider the launch of a company interested in expanding into South America.

There are several trade pacts in South America, but perhaps the most dominant is Mercosur, the commercial agreement between Brazil, Argentina, Paraguay and Uruguay (Chile and Bolivia are associate members). Collectively, these countries represent over 65% of the population in South America, with the vast majority of the inhabitants concentrated in the Southern Cone (approximately 200 million people).

The combination of Mercosur and the heavy population density from Rio de Janeiro southward compels any company wishing to achieve an immediate market presence to have a distribution network in the region. Because of the benefits inherent to Mercosur and the skewed demographics that lean toward the southern region of the trade area, the free zone of Montevideo, Uruguay offers an ideal location for distribution-related activities; even so, it is much more prudent for a company to outsource its distribution requirements in Mercosur than to set up its own network.

First and foremost, Montevideo is a free zone and is subject to the customs regulations of Uruguay. This requires not only local market expertise but also the licenses and permits necessary to operate in the zone. Second, physical plant is at a premium, with construction costs and lead times major considerations. Apart from the physical plant and manpower requirements, the company in question would also have to develop its own distribution network, not an easy task in a region that is larger than the contiguous United States.

If an organization chooses to set up its own distribution network, chances are that so many resources will be consumed in the process that little energy or money would be left over to build a brand and generate revenue. Also, the impact of the fixed costs associated with the distribution function would more than likely price the company out of the market. The 3PL model, on the other hand, offers immediate access to physical plant, a variable cost structure, local expertise and access to trucking networks that extend from São Paulo to Buenos Aires and west to Santiago.

SUMMARY

One could go on for hours extolling the virtues of 3PL in a global environment obsessed with flexibility, operational execution and superlative financial results. In fact, the same could be said about the importance of contract manufacturers to contemporary supply chains. The fact is that a company has to seek the business model (be it virtual or otherwise) that allows it to achieve all of its strategic and financial goals.

Much like any undertaking, the 3PL model carries its share of risks, but when properly studied and carried out offers benefits that most companies could never achieve operating independently. When taken within the scope of financial performance, the income statement and balance sheet appeal of the 3PL model makes the analysis even more compelling.

As businesspeople gain an appreciation for important trends such as globalization and outsourcing, they are in a much better position to define strategies for their own organizations. This knowledge, combined with an understanding of the events that have shaped modern SCM, creates an environment in which executives can take the best that the past has to offer and develop new methods that advance the SCM discipline. Because inventory management can be considered the inspiration for much of the rationalization of supply chains, a study of different methodologies is essential to finding better ways to balance inventory investment with profitability.

NOTE

1. *APICS Dictionary,* The Educational Society for Resource Management, 1996.

7

MUSICAL INVENTORIES

Although many definitions can be offered to explain the essence of supply chain management (SCM), the financial view of the subject centers on creating a balance between profitability and asset utilization. While most industries continue to experience downward pressure on margins, the tactical contribution of SCM to profitability must focus on reducing costs in all processes and activities. As noted in the introductory chapters of this book and referred to throughout the treatise, SCM must also contribute to a company's return on assets. Far from being a revolutionary idea, organizations have focused on these variables since the introduction of the DuPont formula in the early years of the 20th century. The only difference now is that companies must execute the formula in a much more cluttered, international landscape.

Given the intense nature of competition in global markets, it should come as no surprise that companies have devised several ways to not only reduce costs but also take assets out of their operating equation. The discussion on outsourcing is testament to this phenomenon, and it seems that there is no end to managers' creativity in getting assets off their books. Inventory management is of special concern to international companies and focuses on not only finished goods but also raw materials and work in process. The balance of this chapter is dedicated to an analysis of several operating models, each of which seeks to create a balance between the needs of the market and the goal of minimizing inventory levels.

Most people can recall playing "musical chairs" as children. There were always more kids than chairs, and as the music played, everybody danced in a circle around the seats. When the music stopped, the players scrambled for a seat, and any children left standing were out of the game. It may be both amusing and instructive to consider musical chairs as a metaphor for the modern-day management of inventories in the supply chain.

Up until fairly recently, the goal of companies was not necessarily to reduce inventories across the supply chain, but merely to make sure that inventory values did not end up on *their* books. If other companies in the chain got stuck with inventory, that was their problem. What companies have come to realize, however, is that regardless of whether inventories wind up in the hands of suppliers or customers, the inherent costs associated with them eventually re-surface farther down the chain. Carrying costs, insurance, storage and obsoles-cence all inflate the value of inventories and, unless accounted for in sales prices, will erode the profitability of any company.

It is for these reasons that more evolved supply chain participants now endeavor to not only keep inventories off of their books but reduce them across the entire chain. Business practices like materials requirements planning have evolved to accommodate this shared goal, and entire business models have been developed with inventory management as a key tenet. Just in time, for example, is much more than an inventory reduction tool, but it does carry at its core the minimization of inventory levels. In the retail arena, Efficient Consumer Re-sponse and Quick Response focus on the use of technology and information sharing to drive unneeded inventories out of the model. Lean manufacturing, another example, promulgates the need for velocity in all aspects of an organization's activities. Needless to say, less inventory is conducive to greater speed and is a primary driver of the lean philosophy.

MATERIALS REQUIREMENTS PLANNING VERSUS JUST IN TIME

In the preceding chapters, a great deal of space was dedicated to the importance of materials requirements planning (MRP) to contemporary SCM. Although a functional model, the biggest knock against MRP is its emphasis on carrying inventory to avoid disruptions in the supply chain. Just in time (JIT), on the other hand, has come to the forefront of SCM in recent years due to its goal of zero inventories. While very appealing on paper, the execution of JIT models in global markets is extremely challenging and can be likened to walking a tightrope without a net. A comparison of the principles of MRP and JIT is presented in Table 7.1.

Noting that the DuPont formula was first utilized on a wide scale in the automotive industry, it is probably not a coincidence that JIT also has its origins in this sector. With large investments in raw materials, work in process and finished goods, it's no wonder that automotive executives have worked for years to devise methods to reduce inventories any way they can. However, the value of JIT has been somewhat discounted because of managers' obsession with eliminating inventories. The reality is that JIT is much more than a mere in-

Table 7.1   MRP Versus JIT

MRP	JIT
Carry inventory	Zero inventory
Carry safety stock	No safety stock
Use of long-range forecast	Daily consumption
Forecast-based production	Demand-based production
Use of purchase orders	Delivery schedule

ventory exercise. The JIT philosophy encompasses an entire body of thought, bringing value at an operating level as well as influencing a company's corporate culture. To summarize the finer points of JIT that were first discussed in Chapter 3, the discipline focuses on:

1. Reduction of setup times and lot sizes
2. Zero defects in manufacturing
3. Commitment to continuous improvement of all processes and elimination of waste (waste is defined as any activity that does not add value to the overall process)
4. Employee involvement and effective use of human capital

From a wider vantage point, one should note that the additional elements of JIT go beyond inventory management and are consistent with the entire lean manufacturing philosophy. Extending the reach of JIT beyond lean thinking, its principles are also congruous with SCM's goals of effective lead time management and landed cost control. The first point, for example, can represent a high percentage of cumulative lead time, with the setup of production lines sometimes consuming an entire work shift. Of equal import, smaller lot sizes drive the level of inventory investment, beginning with the acquisition of raw materials, the value added to work in process and, finally, finished goods. Also, the size of production runs and how long they take to complete are components of cumulative lead times. Obviously, the smaller the run, the faster goods can be shipped out to customers.

Continuing on, the second point can have a devastating effect on supply chains. Stopped production runs or the return of defective merchandise will put any supply chain in reverse, cost thousands of additional dollars and offer no benefit to an organization. Taken individually, as well as in conjunction with other process improvement initiatives, proper management of these items makes a tangible contribution to the removal of wasted time, effort and money across the supply chain.

The last two points of the JIT value proposition are more enterprise-wide in nature, a trait that can bring benefit to the entire business model and not just inventory management programs. In a global model, continuous improvement implies uprooting the source of bottlenecks or challenges, taking an "upstream/ downstream" approach to problem solving. This means that organizations must harness the expertise and knowledge of all supply chain participants via a team approach, seeking to deal with core illnesses instead of the superficial treatment of their symptoms.

An excellent example of how JIT practices remove waste from enterprise-wide processes is the treatment of purchase orders. In large-scale operations, literally thousands of purchase orders can be sent out in a month's time. With this type of volume, it is easy to imagine the amount of administrative effort required to issue and follow up on product quantities, prices and delivery dates. In the lean school, the question is not to determine how best to manage the purchase order process but, rather, how to eliminate the need for purchase orders entirely. JIT practitioners do not issue purchase orders; they work off of a delivery schedule that is adjusted as demand dictates. The amount of time and human effort saved by working off of schedules permits buyers to dedicate resources to managing relationships instead of chasing paper. In this sense, the supplier dynamic becomes much more strategic and less administrative in nature.

These concepts go hand in hand with the second element of the fourth point, the effective use of human capital. Although rife with challenges, global supply chains are populated by people with diverse backgrounds and vast experience. The inability (or unwillingness) to harness this human capital will invariably result in a compromised business model and leave key players isolated from the process.

When taken in kind with the SCM goals of effective inventory management, landed cost control and lead time rationalization, JIT can be considered a pre-cursor to the SCM philosophy. As a part of the overall lean manufacturing school of thought, JIT should be viewed as one of the most important elements of modern supply chain thinking. Like many business practices, however, it does not come without a caveat. Businesspeople must be cognizant of the fact that JIT models work best in a domestic environment or at least in an interna-tional model characterized by suppliers in close geographic proximity to the manufacturer. A comparison of the characteristics of a domestic JIT model and an international operation brings this point to life, perhaps leading the reader back to the benefits of an evolved MRP model.

JUST IN TIME AND INTERNATIONAL TRADE

As the name would imply, the heart of a JIT operation lies in the ability to deliver raw materials to the point of production at the exact time they are needed and in the precise quantities desired. What it does not imply, however, is that suppliers farther up the chain hold stock to create the illusion that the manufacturer is not carrying inventories. This has been the case in many instances, with the manufacturer technically not having raw materials inventories on its books but with inventories in the supply chain nonetheless.

Following the lean mentality, if a supplier holds inventory, the carrying costs of those goods eventually find their way into the selling price to the manufacturer. If not, the business becomes financially unviable for the vendor, which will either have to raise prices or, in a more dramatic play, seek other more profitable business opportunities. Thus, whereas the manufacturer may make up some ground by reducing assets on the balance sheet, the income statement suffers due to an increase in cost of goods sold. Looking again to the need to balance profitability with asset utilization, the exercise boils down to a case of "six of one and half a dozen of the other."

It is for this reason that the sharing of demand information with suppliers has become such an integral part of the JIT model. Perhaps a forerunner of collaborative planning, forecasting and manufacturing, this component of JIT is really the starting point of the entire operation. If a tier I supplier does not have visibility into future requirements, it is impossible to begin planning its own JIT operations with tier II and tier III vendors. Without this requisite line of sight, the cascading effect ripples up the supply chain, creating stocks of raw materials inventories along the way. This defeats the purpose of JIT and only hides the already nebulous costs of having inventory scattered among multiple suppliers.

A common misconception of JIT operations is that companies do not use a forecast, substituting actual demand for guesswork. This is not exactly the case. JIT operations begin with a forecast (they have to start somewhere) that is expressed on the basis of *daily consumption.* Production planning is not fixed under JIT, but is adjusted to reflect real demand to within a day or even hours of actual manufacturing. The adjustment process continues between manufacturer and supplier until final amounts are agreed upon, produced and delivered to the production line. This is a major departure from the MRP philosophy that locks in production planning well ahead of manufacturing dates, thus creating the inventories intrinsic to the model.

Domestic operations have been successful in executing on the JIT model due to the closeness of suppliers to manufacturing sites, better visibility and less variation in supply chain processes. In fact, if one were to seek the reason for the success of domestic JIT operations, an argument could be made for the geographic structuring of supplier/manufacturer relationships. Specifically, most domestic JIT scenarios are characterized by operations where the supplier is a reasonable distance by truck from the client's facilities or, in some cases, even within view of the plant.

With electronic data interchange (EDI) or Web-based connectivity, it is feasible to place an order with a supplier and have the material sequenced to the production line in a matter of hours. When that same supplier moves operations to China and attempts to achieve the same level of JIT perfection, this nirvana becomes a fiasco that can take weeks to resolve.

In the section on globalization, it was stated that the World Trade Organization and free trade agreements have heavily influenced the growth of industrial campuses. These agreements are the primary way in which governments influence the structure of global supply chains. From an operational perspective, the need for JIT operations to have suppliers close to their manufacturing sites has also been a major impetus in the formation of these campuses. There are hundreds of industrial complexes around the world, and as long as globalization and operational exigencies dictate supply chain anatomy, they will continue to proliferate. Thus, the combination of governmental incentives and tactical necessity has created a structure that is complementary to the JIT model. As industry and government endeavor to work together, these complexes will continue to play a prominent role in supply chain structuring, creating both opportunity and challenges for management teams around the world.

Even though the advent of industrial campuses complements the JIT model, not all raw materials can be sourced domestically. While companies attempt to purchase materials locally, there are many factors that require organizations to procure materials offshore. As governments work to attract industry, the business community needs time to ramp those industries up to world standards. Specifically, as governments offer incentives for local content and labor, entrepreneurs must find financing, build plants, train personnel and get processes running.

Once operational, there are still variables such as product quality, production capacity, manufacturing lead times and cost that must be weighed against competitive imports. Businesspeople must recognize that this process is evolutionary in nature, and while JIT operations prefer local sourcing, it takes time to get newly formed domestic industries up to snuff. This transition from international to domestic purchasing is another factor that supply chain managers must consider as their processes evolve and change.

The combination of governmental incentives and operational necessity will continue to promulgate the growth of supply chain frameworks that support JIT operations. One must be cognizant of the fact that although operations can be improved through local sourcing, variances will still exist between planned and actual results. With this reality in mind, it would be wise for businesspeople to revisit the benefits of MRP systems and perhaps seek a middle ground that combines the best of JIT and MRP. This hybrid approach, which is already being done by many companies, offers the benefit of reduced inventory levels while assuring that product is available in the right place, quantity and time.

A HYBRID MODEL

One last look at the concept of manufacturing planning and control (MPC) and its component master production scheduling reveals some interesting implications and opportunities for SCM. Three concepts integral to MPC that may be subject to enhancements by the JIT philosophy are freezing, time fencing and consuming the forecast.

Freezing is a production planning practice whereby no changes can be made to the production plan (and hence exploded MRP requirements) inside of a specified period. In many organizations, it is not unusual to see a frozen period in the range of 8 to 12 weeks. For international organizations that do not have a lot of confidence in their supply chains, the frozen period can be much longer. This exercise has implications for MRP due to the fact that raw materials inventories are built up in anticipation of upcoming production, regardless of what the real demand turns out to be.

Time fencing is a continuation of freezing in that measurement periods are broken down by weeks, with changes to the production plan only allowed outside of a certain "fence." *Consuming the forecast,* conversely, is a practice that implies replacing forecasted amounts with actual orders. As sales orders come in for weeks outside of the frozen period, adjustments are made up or down to the forecast based on the collective volume of all orders received for those periods.

One major difference between MRP planning and JIT is that the former defines periods in weeks and the latter in days. It is the expression of demand in days that allows JIT practitioners to place orders with suppliers literally on the same day production will take place (if, of course, the supplier is close by). Another difference is that JIT normally does not have frozen periods, at least not for weeks at a time. This practice delays or postpones the buildup of raw materials inventories to the benefit of the buyer's balance sheet. Finally, JIT is supposed to be based on actual demand, so consuming the forecast should not be a consideration (certainly for periods closest to production). Given this scenario, how do supply chain managers build greater flexibility into their models while assuring product availability?

A possible solution to this dilemma is to continue to utilize the MRP component of the MPC model, but express demand in days rather than weeks. This not only allows for greater precision in planning but also creates a situation where the level production of all products can be achieved. Also, if companies can attain the dual goals of reducing cumulative lead times and keeping them stable, the possibility exists to reduce the frozen time fence and as a result the buildup of inventories.

Finally, if it is not feasible to execute orders with suppliers on a daily basis, consumption of the forecast could be a viable alternative. Use of this concept in conjunction with a reduced frozen period allows for greater exactitude in determining raw materials requirements, with purchases based on actual demand rather than forecast. Although not perfect, this option does offer the potential of greater accuracy in aligning inventories with order-based requirements.

Without question, the linchpin to the above or any other supply chain exercise is the accuracy of the forecast. If projections were accurate to begin with, there would be no need to carry inventories or safety stocks. Unfortunately, the human condition is an imperfect vessel brimming with uncertainty, and as long as people are completing forecasts (aided by technology or otherwise), there will be errors. There is hope, however, based on the length of the forecast period itself.

An axiom of forecasting is that the shorter the period under projection, the greater the probability for accuracy. A simple example illustrates this point. Most people know with certainty what they will be doing tomorrow. It is much more difficult, however, to predict what one will be doing in six months (compensating for bad forecasts, no doubt!). Understanding that forecasts correspond to planning periods and that the length of the period is a function of the longest lead time for a given product or component, it is fair to say that if lead time can be reduced, so can the forecast period.

Again, the shorter the forecast period, the greater the probability of accuracy. This concept involves logic and mathematical modeling that are outside the scope of this discussion. Suffice it to say, however, that lead time management and its impact on inventory levels once again makes its way to the forefront of SCM. These ideas, when combined with the possible solutions presented for reducing min/max levels, postponing order points and diminishing the need for safety stock, make a powerful argument for the improvement of supply chain performance.

JUST IN TIME AND VENDOR-MANAGED INVENTORIES

Even with the possibility of employing a combination of MRP and JIT, supply chain managers are still seeking ways to reduce inventories up and down the supply chain. A pure JIT model certainly addresses the issue of inventory elimination, but the risk is just too great when dealing with suppliers, production variances and capricious clients in multiple countries. Like any business practice, inventory management is in a state of constant flux, with companies always looking for new methods and tactics to improve performance. Vendor-managed inventory (VMI), a fairly new practice for global operations, borrows from the past, benchmarks Efficient Consumer Response/Quick Response and employs new ways to bring inventory benefits to suppliers, manufacturers and, ultimately, the end user.

Although a newly coined term, the application of VMI in its original form is already somewhat misconstrued and used out of context. Now employed in regard to any type of inventory, the original application of VMI was limited to a raw materials and production environment. While recognizing the various iterations of VMI, the fundamentals of the concept are as follows:

1. Multiple suppliers occupy a facility in close proximity to the manufacturer's site, retaining title to the goods until they are consumed in the production process.
2. Because the supplier retains title and is responsible for the well-being of the goods, the Incoterms (shipping terms) are in many cases either delivered duty paid or delivered duty unpaid.
3. The supplier is responsible for replenishment and in some cases also determines the min/max level.
4. The manufacturer issues no purchase orders and "self-bills" based on actual consumption.
5. In an international model, raw materials are stored in a bonded warehouse close to the production facility to either delay or eliminate customs duties.
6. Daily drawdowns on inventory based on actual demand are the norm.

The VMI model solves the issue of inventory availability while still keeping inventories off of the manufacturer's books. However, the logical response to this is that the costs inherent to carrying inventories revert to the supplier along with all of the consequences mentioned earlier in the chapter. The components of VMI that address this issue are a truly collaborative attitude between buyer and seller, the extensive sharing of production planning information and the direct involvement of the supplier in determining inventory levels.

Perhaps the most important aspect of VMI that sets it apart from more traditional inventory management practices is the nature of the relationship between supplier and customer. Because the vendor holds inventory until it goes into production, it is in the vendor's best interest to focus on the customer relationship management facet of the program. In order to avoid having either an excess or shortage of raw materials, vendors must be in daily contact with their customers, talking with planners, buyers and even salespeople to have the pulse of planned production at their disposal. Variances between forecast and actual consumption must continually be reduced over time as collaborative efforts work toward bringing demand-based information to the front lines of the operation.

This is a major departure from traditional relationships where vendors plan production based on purchase orders received well in advance of due dates. The use of purchase orders allows for a much more passive approach to the vendor side of a business relationship. As long as the supplier delivers a "quality" product in the quantity ordered on the date requested, all is well. In the VMI model, the onus is on both the supplier and customer to manage the relationship proactively, thus avoiding the pitfalls of traditional inventory management programs.

VENDOR-MANAGED INVENTORY OPERATIONS

The fact that the vendor holds title to the merchandise is but one factor that changes the essence of the buyer/seller relationship. Title transfer has clear balance sheet ramifications, but in an international production model carries substantial operational implications as well. It should not be lost on the reader that even in the most contemporary of inventory management programs success depends on two operational activities that have been discussed throughout this book: lead time offsetting and inventory accuracy.

While critical under the MRP model, the accuracy of both lead times and inventory levels in the case of VMI is even more important. To summarize, variances in lead times reverberate through the organization, eventually leading to disruption on the production floor. Conversely, inaccurate inventory counts will either precipitate or delay replenishment based on bogus information, again with far-reaching supply chain consequences. A combination of varying lead times and inaccurate inventories in an international VMI model is fatal to the operation.

Lead time offsetting and inventory management are fundamental to any successful vendor/customer relationship, but in the VMI model responsibility for both ultimately lies with the supplier. As such, it is incumbent upon the vendor, with constant cooperation from the customer, to focus on reducing variances in both lead times and inventory counts.

MIN/MAX LEVELS

As alluded to in the third principle of VMI, the model dictates that the vendor establishes the min/max level of inventories. It is for this reason that the supplier and customer must work so closely together on forecast and actual consumption. If the min/max is out of line with actual requirements, there will either be too much or too little inventory at the VMI facility. In the case of the former, excess inventory will take up valuable shelf space; in the latter case, line stoppages and increases in work in process will become the norm.

In addition to the need for min/max levels to be aligned with actual production numbers, the accuracy of the counts at the VMI facility must be 100%. Accuracy is so important for an international model because replenishment shipments are executed based on what the vendor believes it has in inventory and the time needed to get more materials into the facility. If the inventory level is not accurate, the result will be the same as in the discussion on min/max levels. Specifically, if the inventory management system shows more product than is actually in the facility, replenishment orders will arrive late, causing lines to go down, work-in-process inventories to grow and finished goods delivery dates to be missed. On the other hand, if the system shows less than the actual amount on hand, orders will be shipped too early, creating a glut of raw materials at the VMI operation. Neither of these situations bodes well for the health of the vendor/customer relationship. It should be clear that a combination of unrealistic min/max levels and low inventory accuracy in a global production model can put a factory out of business.

The importance of lead times and inventory accuracy also creates waste-related concerns in the VMI facility. Bearing in mind that an international VMI site is bonded, the operator must procure government approval to run a facility. Part of the approval process involves determining the exact amount of space the operation will require. In a domestic VMI operation, any additional space requirements are a matter of adding on to the existing building. In a bonded facility, any additions require further government approval, a process that is not known for high levels of expediency. Thus, if inventories grow due to a lack of confidence in lead times or inventory accuracy, an operator may be in the unenviable position of not having anywhere to store goods. For a lean VMI operation, underutilized or unneeded space is considered waste, and the operator must find ways to reduce the space requirement rather than expand the facilities. Once again, the enterprise-wide ramifications of inventory management seep into all aspects of an operation.

VENDOR-MANAGED INVENTORY AND FINANCIAL CONSIDERATIONS

The accuracy issues discussed thus far also carry financial implications for the vendor/customer relationship. As noted in the fourth point, the customer not only avoids the use of purchase orders in the VMI model but also self-bills. Taken together, the elimination of purchase orders *and* invoices affords huge gains in productivity. The administrative gains from eliminating invoices, however, are dependent on the ability to account for all of the raw materials consumed in production over a predetermined period.

Albeit in a different context, inventory accuracy is once again critical to the overall operation. In this instance, production has already been completed and title has passed from the vendor to the manufacturer. Now it is time to get paid. However, if there are any unresolved issues pertaining to the inventory, in particular the ability to accurately account for consumption, the customer will not pay, which unnecessarily delays collection of receivables.

In any business model, the accuracy and availability of raw materials inventory are basic to supply chain velocity. In terms of a VMI operation, its very survival depends on it. However, the challenges of operating a successful operation are not just limited to what goes on in the warehouse.

LEAD TIMES, INCOTERMS AND VENDOR-MANAGED INVENTORIES

The issue of lead time actually ties into the second VMI principle, the use of Incoterms. Sometimes treated as a footnote to international negotiations, the Incoterms actually drive the dynamics of the relationship between buyer and seller on two important points: risk of loss or damage to the goods and responsibility for transportation and related expenses. Independent of the business model, it must be noted that Incoterms do not consider transfer of title; they pertain only to the obligations of the seller in relation to *delivery of the goods.*[1] However, this point does not relieve the vendor of responsibility for the well-being of the merchandise or the cost of transportation to the production facility.

In a VMI model, the preceding points have two implications. First, because the vendor owns the merchandise up to the production process, it makes sense to adjust the Incoterms to shift responsibility to the vendor for risk of loss or damage and transportation expenses. Simply stated, if the vendor owns the merchandise, the vendor should be responsible for its well-being. In more traditional purchase-order-driven models, the vendor relinquished responsibility farther upstream in the supply chain, using Incoterms like ex works, free carrier or free on board. In order to align Incoterms with title transfer under VMI, responsibility moves to the vendor via Incoterms like delivered duty unpaid and delivered duty paid. In this scenario, should anything happen to the goods in the form of damage, loss or theft, it is technically the responsibility of the vendor.

Second, use of the delivered duty unpaid and delivered duty paid Incoterms should not be overlooked from a landed cost perspective. Under these terms, the sale price quoted to the customer includes not only unit price but also any transportation expense associated with getting the goods into the production facility. As discussed in previous chapters, this could include origin pickup, consolidation, international airfreight, documentation, customs clearance and local delivery. If a vendor moves from an Incoterm like ex works to delivered duty unpaid without accounting for those additional costs in the sale price, the vendor will lose money before the first unit is ever shipped.

Finally, because the vendor's responsibility is heightened under delivered duty unpaid and delivered duty paid, the level of logistics expertise required of the vendor increases commensurately. With ex works, for example, the vendor makes goods available to the customer at the vendor's facility and from that point forward washes its hands of any transportation-related liability. Although it makes sense for a supplier to monitor the flow of its shipments regardless of the Incoterm used, reality dictates that the buyer be more vigilant under this type of Incoterm. With a delivered duty paid Incoterm, the vendor is responsible for the goods and pays the freight and would therefore be wise to employ a third-party logistics company capable of handling that responsibility.

All of the operational requirements discussed thus far must be carried out with +99% accuracy in order for the VMI model to function effectively. Some may consider these levels too unrealistic for an international model, but it is actually these same demands that make the model successful. With so much at stake from both an operational and financial perspective, it would be foolish of both the vendor and customer to not work together to reduce lead time, inventory and production variances. This emphasis on details and constant collaboration extends well beyond an inventory management environment, all the way up the supply chain to its origins.

While all of the operational details inherent to a successful VMI operation can be articulated, the most important component of the program is more subtle. From the outset, the fortunes of a VMI model rely on the philosophy and attitude that both vendor and manufacturer apply to their relationship. In the past, many vendor/customer relationships have been characterized by a constant game of "one upmanship," with each entity seeking ways to take advantage of the other. If a manufacturer canceled shipment of raw materials well after an order was placed, that was the vendor's problem. Conversely, if a vendor loaded up a customer with more raw materials than production called for, it was not the vendor's concern. The VMI philosophy forces both vendor and manufacturer to realize that any supply chain disruption affects all involved, not just the party holding the inventory. Each is equally responsible for variance reductions in the areas of product quality, lead times and inventory management, with an understanding that all involved eventually share unnecessary supply chain costs.

As detailed in Table 7.2, the juxtaposition of the JIT and VMI philosophies creates some very interesting contrasts. Most notably, JIT pushes the model toward zero inventory, while VMI has inventory built into it. It is also of interest to note, however, that each school promotes continuous improvement, the elimination of waste and intense supplier management. Paradoxically, the JIT model works because there is no inventory being held, whereas the VMI model works because there is inventory being held. Which model functions best is a question of corporate culture, supply chain structure and industry-specific characteristics.

Table 7.2   JIT Versus VMI

JIT	VMI
Zero inventory	Supplier owns inventory
No min/max levels	Supplier sets min/max levels
Delivery schedule	Supplier offsets lead times
Supplier bills for raw materials	Manufacturer self-bills
No purchase orders	No purchase orders

As Thomas Jefferson said, "the price of freedom is constant vigilance." For both JIT and VMI, the cost of success is constant vigilance as well.

INCOTERMS: CORNERSTONE OF THE BUYER–SELLER RELATIONSHIP

First established in 1936 by the International Chamber of Commerce in Paris, France, Incoterms (International Commercial Terms) form the operational foundation of any cross-border transaction. Since their inception, the goal of the Incoterms has been to provide a standard that addresses the responsibilities of the seller as they relate to the delivery of merchandise to an international buyer. As articulated in the Introduction of the 2000 edition of *Incoterms,* the scope of these 13 trade terms is limited to:

> Matters relating to the rights and obligations of the parties to the contract of sale with respect to the delivery of the goods.

More specifically, Incoterms cover two critical clauses in any well-prepared contract for sale. First, use of a specific term clearly defines at what point in the logistics chain responsibility for loss or damage to the goods shifts from the seller to the buyer. Second, Incoterms also clarify at what point transportation and related expenses (local pickup, international airfreight, customs clearance, duties, etc.) shift between the parties. Given the critical nature of these two points to a successful business relationship, an understanding of the true ramifications of the Incoterms must be established well before shipments are effected.

Since the Incoterms deal in part with the burden of expense associated with the movement of goods, they have a considerable impact on landed costs. As a percentage of total cost of ownership, transportation and related expenses can represent up to 20% of the landed expense. Without clear definition of who pays for what, phantom costs will continuously surface, eroding the gross profit of both buyer and seller.

EFFICIENT CONSUMER RESPONSE AND QUICK RESPONSE

The retail sector is by no means free of inventory concerns and has applied its own best practices to keep waste out its supply chains. The best application of this mentality, and in contrast with other models, has been the prudent use of technology to bring substantial benefits to collaborative planning.

As a variation on a now familiar theme, techniques similar to those found in VMI and JIT have come into practice for finished goods under the monikers Efficient Consumer Response (ECR) and Quick Response (QR). Although the same in principle, ECR and QR are different from a VMI model for a couple

---

Prudent use of the Incoterms can also affect the transportation component of cumulative lead times. Issues that deal with mode of transport (air, ocean, rail, truck or multi-modal), the definition of "usual" shipping practices and the meaning of "delivery" are all meticulously covered in the publication. In a world where time to market and velocity are sources of competitive advantage, comprehensive knowledge of the Incoterms is vital to a company's success in global trade.

It is important to point out that the Incoterms per se do not carry the force of law. Incoterms are standards that are intended to be part of a sales contract, the intent of which is to define commonly used trade terms. If, however, reference is made to the *Incoterms 2000* in a binding contract for sale, interpretation of the responsibilities relating to delivery of the goods will be pursuant to the Incoterms. For this and many other reasons, it is prudent to include reference to the *Incoterms 2000* in any international sales contract. As an additional note on the enforceability of contracts using the Incoterms, the 2000 publication is consistent with and makes reference to the 1980 United Nations Convention on Contracts for the International Sales of Goods.

Although the Incoterms are very clear with regard to scope, their use continues to generate a great deal of confusion between buyer and seller. For this reason, it is equally important to articulate what the Incoterms do not cover. For example, the Incoterms explicitly state that their scope does not consider transfer of title (different from responsibility for loss or damage), property rights, financing or breach of contract. In this context, Incoterms only cover the two clauses previously mentioned, and the other important details of a binding sales contract are covered under separate clauses.

Tactical knowledge of the Incoterms is the cornerstone of any international operation. Regardless of the departments in which employees work, a lack of understanding of the Incoterms will eventually lead to waste, longer cycle times and extremely annoyed customers.

Source: *Incoterms 2000*

of important reasons. First, ECR and QR apply to finished products in a consumer goods model. Applicable to both grocery and hard consumer goods (electronics, etc.), this type of merchandise is in the last stages of its supply chain journey, just prior to getting into the hands of the final user.

Another major difference between ECR/QR and VMI is that the retail sector has historically used technology much more effectively than other industries have. The application of standards-based bar code technology in the retail sector has allowed for much more effective timing of supply with demand, inventory management and a complete reversal of the cash-to-cash cycle. Without bar code standards like the Universal Product Code (UPC), none of the fundamentals of ECR/QR would be possible, making the already slim margins in retail that much more difficult to achieve.

ECR/QR is made possible by point-of-purchase (POP) technology that communicates inventory updates to suppliers at the exact moment purchases are made in a retail outlet. As goods are scanned through a cash register, informa-

---

GLOBAL TRADE AND THE USE OF
RADIO FREQUENCY IDENTIFICATION

There are two reasons why bar coding has been successful in the retail arena over the last 30 years. First, industry players have developed and adopted standards that allow all involved to speak the same technological language. Second, the costs associated with bar coding have been driven down to the point where they not only are justifiable but actually create net savings in the supply chain.

While there is no disputing the value of bar coding to retailers, their tier I suppliers and, ultimately, the consumer, universal application of the technology across industry sectors from raw materials to finished goods has been limited. The list of excuses from the business community for not adopting bar code standards is as long as the software code written to support the technology. That being said, immediate action must be taken to create the visibility needed to effectively manage global business activities and create the opportunity for massive productivity gains.

One technology that seems to hold great promise is radio frequency identification (RFID). RFID uses a chip embedded in even the smallest of products that permits the tracking of goods at any point in the supply chain. Unlike bar coding, RFID does not require line-of-sight reading, but rather transmission of a signal from the chip to receivers strategically located in places as diverse as factories, truck terminals, customs entities and points of purchase. By no means ubiquitous, current uses of RFID technology can be found in tracing the whereabouts of rail cars, automatic payment of highway tolls and managing live inventory in cattle yards.

tion on purchases is fed back to suppliers, setting off upstream activities based on predetermined lead times. While admittedly more compelling in a domestic environment, real-time visibility is the tool that has made ECR/QR as effective as it is. POP technology has allowed powerhouse retailers to dictate the terms of purchase to their suppliers (who are no small fry either) and pay for goods only after they have been scanned at the cash register and cash is received. Thirty years ago, this practice would have been known as consignment; today it is called ECR/QR.

Perhaps the use of the term consignment to describe an ECR/QR model is a bit harsh as there are benefits to both supplier and retailer in this model. First, the adoption of standards-based bar code technology has created productivity gains that would not have been achieved otherwise. POP information echoes through the entire supply chain, providing information that is invaluable to suppliers for their own raw materials purchases, production planning and distribution activities.

Apart from the issues of cost and standards adoption, realization of the potential of RFID also depends upon the coordinated involvement of business, government and academia. RFID has a head start in this regard, with endorsements by the U.S. government, the Uniform Code Council, Inc., direct involvement of MIT's Auto-ID Center and a pilot program with business heavyweights like Wal-Mart, Home Depot and Gillette. First indications are very promising, and it is estimated that cost-effective use of RFID could be seen on a large scale in the next decade.

Although RFID offers huge benefits in the areas of product visibility and understanding consumer behavior, supply chain managers should already be thinking of future applications for the technology. In an international context, for example, chips could be programmed with information on country of origin of products or the Harmonized System number. Given the lethargic nature of many customs processes around the world, this use of RFID could shave several days off of transit times while providing valuable landed cost information to businesspeople. Because hard-copy documents continue to play a role in global trade, chips embedded in the documents themselves could help match cargo with corresponding documentation requirements, offering almost boundless productivity gains and reducing the advent of lost shipments.

The thought process associated with the application of RFID is as young as the technology itself. The work of the above-mentioned entities, in conjunction with the creativity of business thinkers, will accelerate its use to the benefit of companies and consumers around the world. Even with all this potential, it will be time, hard work and the willingness of business to accept technology standards that will write the history of RFID.

As retail becomes more international (reference the global battles between companies like Wal-Mart and Carrefour), supply chain visibility will move to the forefront of competitive advantage by not only improving margins but by keeping inventories out of the supply chain until absolutely necessary. Suppliers benefit from this exercise because the amount of time they have to hold inventory in the supply chain is reduced through the better timing of supply with demand. In this sense, ECR/QR becomes a virtuous circle, the execution of which will only improve over time.

One can see that there are both similarities and differences between inventory management techniques found in MRP, JIT, VMI and ECR/QR. It is also apparent that each school of thought can apply benefits garnered from the other models, leading the inventory management discipline to better utilization of current assets. Apart from shared techniques, the lesson to be learned is that the adoption of standards-based bar coding is the only answer in the quest to create real-time visibility across geography, industries and function.

This point is a subject for another book, but suffice it to say that as long as supply chain entities operate disparate systems with innate connectivity issues, the unhealthy game of musical assets will continue merrily along. In today's cutthroat environment where no quarter is given (nor should it be asked for), any organization left standing when the music stops may be out of the game for good. For this reason, supply chain entities would be well advised to take a page out of the retail book and adopt a platform that will produce the same benefits that retailers have enjoyed since the 1970s. With real-time visibility and much better inventory accuracy, the use of bar codes would certainly make a VMI model more palatable for the supplier community.

NOTE

1. *Incoterms,* International Chamber of Commerce, Paris, 2000.

8

SIX SIGMA APPLICATIONS IN GLOBAL BUSINESS MODELS

The common thread between all of the aforementioned business models is that they have adopted best practices from their predecessors while developing new tactics that are better suited to current markets and industries. Truly innovative breakthroughs in global commerce models are rare, while the ability to apply existing methods, discard outdated activities and develop new tactics is a much more common event in business today.

There has been no shortage of operational panaceas during recent years, all of which have been promoted as saviors of industry. Predictably, some have fared better than others. Most have faded to footnote status, however, due to the fact that they were based more on consultants' hype than any quantifiable value brought to an organization. While a detailed study of these methodologies is a conversation for another day, it appears that the models most adaptable to global business are those that create measurable links between enterprise-wide execution and financial performance.

Given the above, it is no surprise to see remnants of the total quality management (TQM) movement manifest themselves in more contemporary programs. Statistical process control and the use of trend charts, for example, are still very much a part of many companies' quality and continuous improvement programs. Whereas TQM was knocked for its internal focus on production processes as opposed to client needs, it is interesting to observe that the fundamental tools of the model are still of value today. The reason why they are still in use is that, when taken in conjunction with newer practices, they collectively help to create the vector view alluded to in this book.

One example of a contemporary methodology for tying execution to performance is the balanced scorecard approach developed by Kaplan and Norton.[1] With a clear orientation toward client needs, the balanced scorecard tool set aids companies in measuring business processes from a customer, financial, process and development/learning perspective. When properly designed and executed, use of the balanced scorecard can be a powerful tool for companies engaged in global business.

SIX SIGMA AND GLOBAL BUSINESS MODELS

As mentioned in an earlier chapter, the bane of international operations is process variation. Whether in a production, logistics or administrative environment, deviation from established performance standards will ultimately result in more inventories, higher landed costs, longer lead times and/or weaker financial performance. With this point a constant reminder for business managers, it would be wise for organizations to focus on tactics that reduce variation and its myriad ways of plaguing operations. Taken in hand with the lean philosophy, the one–two punch of increased velocity and reduced process variation is exactly the goal that supply chain managers should be pursuing.

Much more than a historical footnote, it was actually the TQM movement that first adopted the idea of reducing process variation. Then, as now, variation was defined as any difference between the planned and actual outcome of an event. Pioneers like W. Edwards Deming focused on the use of the standard deviation, limited at that time to a production environment, to first baseline and then help to reduce variation in product quality. Of equal historical importance, it is instructive to observe that the use of the standard deviation was first developed in 1893 by mathematician K. Pearson.[2] As mentioned earlier, it seems that the best tools are those that transcend both time and fad with characteristics that make quantification of process performance a reality. To borrow from the old Levi's tag line: "Quality never goes out of style." In business, neither does basic but solid math.

Six Sigma is a methodology that promotes enterprise-wide continuous improvements through the use of the standard deviation and other analytical tools. First introduced by Motorola in the late 1980s, Six Sigma is composed of tools designed to reduce variation in all business processes. Later adopted by equally high-profile companies like General Electric and Allied Signal, success stories related to Six Sigma abound in the business press and can be found in annual reports around the globe. Because of its client orientation, ability to reduce process variation and focus on cycle times, international business operations are a prime target for the application of Six Sigma.

The name Six Sigma actually finds its origins in the Greek letter "sigma," the symbol in mathematics that signifies standard deviation. The mathematical relevance of the standard deviation is that it measures spread (or dispersion) from the mean value of a population or sample. The business application of Six Sigma lies in its ability to first establish a mean (similar to average) value for a process and measure the spread from the mean of individual values. Of equal commercial significance, it has been proven that 68% of all values fall within one standard deviation of the mean, 95.5% fall within two standard deviations and 99.7% fall within three standard deviations of the mean. As shown in Figure 8.1, the term Six Sigma is used to reflect the fact that some results fall below the mean and others beyond it (hence the name Six Sigma as opposed to Three Sigma).

If customer requirements can be quantified, they can then be compared with the actual outcomes of a process. It must be stated, however, that just because 99.7% of all values fall within three standard deviations of the mean, it should

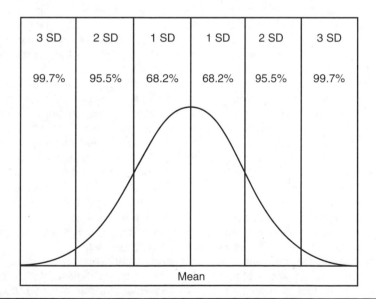

Figure 8.1 Standard Deviation

COMMERCIAL APPLICATIONS FOR
THE STANDARD DEVIATION

When applying the principles of mathematics to business, it would be difficult to find a more versatile tool than the standard deviation. Sometimes confused with the arithmetic mean (average), the standard deviation measures the dispersion of data points in a population or sample. Technically, the standard deviation is defined as the square root of the sum of the squared differences between data points and the average value of those data points. Sounds impressive, but what does it mean?

The standard deviation actually begins with an average value for a data set, and then the individual values are subtracted from that average. All differences are then squared to account for any negatives and are then summed. From that point, the square root of the total value is calculated to arrive at the standard deviation. This figure is what is of most interest to mathematicians and businesspeople alike, as it defines the spread of data from the average.

Averages are important to the standard deviation because of a phenomenon in mathematics known as central tendency. Because averages are derived from all the values in a population or sample, the natural tendency is for the majority of individual data points to cluster around the average value. What the standard deviation reveals is exactly how dense the cluster of data points is. The goal of businesspeople is to make sure that individual outcomes in any process are as close to the mean (or, more importantly, customer specifications) as possible. The relevance of the standard deviation in this endeavor is that once a process can be measured, actions can be taken to bring outcomes within the specification limits agreed upon with a customer. An example of lead time management can be used to illustrate the application of the standard deviation in process improvements.

For analysis purposes, assume that a seller and buyer agree that the lead time for ocean shipments from Asia to the United States is 23 days door to door. As actual outcomes transpire, the standard deviation from the target transit time is calculated, showing the spread from the 23-day target. For example, if after tracking 100 shipments it is determined that the standard deviation is three days, it can be said that 68.4% of the shipments arrive either three days early or three days late (one standard deviation from the mean). Using the same logic, it can also be stated that 95% of the shipments are either six days early or six days late. For shipments that arrive in exactly 23 days, the objective is to continue to hit the transit time agreed upon. Of equal importance, businesspeople must analyze the late shipments and determine methods to bring as many as possible to the target date.

As one can see, standard deviation measures variation in processes. Once the operational definitions of any business process are defined, this tool can be used to isolate both compliance with and variation from a target. It is for this reason that the standard deviation has so many applications for business and should be used as a basic tool in process improvement initiatives.

Table 8.1   Sigma Levels

Defects per Million Opportunities	Sigma Level
841,300	0.5
691,500	1.0
500,000	1.5
308,500	2.0
158,700	2.5
66,800	3.0
22,700	3.5
6,200	4.0
1,300	4.5
230	5.0
30	5.5
3.4	6.0

not be deduced that process performance is at a 99.7% level. Actually, if the mean value is not consistent with customer expectations, many of the individual values that are within three standard deviations will still be outside the client's tolerance.

On the other hand, as the mean value approximates the customer's requirements, more and more individual values will fall within the specification limits. If all of the values fall within the specification limits imposed by the client and are inside three standard deviations from the mean, the process is performing at a 99.7% or Six Sigma level. Expressed differently, achievement of Six Sigma means that only 3.4 defects will be found in every million opportunities. Although an admirable achievement, it is when processes are not operating at this level that is of greatest interest to practitioners of Six Sigma thinking. To that end, Table 8.1 shows a summary of Six Sigma levels associated with numbers of defects.

THE PRINCIPLES OF SIX SIGMA

Because Six Sigma is as much philosophical as it is tactical, an understanding of the tenets of the program is necessary to harness its full potential.[3] As related in many fine publications on the subject, the fundamentals of Six Sigma are:

1. **The voice of the client speaks the loudest**: All Six Sigma initiatives are driven by client needs, described as critical-to-quality characteristics.
2. **Process orientation**: For Six Sigma disciples, the process is the product, with all outcomes the sum of many inputs.

3. **Data carry the day**: With such an emphasis on quantification, all Six Sigma initiatives and decisions must be based on quality information.
4. **Managerial ownership**: While Six Sigma does promote delegation and the involvement of content experts in projects, it also insists that the highest levels in management not only promote but also participate in the work.
5. **An environment without barriers**: The Six Sigma philosophy promulgates the removal of any organizational, functional or cultural barriers that may have a negative effect on the probability of success.
6. **No fear of failure**: If people spend so much time fixing mistakes, Six Sigma practitioners believe that they should not fear making mistakes as they introduce better ways of doing business. In the Six Sigma world, it is recognized that issues will occur along the way to excellence.

PROCESS VARIATION AND FUNCTIONS

The math behind Six Sigma can get fairly complicated, but the best way to understand what drives process outcomes is to gain a conceptual understanding of functions. In its simplest mathematical format, Six Sigma can be boiled down to:

$$Y = f(x)$$

In prose form, the above is read as "Y is a function of x." In other words, when dealing with any type of process, the end result, or output (Y), depends on all of the inputs (x) that go into that process. In the Six Sigma vernacular, Y is referred to as a critical-to-quality characteristic, which is an attribute that clients desire in the products or services they purchase. The power of Six Sigma lies in its ability to be applied to any type of process in an organization. The common ground among all projects is that the goal is to reduce variation in the process being analyzed.

While TQM focused its variance reduction efforts on production environments, successful Six Sigma projects have been recorded in areas such as accounts payable, order fill rates and billing accuracy, among others. One of the attractive components of Six Sigma is that it allows teams to first prioritize the importance of potential projects and then use the same methodology to measure variation, regardless of the department or function. The way in which Six Sigma links cause-and-effect relationships with the standard deviation's method for measuring process variance is by using *defects per million opportunities,* or DPMO, as a baseline.

DEFECTS PER MILLION OPPORTUNITIES

In the language of Six Sigma, a defect is defined as any characteristic of a product or service that does not comply with predetermined client specifications. The client can be either internal to the enterprise or external in the form of end users. Thus, a defect could be a cable television installer who does not arrive at a residence within a two-hour guaranteed window or a part coming off a production line that is out of gauge for the next step in the process. How a defect is defined depend on the business a company is in, as well as the demands of its clients. What stands out in this phase of the Six Sigma analysis is that defects are measured against every *one million* opportunities. In the early days of mass production, defects were measured against every *one thousand* opportunities. This shift is clear evidence of how sophisticated customers have become and that they are much less tolerant of errors in any aspect of their commercial relationships.

Because there are so many types of variances in a business application, the original developers of the Six Sigma methodology put all defects on an even playing field via the DPMO methodology. The manner in which this is done involves five simple but important steps. First, team members must identify the type of "units" they are measuring. A unit must be defined as the distinguishing feature of a product or service acquired by a client. It could be pieces in a production lot, warehouse orders, invoices or any type of product or service. Regardless of what the item is, the key characteristics in selecting a unit to be measured are that it can be consistently identified and that it be discrete.

The second step is to identify how many potential opportunities for defects exist in the process of delivering a product or executing a service. For example, in the process of issuing invoices, how many opportunities exist to make a mistake? Billing address, items purchased and amount billed are but a few ways in which erroneous information can infiltrate the process and should be counted as defect opportunities. In the case of warehouse orders, short shipments, wrong merchandise and damaged goods must be accounted for as defect opportunities as well. The key in this step is to analyze a process to the point where all potential ways to make a mistake are identified for subsequent use in the DPMO conversion.

The next step in the DPMO process is to identify the total number of units to be considered. Following the above examples, this could be 1,000 pieces coming off a production line, 500 warehouse deliveries or 2,000 invoices sent to customers. What is important is that there be a sufficient number of units to accurately portray the characteristics of the process. If there are a small number of units to be accounted for, the entire population can be analyzed. If not, then a sample should be taken in a manner that follows well-known statistical practices. With this information, analysts can move on to the fourth stage in determining DPMO, compilation of the number of actual defects.

Identifying real defects can be done in a variety of ways. The first objective, of course, is to establish what a customer's expectations are. This is the point in the client relationship where demands move from the abstract world of "we need better customer service" to the quantifiable "we expect deliveries within two days of placing an order." Once that expectation is agreed upon, measurement against the standard can begin. From that point, defects can be exposed through customer complaints, product returns, customer surveys or even unpaid invoices.

When the unit of measure is established, defect opportunities isolated, number of units under consideration determined and actual defects accounted for, analysts can move on to determining the number of defects per million opportunities found in a process. It is at this time that practitioners establish a baseline for performance and begin to use the Six Sigma tool set to improve performance. The DPMO formula is

(Total number of defects × 1 million)/(Defect opportunities × Units measured)

DPMO Illustrated

A U.K. publisher will be used as an example to demonstrate the DPMO exercise in an international context. In recent months, the publisher has received increasing complaints from offshore clients regarding crossed shipments, missing product and damaged goods. An exporter to 20 countries around the world, the publisher considers order accuracy a form of competitive advantage and launched a Six Sigma project to root out the cause of these problems. In concert with outside consultants, an internal team of content experts was formed from the sales, order management and shipping departments. The unit to be measured was labeled "the flawless order" and was interpreted as meaning the correct merchandise shipped in the quantity ordered, on time, billed correctly and received without damage.

Based on sampling methodologies provided by the consultants, it was decided to use a sample size of 723 shipments. Defect opportunities were broken down into the following categories:

1. Customer received the wrong product
2. Customer was shipped less than ordered
3. Customer was shipped more than ordered
4. Goods arrived late (more than one business day beyond the due date)

Table 8.2   DPMO Calculation

Defect Opportunities	Defects per Opportunity
Wrong merchandise	55
Short-shipped	38
Overshipped	25
Late arrival	34
Damage to goods	24
Incorrect invoice	49
Total	225
DPMO	**51,867**
Sigma level	**3.1**

5. Goods arrived damaged (wet, visible scratches, pages torn, etc.)
6. Incorrect invoice

With this information, the Six Sigma team undertook the most difficult part of the project: identifying the orders that had one or perhaps multiple defects. Results of the study can be found in Table 8.2.

After compiling all of the necessary data, the Six Sigma team was ready to determine both the DPMO figure and its corresponding sigma level. Plugging the numbers into the formula revealed the following DPMO information:

$$(225 \times 1 \text{ million})/(6 \times 723) = 51,867$$

This calculation is important for two reasons. First, it states that in the "flawless order" process the publisher can expect to generate 51,867 defects out of every million opportunities. Returning to Table 8.2, the number also allows the publisher to calculate the Six Sigma level associated with current process performance. Seeking the closest approximation to 51,867, it can be said that the publisher's Six Sigma level for flawless orders is in the neighborhood of 3.1.

Although a far cry from Six Sigma status, at least the publisher knows what is important to its clients, has quantified performance and has established a baseline for improvement. The publisher will be left to its own designs at this time, but it is fair to say that the real work of Six Sigma has just begun.

DMAIC

The math behind Six Sigma only tells part of the story. Most methodologies for improving business processes begin by establishing a baseline measurement from which to work. That is certainly the case in Six Sigma with its use of the standard deviation and DPMO calculation. Where methods often fail, however, is in providing the tools necessary to move off the baseline and advance to long-lasting gains for a company. Six Sigma is unique in the sense that it is founded upon universally accepted mathematical principles, but also provides a framework and tool set that help to translate good intentions into monetary benefit. The real potency of Six Sigma is found in its ability to identify and prioritize projects, create a process improvement road map and provide a battery of techniques that are a powerful force against process variation. The primary method through which this is done is known as DMAIC, or *define, measure, analyze, improve and control.*

It should be pointed out that the depth and breadth of Six Sigma projects vary from company to company. Depending on the type of business, demands of clients and current health of the enterprise, many different initiatives can be undertaken.[4] Many sigma projects revolve around discrete process improvements. As companies find major issues in areas such as accounts receivable and the shipping dock, they will focus a Six Sigma effort on improving that specific area. Other companies may find that certain functions are so dysfunctional that they are compelled to redesign the entire process from scratch. In a third instance, the entire enterprise falls under the guise of Six Sigma, seeking to design and integrate multiple processes across the entire enterprise. Regardless of the scope of a given project, the DMAIC road map should be used consistently from project to project. A full-blown methodology within itself, volumes have been written on the execution of DMAIC.

For purposes of this book, treatment of the subject will be limited to its general framework and emphasis on discipline during all phases of a project. The discussion will also focus on ten key tools that can be used at various phases of the DMAIC process, all of which have individual applications in the field of supply chain management. While the Six Sigma methodology is meant to be applied to a project in its entirety, daily adherence to the goal of eliminating waste through variance reduction is equally powerful. Armed with this mentality, businesspeople can undertake long-term Six Sigma projects while applying individual techniques to everyday challenges.

Define

The *define* phase of Six Sigma is a multi-step process that allows management to not only identify problem areas in a company but also prioritize the importance of potential projects. While projects will have different priority levels within an organization, the basic requirements for any project to be considered are that they be relevant to the client, feasible given the resources at hand and bring quantifiable financial benefit to the company.

A simple brainstorming exercise among team members will uncover a plethora of opportunities to be evaluated. Depending on the business activities of the customer, problems can range from "too many engineering changes after sending out a prototype" to "too much wait time in the insurance claims resolution process." Once opportunities have been identified, they must then be prioritized in order of importance. After projects have been identified and prioritized, the work of organizing the project can begin.

The first step of the project team is to prepare a charter that articulates a problem or opportunity, the business case and a goal statement. Based on that information, the charter also presents the scope of the project, names of team members, resource requirements and any potential constraints the team may face. Finally, the charter lists a preliminary sequencing of events by target and actual dates.

The second step of the define phase is to identify customer needs. This is one of the most critical phases of the entire methodology, as these requirements lead to the definition of critical-to-quality characteristics against which actual performance will be measured. Returning to the role of the standard deviation in Six Sigma, it is the identification of variance between actual and desired outcomes that enables practitioners to apply improvement techniques. Comparison of the upper and lower specification limits set by the client with the mean and standard deviation is what determines if quality is within tolerance. For this reason, determination of actual customer requirements must be achieved during the define stage.

The final step in the define stage is the preparation of a process map that visually describes the subject under analysis. Different mapping techniques can be used, but the goal is to gain a high-level understanding of who all of the players arc in a process and what the flow of goods, documentation, information and funds looks like. Once a graphical representation of the overall process is prepared, team members may choose to create more detailed process flow maps of specific functions within the overall process. It is at this time that bottlenecks, rework loops and wait time may begin to manifest themselves.

After identifying a project, creating its charter and mapping high-level processes, the project team is ready to move on to the second phase of DMAIC, measure.

Measure

Once client requirements have been established, the measurement of processes can begin. The *measure* phase can be the most trying of the whole exercise, given the level of difficulty in gathering up-to-date and relevant data. Recognizing the problems inherent to organizing information, the team must be realistic regarding the accuracy of information, its source, how easy it is to gather and, finally, how it can be interpreted for purposes of the project. For supply chain projects that are international in scope, these considerations can create serious constraints for the project team and must be dealt with early on. In addition to these parameters, team members must focus on measures that not only are important to the client but also can be defined quantitatively. A statement like "better customer service" is never acceptable as a measurement criterion, whereas "installation of full service within 45 minutes of technician arrival" is.

Most continuous improvement methodologies have a mechanism for establishing baseline performance. Six Sigma departs from traditional methods, however, in that it not only measures current performance but also insists on identifying the cost of poor quality (COPQ) associated with that level of execution. This unique requirement of Six Sigma is the primary link between performance and cost. Since one of the principles of Six Sigma is to bring financial benefit to the company, current performance and corresponding COPQ must always be identified.

The number one method used to verify current performance levels is the two-step process of the DPMO calculation and determination of the sigma level. Returning to the example of the U.K. book publisher, recall that the result was 51,867 DPMO and the sigma level 3.1. Armed with this information, the project team can begin to determine the COPQ associated with that sigma level. Once a monetary cost has been associated with current performance, team members can begin to analyze ways to reduce variation and eliminate waste.

The COPQ for the U.K. publisher must be determined within the context of the critical-to-quality characteristics identified by clients and the way in which defects can occur. In terms of critical-to-quality characteristics, a flawless order was understood to mean "the correct merchandise shipped in the quantity ordered, on time, billed correctly and received without damage." Defects could occur by shipping the wrong merchandise, over/undershipping, shipping late, invoicing incorrectly or the client receiving damaged goods. At this juncture, the COPQ exercise must determine what it costs the U.K. publisher to prevent mistakes from happening, as well as to fix them should they actually occur. For example, if the publisher is forced to do an additional quality check on all orders prior to shipping, what is the cost of that extra step in the process? Also, if a customer receives the wrong goods, the publisher has to pay the freight for the correct order to go out as well as to return the wrong books. What is the cost associated with that type of error? Finally, the COPQ must account for the expense of crediting and reissuing invoices and preparing new orders in the warehouse. All things considered, what is the total cost of preventing bad orders from getting out or fixing the mistakes that do slip through?

As one can see, calculation of the COPQ of a given service level pushes the abstract idea of customer service into the real world of dollars and cents in a major hurry. In a global model where the waste associated with COPQ can run into millions of dollars, the ability of Six Sigma to identify and remove waste becomes increasingly manifest.

Analyze

It was stated earlier in the chapter that process variation is driven by the cause-and-effect nature of functions. Given that Y is a function of x, the quality of an outcome depends upon the interaction between all of the dependent and independent variables that go into creating that outcome. It is the job of the project team in the *analyze* phase to study both data and processes to determine where variance occurs, paving the way for process enhancements in the improvement stage.

It is at this time that many of the techniques found in the Six Sigma toolbox show their greatest value. Given that team members are analyzing tasks, looking for trends, problem clusters and overall waste, proper use of these tools will reveal telling information about the health of a process. Discussed in greater detail in Chapter 9, Pareto charts, histograms, run charts, Ishikawa diagrams and scatter diagrams can all be used to define the composition and state of current processes. In the early phases of the analyze stage, detailed process mapping techniques are also employed to provide team members with a visual representation of the task at hand. From that point, the aforementioned tools are brought in to help team members establish hypotheses about potential sources of variation and waste.

Completion of the detailed process map facilitates the application of other tools designed to isolate trends, cause and effect, frequency distributions and correlations. The outcome of that analysis allows team members to move beyond hypothesizing and substantiate their claims as to the source of problems. As hypotheses on the cause of variation are proven, they are carried over to the improve stage of DMAIC, where new methods will be designed to improve performance.

Detailed process maps can be very helpful in the search for waste. This tool ties in neatly with the lean manufacturing mentality insofar as a good process map will expose points in a process where rework, wait time, bottlenecks, decision points and redundancy occur. The sworn enemy of lean thinking, use of this Six Sigma tool augments efforts to identify waste and is complementary by nature. In terms of benefits for global business models, the pollination of the lean mentality with Six Sigma tools may be the most potent methodology out there today.

Improve

If there is a potential gap in the DMAIC methodology, it can be found between the analyze and *improve* stages. This likelihood exists due to the fact that it is oftentimes easier to identify problems than it is to fix them. Change is always met with resistance, and it is interesting to observe how people are willing to expend an infinite amount of energy pushing back against change but very little embracing it. Apart from the human dynamic associated with change, the solution has to be right for the client. With the voice of the customer in the team's ear, team members also must be cognizant of cost constraints associated with implementation, how long it will take and what new skill sets will be required of employees to make it stick.

As sigma teams become convinced of the overall value of their solutions, mechanisms must be built into process design that minimize the probability of variation. Taken from Japanese lean applications, poka-yoke is a technique that does not permit the next step in a process to take place until the preceding step is done correctly. Also know as foolproofing, poka-yoke can be used as effectively on the production floor as in a back-office administrative function. For example, a machine tolerance that will not allow the force-fit of a component onto a chassis is an example of poka-yoke. In a documentation environment, order management systems that do not allow an order to be closed until all country-specific documents are accounted for is another example of poka-yoke. In either case, the process or system will not allow the next step to happen until the prior steps are done correctly. The impact of this technique on customer satisfaction and COPQ make it a must-have for any improvement project.

While Six Sigma provides tools to minimize the probability of failure in both human and process design areas, success ultimately depends on the creativity of team members in devising new solutions. The journey to creativity in the improve stage begins with a broad view of the business model and a willingness to jettison conventional thinking. In order for this to happen, people have to ask the right questions about the problems they are trying to solve. Oftentimes, the question to ask is not "What can we do to fix this step in the process?" but rather "What can we do to eliminate the need for this step in the first place?" Think back for a moment to the lean section on just in time and how the process eliminates the need for purchase orders. One can be sure that just in time did not start out this way and that it was the creative thinking of a team that brought this quantum improvement in supply chain management forward.

Recall that a goal of just in time is to reduce inventories through smaller lot sizes. This is an admirable objective, but a side effect of smaller lot sizes is more purchase orders. The purchasing department may be buying in smaller quantities that are in line with actual demand, but the administrative burden of dealing with the more frequent placement of orders may defeat the original benefit. Whereas a company can remove waste in the factory by reducing lot sizes, it may be creating more waste in the office by the need to process extra purchase orders. When employees observe the administrative swelling caused by the increase in orders, a conventional response is to hire more people in purchasing. Lean thinkers address the issue not by asking how to handle more purchase orders but by identifying how to eradicate the need for them entirely. The solution? Putting suppliers on a delivery schedule that is adjusted to accommodate real demand as delivery dates approach.

It is precisely this type of thinking that is required in the improve stage of DMAIC. Once again, Six Sigma methodologies applied to the body of lean thinking create extremely powerful applications for all facets of supply chain management.

Control

The biggest criticism of any continuous improvement project is that five minutes after the consultants walk out the door, things go right back to the way they were. That is a legitimate claim because process implementation can be likened to a large rubber band. When held in one's hands, the rubber band can be twisted and manipulated into almost any shape. However, once the pressure is released, it springs right back to its original shape. The objective of the *control* stage of DMAIC is to make sure that the process works right and that it holds its intended shape.

One way to maintain control over both pre- and post-process implementation is to limit the scope of the project. Limiting the scope of an initiative in the project charter decreases the probability of "process creep." Another way to maintain control is to take implementation in phases, beginning with a pilot program. A pilot program incorporates all elements of the overall implementation but on a much smaller scale. This approach allows for unexpected consequences to be exposed, additional resources to be marshaled and processes to be tweaked. Once a track record has been established and people start to see tangible results, the process implementation can be expanded.

When a team is working on a global supply chain project that cuts across function, geography and language, it is advisable to limit the scope of a project and start with a pilot program. A good idea that is badly implemented is oftentimes worse than what people worked with before. Also, in the incredulous world of improvement initiatives, it doesn't take much for people to unjustly label a good project as just another management scheme du jour.

At the end of the day, control is about anticipating potential problems and being in a position to address them quickly. That means picking up on variations in new processes and bringing them within specified limits rapidly. Control also means gaining momentum by sharing productivity gains with the entire organization. The more people can see tangible benefits from a process, the more they will participate in its proliferation. It is the communication of challenges and benefits inherent to improvement projects that keeps people interested and willing to contribute. In the control stage of DMAIC, the team has come too far to watch its initiatives fade to footnote status in the growing volume of managerial magic tricks. Continued discipline, perseverance and communication through the last stages of the control phase are absolutely necessary to round out a project.

SUMMARY

As a stand-alone methodology for process improvement, Six Sigma offers practitioners the means to improve customer relations, minimize defects across operations and reduce cycle times. With a foundation built solidly on the math of the standard deviation and DPMO calculation, companies are also able to isolate areas of the business where variation and waste run the most rampant. As sigma levels are linked to the expense of defects via the COPQ technique, the monetary consequence of process variation is also identified. While Six Sigma has many attractive features, it is this linking of performance with COPQ that is perhaps its most salient component.

When the Six Sigma methodology is applied in companies that adhere to the lean principles and understand the dynamics of international supply chain management, the benefits that accrue to these organizations are truly maximized. A consistent theme throughout this book, it is the understanding of business history, adoption of modern commercial philosophies and application of relevant tools that offer the best hope for companies to prosper now and in the future.

NOTES

1. Robert S. Kaplan and David P. Norton, *The Balanced Scorecard: Translating Strategy into Action,* Harvard Business School Press, 1996.
2. M.G. Kendall and W.R. Buckland, *A Dictionary of Statistical Terms,* Longman Group, 1971, p. 186.
3. This section is adapted in part from Pete Pande and Larry Holpp, *What Is Six Sigma?,* McGraw-Hill, 2002; Greg Brue, *Six Sigma for Managers,* McGraw Hill, 2002; and Peter Pande, Robert Neuman, and Roland Cavanagh, *The Six Sigma Way Team Fieldbook,* McGraw-Hill, 2002.
4. Peter Pande, Robert Neuman, and Roland Cavanagh, *The Six Sigma Way Team Fieldbook,* McGraw-Hill, 2002, p. 14.

9

SIX SIGMA TOOLS FOR SUPPLY CHAIN MANAGEMENT

The power of Six Sigma lies in its ability to apply proven techniques to a problem or opportunity within a comprehensive project management framework. Because of the variation inherent to international operations, this methodology is ideal for companies operating a global business model.

Six Sigma is different than other continuous improvement methodologies for a variety of reasons. First, the discipline insists on creating what is known as "operational definition." Carried out in the early stages of a project, operational definition takes what are oftentimes qualitative client requirements and translates them into quantitative characteristics known as critical-to-quality characteristics. Recognizing that the voice of the client speaks the loudest, the sigma tool set contains techniques that allow team members to put a measurable value on abstract customer needs. Once operational definition and critical-to-quality characteristics are established, it is from this point that variance from a predetermined standard can be measured.

Apart from its comprehensive methodology and vast problem-solving tool set, the greatest contribution of Six Sigma is its capacity to link the cost of poor quality to variations found in processes and products. Thus, as variation is reduced and the quality of products and processes improves, team members enjoy the dual benefit of watching customer satisfaction improve and cost of poor quality go down. It is the ability to first identify critical-to-quality characteristics and then measure the costs of not complying with those requirements that makes the Six Sigma methodology so appealing.

Ideally, the Six Sigma methodology should be applied in its entirety to well-defined and feasible projects. Whether engaged in process improvements, process redesign or enterprise-wide efforts, the powers of Six Sigma are best exploited when used in a comprehensive fashion. While this is a defining characteristic of the system, it is also important to realize that Six Sigma is as much a philosophy as it is a set of improvement techniques. Not unlike any other philosophy, Six Sigma is built upon a base of core values that manifest themselves every day. In the sigma world, that daily manifestation is found in the quest to remove waste and improve cycle times by reducing process variation. Therefore, while companies should focus on applying sigma tools in the project format, they can also be used every day to bring incremental improvements to an organization.

It is the combination of adherence to the Six Sigma philosophy and tireless application of its techniques to business problems that will exact its greatest benefits. Of course, knowledge of when and how to use the sigma tool set is what opens the door to continuous process improvement. While there are many tools that can be used in a Six Sigma project, the focus of this chapter is those techniques that have applications throughout the life of a project, as well as in a daily business setting.

FIVE WHY ANALYSIS

Many of the techniques found in the sigma tool kit are designed for specific phases of the DMAIC process, while others can be use at any time throughout the life of a project. Applicable to both high-level brainstorming sessions and process-specific analysis, the five why analysis conditions people to question any facet of a company's operation at least five times. First adopted by Japanese lean thinkers and picked up in the United States by Motorola, five why analysis assists team members in many endeavors, including identifying potential projects, pinpointing areas of waste and focusing on root causes of problems. Whether in the early stages of a project or in the finer areas of process analysis, the five why approach is designed to prepare team members for use of other sigma tools that lead to process improvements.

Let's look at an example of a five why exchange that took place between a sigma team and a group of buyers. The company in question is Buchanan Automotive, a Columbus, Ohio–based auto parts manufacturer that imports raw materials from Asia. Its inventory levels are growing rapidly and company management does not understand why. Conducted during an early brainstorming session, the flow is indicative of how five why analysis can point team members in interesting directions.

Question #1: Why are inventory levels so high?

Answer: Because raw materials purchases are out of line with the forecast and production planning.

Note: From the answer to the first question, there is reason to believe that raw materials are to blame for increasing inventories. For the moment, at least, work in process and finished goods are left aside.

Question #2: Why are raw materials purchases out of line with production planning?

Answer: There have been some quality issues with components that have caused work in process to increase, but mainly because buyers are paranoid.

Question #3: Why are buyers paranoid?

Answer: Lead times are not reliable, so in order to avoid shutting lines down, they are placing their orders earlier and in greater quantities.

Note: The discussion now may indicate that the problem is not with inventories per se but nervousness in the system based on unreliable lead times.

Question #4: Why aren't lead times reliable?

Answer: Too many customs delays at destination.

Question #5: Why are there so many customs delays?

Answer: Many suppliers do not provide commercial documentation when they tender cargo and there are too many mistakes when cargo is received.

Note: While the investigation is just beginning, the project team has uncovered potential areas of concern and can begin to hypothesize about causes. In this case, further process review may validate or reject where the five why analysis has led the team thus far.

This simple exchange is also proof that the people closest to an activity are the ones with the greatest amount of knowledge about a product or process. Had the members of the sigma team not taken the time to talk with the buyers, they may have never arrived at the decision they agreed upon.

SIPOC PROCESS MAP

The acronym SIPOC stands for *supplier, input, process, output and customer* and is used primarily as a high-level process map. SIPOC maps are particularly useful in the define stages of a Six Sigma project for two reasons. First, the structure of the map emphasizes the importance of causal relationships in any business activity (inputs go into a process and create outputs). Second, the SIPOC methodology identifies all players in a process and their role in delivering a product or service.

Preparation of the SIPOC map actually begins with the process itself. Because it is a high-level map, steps in a given process are normally limited to half a dozen key activities. As each process step is identified, team members work backward to determine what the initial *input* is into that step, as well as who the *supplier* of the input is. Then moving forward, the *output* of the process is identified, as well as who the *customer* of that output is. Requirements associated with each process step are listed on the far right.

Table 9.1 displays an SIPOC process map that was developed from the preceding five why analysis. The Buchanan team decided to focus on inbound materials flows due to the fact that the answers provided pointed to upstream problems (supplier inputs) that were causing faulty outputs (timely deliveries). The team hypothesized that while growing inventories were symptomatic of a problem, the real illness may be associated with the management of inbound flows of raw materials from China to the plant in Columbus, Ohio.

Normally, SIPOC maps are used in the define stage of a project to help team members visualize inputs and outputs of a process on a high level. As projects move into the measure and analyze stages, more detailed process maps are utilized to quantify the existing state of a process. In some cases, however, SIPOC maps reveal enough about a process to shine a spotlight on suspected root causes via a detailed process map.

After preparing the SIPOC map of inbound materials flow, a specific activity in the process stuck out in the minds of the team members. Isolated in Table 9.2, step two in the SIPOC process required the supplier at origin to contact a third-party logistics (3PL) provider for a local pickup. The output of the process was the collection of both cargo and commercial documents by the 3PL firm. If the five why analysis revealed that documents were either missing or contained errors when they arrived at U.S. Customs, the team wanted to know the precise nature of the interaction between the supplier and 3PL firm at origin. It was for this reason that the team decided to take an early look at the inbound process via a more detailed process map.

DETAILED PROCESS MAPPING

As the name would indicate, detailed process maps are intended to bring more detail to an analysis and isolate areas of potential process improvements. Used

Table 9.1   SIPOC Process Map: Inbound Materials Flow from Asia to Columbus, Ohio

Supplier	Inputs	Process	Outputs	Customer	Requirements
Buchanan Automotive	Materials requirements plan	Purchase order released	Raw materials order	Columbus, Ohio plant	
Supplier's logistics department	Pickup request	Asia supplier contacts origin 3PL firm for pickup	Documents and cargo picked up	Columbus, Ohio plant	Documents and cargo ready for export
3PL firm at origin	Cargo is labeled, consolidated and sent to airline	Origin 3PL exports goods	Export shipment	Columbus, Ohio plant	Airway bill, invoice and packing list matched via 3 Cs methodology
3PL firm at destination	Airway bill, invoice, packing list and customs entry	Cargo arrives and clears customs	Entry presented to customs	Columbus, Ohio plant	Classification and valuation of goods
Local trucker	Customs release and delivery order	Local delivery	Delivery to plant	Columbus, Ohio plant	Customs release document (delivery order)

Table 9.2   SIPOC Process Map for Step Two: Supplier and Origin 3PL Firm Interaction

Supplier	Inputs	Process	Outputs	Customer	Requirements
Supplier's logistics department	Pickup request	Asia supplier contacts origin 3PL firm for pickup	Documents and cargo picked up	Columbus, Ohio plant	Documents and cargo ready for export

during the define and analyze stages of a project, process maps are intended to identify the disconnects, bottlenecks, redundancies, rework loops and decision points that create waste in a process. Because of the discrepancies between the five why exchange and what the SIPOC map showed relative to the supplier/3PL firm interaction at origin, the team zeroed in on that process. In the case of the inbound materials flow process, some interesting issues were uncovered.

Figure 9.1 shows that the process splits after the 3PL firm is contacted by the supplier for a pickup. If both the cargo and documents are ready, the process proceeds normally and goods are prepared for export. Conversely, if the cargo is not ready, a delay is incurred and the 3PL firm will have to return at another time to collect the shipment (and charge for another pickup). The scenario that was of greater interest to the team, however, was when cargo was ready but documents were not provided by the supplier. At this juncture in the process, the 3PL firm reaches a decision point: either hold the cargo and wait for the commercial invoice and packing list or simply ship the cargo without documents and hope to get them later. In lieu of any specific instructions from the importer in Columbus, the 3PL firm opted in most cases to ship the cargo without documents, hence creating the downstream customs delay first revealed

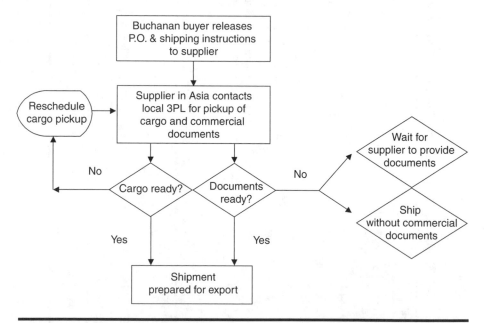

Figure 9.1 Detailed Process Map for Inbound Flow of Documents and Merchandise

in the five why analysis. Either option beyond the decision point was a losing proposition given that both scenarios created delays in the process. The only difference was that waiting for documents created origin delays, while shipping without them precipitated problems at destination.

Needless to say, the team working on this project still has a great deal of work to do. As the team members move through the DMAIC process, they will be compelled to use tools like standard deviation, trend charts, Pareto analysis and histograms that will lead them to the process improvements they seek. At this point, however, the value and application of five why analysis, SIPOC process mapping and detailed process mapping in setting the course of Six Sigma process should be evident.

CRITICAL-TO-QUALITY TREE DIAGRAM

Under most circumstances, the SIPOC diagram is designed to provide the team with a visual representation of a process and is the last step in the define stage. In some cases, an SIPOC map does illustrate blatant areas of concern, and it is at that time when a detailed process map is prepared. Once identified by the detailed process map, problems can be quickly rooted out and immediate gains achieved. Even if a team is fortunate enough to harvest incremental gains early in a project, it must continue through the entire methodology. This is particularly true during the measure stage, when critical-to-quality characteristics (CTQCs) are defined, sigma levels determined and cost of poor quality calculated.

Critical-to-quality (CTQ) trees are what translate voice of the customer needs to specific and measurable product/service characteristics. Based on outputs that are identified in the SIPOC diagram, CTQ trees not only identify a need but also describe what the drivers of the need are. Based on this cause-and-effect relationship, the CTQ tree is then able to quantify what the CTQCs of a customer requirement are. It is this transition from the abstract to absolute that makes the CTQ tree exercise important to an overall project.

Figure 9.2 illustrates a CTQ tree diagram for a company that is experiencing invoice problems from its suppliers. Although willing to pay, the company in question continuously receives invoices from vendors that are late or contain the wrong information. As part of a lean supplier management initiative, the customer is trying to rationalize the billing process and keep days payable outstanding at 21 days.

Beginning on the left-hand side of the diagram, the need is defined as timely and accurate receipt of invoices from suppliers. Although a valid requirement from the rare customer that wants to pay its bills, at this time it still lacks

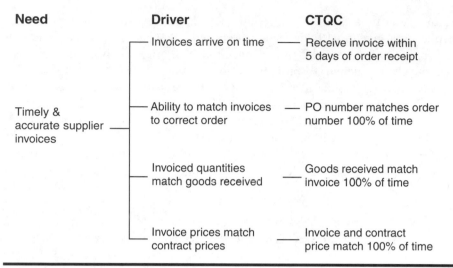

Figure 9.2 Critical-to-Quality Tree for Invoicing Process

definition. In an effort to identify the drivers behind the need, the customer has defined four areas: invoices arrive on time, the ability to match invoices to corresponding orders, quantity received matches what is on an invoice and the price billed matches the contract price. This is an important step in the process insomuch as general requirements are being supported by specifics. With this level of information, the customer is now ready to quantify exactly what its CTQCs are.

With regard to the first driver, invoices arrive on time is defined to mean that the customer receives a bill within five business days of receipt of the order. For ability to match invoice to correct order, the customer has decided that the sales order number from the vendor must reference the client's original purchase order number on the invoice 100% of the time. In order to assure that the client is not paying for goods not received, the third driver calls for a 100% match between billed and received merchandise. Finally, the fourth driver is concerned with accuracy between the price for a component on the invoice and the original contract price. In this instance, accuracy of billed versus contract pricing must be 100%.

Although it has established high CTQC standards, the customer feels that, in exchange for its willingness to pay early, it deserves information that is 100% accurate. The client must work with suppliers to achieve this level of excellence, but the CTQ tree has kick-started the process by allowing the client to articulate a need, identify its drivers and assign a value to the services it requires. From that point, continuous process improvements can be uncovered and applied to the accounts payable process.

CALCULATION OF SIGMA LEVELS

Sigma levels were first discussed in Chapter 8 using a U.K. publisher's order management process as an example. Continuing with the discussion of the accounts payable project described in the preceding section, the calculation will be presented again.

The first thing to remember about the sigma level is that it is the ratio of actual defects to the total number of possible defects that can occur. This aspect of the sigma process allows team members to identify not only how problems happen but, when used with other sigma tools, to determine where in the process defects are occurring. When taken within the vector of how and where, the ability to identify opportunities for improvement becomes much greater. Recall the defects per million opportunities (DPMO) calculation from Chapter 8:

(Number of defects × 1 million)/(Defect opportunities × Units measured)

Upon establishing its CTQCs, the aforementioned customer implemented the program with a group of key suppliers. After a six-month period, the customer saw some compliance from vendors, but just was not sure where they stood quantitatively. It was at this point that the customer compiled the statistics necessary to calculate the sigma level for the accounts payable project. As detailed in Table 9.3, those statistics are unit measured, number of units, defect opportunities, types of defects and total number of errors. Based on the information gathered over a six-month period, the result of the DPMO calculation is

(198 × 1 million)/(5 × 895) = 44,245 defects per million opportunities

Note that during the first six months of the accounts payable initiative, the customer and its suppliers achieved a sigma level of roughly 3.150. While not

Table 9.3 DPMO and Sigma Calculation for Accounts Payable Process

Unit measured	Vendor invoice
Number of units	895
Defect opportunities	5
Types of defects	
Invoice arrived late	
Contains incorrect information	
Cannot match purchase order number with sales order number	
Quantity billed does not match product received	
Invoice amount does not match contract price	
Total number of errors	198
DPMO	44,245
Sigma level	3.150 (approx.)

great, it is a young process and, armed with a baseline, the customer can now seek ways to improve specific aspects of the operation. Remembering that a sigma team must search out the how and where of defects, a good place to start would be the five defect opportunities. By identifying the type and frequency of errors among the five defect opportunities, the sigma team can use other tools to drill down to specific problems. From that point, improvement techniques can be utilized to continuously improve upon the DPMO and, consequently, the sigma level.

THE COST OF POOR QUALITY

It has been emphasized in several instances that a benefit of any Six Sigma initiative is the ability to tie process variation to the cost associated with that variance. Once this figure is calculated, sigma teams have a tangible dollar figure that connects the esoteric jargon of statistics to the easily understood language of yen, won and rupees. Prior to arriving at that calculation, however, it is important to categorize the types of costs associated with poor quality:

1. **Internal defects**: Costs that can be traced to defects that are discovered before the customer receives the merchandise. As a customer can be either internal or external to an organization, examples of internal costs include rework, scrap, down lines and multiple inspections.
2. **External defects**: Costs associated with errors that are uncovered after the customer receives the product or service. These costs include return freight charges, refusal to pay, invoice allowances, product replacement and loss of customer goodwill.
3. **Appraisal costs**: Expenses associated with monitoring the quality of a product or service, including inspections, audits and quality control.
4. **Prevention costs**: Costs associated with taking a more proactive approach to quality that includes supplier integration efforts, quality at the source, employee training and equipment maintenance.

Pinpointing the expense associated with defects can be a cumbersome task. This point becomes even more relevant when one recognizes that the supplier and customer incur the same costs. Whether considering the time associated with fixing mistakes, the expense of phone calls and faxes exchanged during resolution or the lost productivity associated with the entire exercise, it is clear that both supplier and customer share in the pain. As such, any calculation that estimates cost of poor quality (COPQ) must be increased by an order of two to account for the losses incurred by buyer and seller.

To wrap up the accounts payable example, it was determined that two full-time employees in the eight-person accounts payable department were dedicated exclusively to auditing and fixing bad invoices from suppliers. Although their presence does bring benefit by reducing the impact of paying incorrect invoices, it can be argued that the cost of their very presence is a COPQ. Taking into consideration two fully loaded salaries, communications expenses, office space, system bandwidth and general administrative expenses, the cost of employing two such people could easily exceed $90,000 per year. Also, if each of the suppliers employs people dedicated to correct and reissue invoices, the COPQ across the entire supply chain increases proportionately.

Apart from the total expense of having employees dedicated to auditing invoices, calculations can be performed that bring a per-hour cost to the exercise as well. Aided by the DPMO and sigma level, any company can do simple calculations for the cost per man-hour of auditing supplier invoices. A rudimentary calculation may consist of the following:

Cost per man-hour × Average hours needed to fix one invoice
× Number of invoices

Based on internal calculations, let's say that a company can determine that its cost per man-hour in accounts payable is $30. This includes not only the fully loaded hourly wage of one person but also the direct expenses allocatable to the entire audit/correction process. It has also been determined that the average time needed to identify, audit and resolve invoice-related problems is 2.5 hours per invoice. Finally, the total number of invoices that must be audited and corrected is 40 per month. With these figures, the company can determine its own COPQ as:

$30 × 2.5 hours × 40 invoices = $3,000 per month or $36,000 per year

Needless to say, it is much easier for a Six Sigma team to approach management with these figure than with a DPMO of 22,700 or a sigma level of 3.5. When a sigma team can express a problem in a financial format, the likelihood of obtaining top management's support in eradicating process variation will be much higher. It is this unique feature of the methodology that makes Six Sigma so appealing and COPQ calculations a requirement for any project.

DEPLOYMENT PROCESS MAPS

Detailed process maps are very helpful in sequencing vertically discrete operations. Deployment process maps (DPMs), on the other hand, track operations

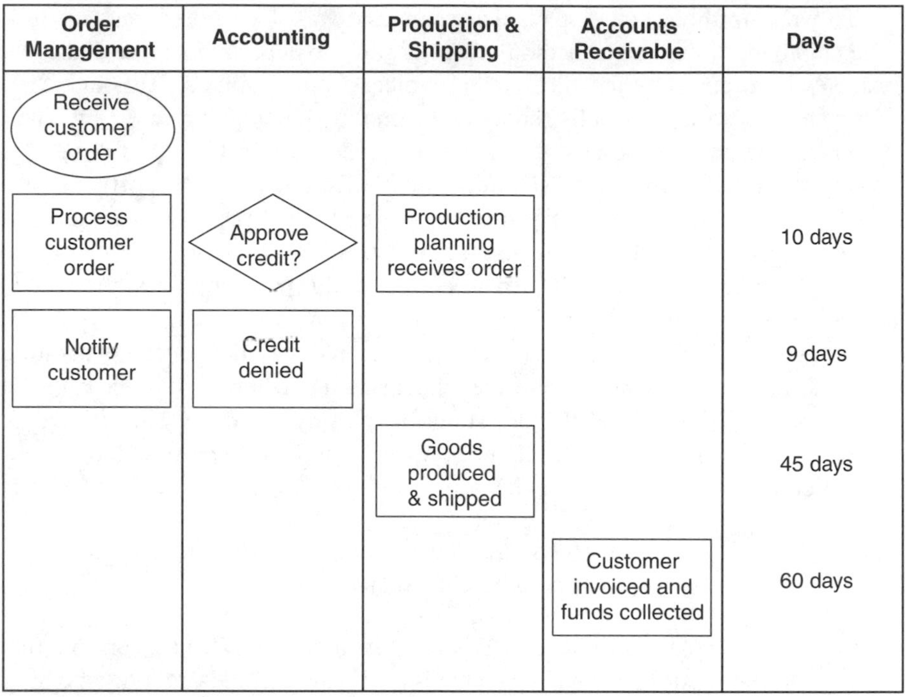

Order Management	Accounting	Production & Shipping	Accounts Receivable	Days
Receive customer order				
Process customer order	Approve credit?	Production planning receives order		10 days
Notify customer	Credit denied			9 days
		Goods produced & shipped		45 days
			Customer invoiced and funds collected	60 days

Figure 9.3 Deployment Process Map for Operating Cycle

or activities as they move horizontally across several departments in an organization. As one would suspect, this view of a process allows team members to zero in on disconnects between functions that create waste, downtime and non-value-added activities. DPMs are most useful when employed to map enterprise-wide processes as they move across an organization and can include supplier and/or customer activities. As such, DPMs are especially applicable when analyzing global supply chains.

Figure 9.3 shows a DPM that has been prepared for the order management process of a Dutch exporter. The exporter is concerned with the amount of time it is taking to process orders, approve customer credit, manufacture the goods, ship, bill and collect money.

The reader may recognize this process as the operating cycle, or the time it takes to sell a product, invoice and collect payment. Because the company in question operates a build-to-order model, the process is mapped from the time a customer places an order through actual collection. Analysis of each department, the steps per department and elapsed time for each step helps a sigma team to identify breakdowns in the process, redundancies and dead time.

The first potential disconnect may be between the order management function and credit approval. A logical question the sigma team may ask is why orders are input into the system before credit approval is sought from another department. Why not have credit approval information available to the order management people before an order is processed? Given that the total time to carry out the two processes is six days, it would certainly be a worthwhile investment of time to answer that question. Once credit is approved, it takes another four days to get the order to the manufacturing department. Conversely, if a customer does not have sufficient credit, notification that the order has been rejected takes an additional three days. In this case, the customer is going to be annoyed not only by the fact that the order was rejected but that it took nine days to find out!

If an order is approved, it is sent on to manufacturing, where it takes an average of 45 days to source raw materials, manufacture the order and ship it out. Because of the build-to-order model, it is understandable that this process takes longer than shipping from finished goods inventory. Even so, 45 days seems long, and a detailed process map of the manufacturing process may be called for. Once the order is shipped, it takes another 60 days to bill and collect money.

A cursory look at this process would indicate that there are several functions that could be executed simultaneously. Also, it is clear that the functions that take the longest are manufacturing and accounts receivable. As mentioned previously, each of those functions requires a more in-depth analysis using the full Six Sigma tool kit.

Without even analyzing each individual function or the myriad handoffs inherent to the process, it appears that the exporter in question has a systems visibility problem. While this obviously requires more study, the use of an enterprise resource planning software suite would allow many of the sequential activities to be done in parallel, with each downstream player (manufacturing, for example) in a position to get moving ahead of time. This ability alone would reduce cycle time by a considerable percentage.

DPMs are best utilized when several departments are involved in a process. They are even more powerful when entities outside of an organization have input into the overall quality of output from a process. The ability to capture disconnects between suppliers, a manufacturer and its customers will almost surely reduce cycle time and allow companies to take orders, sell and collect money in a much more expedient fashion. In the example under analysis, if an order is rejected due to credit problems, the customer should be notified immediately, not nine days later. When an order is accepted, the ability to move from an operating cycle of 115 days to 50% of that number is not at all unreasonable.

VALUE-ADDED PROCESS MAPS

In view of the fact that reduction in cycle times is a primary goal of Six Sigma, the value-added process (VAP) map can be considered one of the most powerful tools in the sigma toolbox. Designed to differentiate between value-adding and non-value-adding activities in a process, VAP maps target waste that manifests itself in the form of time lost on unnecessary or redundant activities.

A VAP map is very similar to a detailed process map insomuch as it is used to sequence events in a process. Of additional value, however, is the calculation of time necessary to execute each individual step in the process. The time to complete individual activities is calculated and appears to the right of each task, and the total cycle time is identified.

When the process map and corresponding task times are calculated, teams then begin to identify areas that can be refined or taken out of the process. Naturally, as activities are improved or eliminated, the cycle time decreases. When the exercise is complete, the process is pilot tested and eventually implemented full scale. In the case of a VAP map, the improvement can be measured immediately and interpreted as the difference between the original cycle time and the time necessary to complete the new process.

Figure 9.4 is a VAP map prepared by an Indian supplier of components and assemblies to the electronics industry. The engineering department of the Indian company is concerned with the design time necessary to deliver components to its customers. It has been taking over six months from the moment the engineers receive a schematic for a new component until a quality product is delivered to the customer. The engineers feel that part of their value proposition should include rapid turnaround from engineering to manufacturing, with a minimum of design changes along the way. Design of a VAP map was the first step in achieving that goal.

The first observation that can be made about the engineering and design change VAP map is that there is no communication between the customer and supplier. Without any input or collaboration from the vendor, the customer simply delivers a schematic and expects to receive a perfect component in return. From that point, the exchange resembles a protracted game of ping-pong, where the prototype is bounced back and forth for endless design changes. The alarming aspect of this exercise is that the process takes 195 days to complete. In a world where product life cycles are less than six months, this extended cycle time is unacceptable.

As the proposed VAP map suggests, if both vendor and customer were to play on the same side of the ping-pong table, they could deliver a component to production in 100 days. Beginning as a collaborative effort in step one, the vendor and customer work together on quality, fit and manufacturability. When

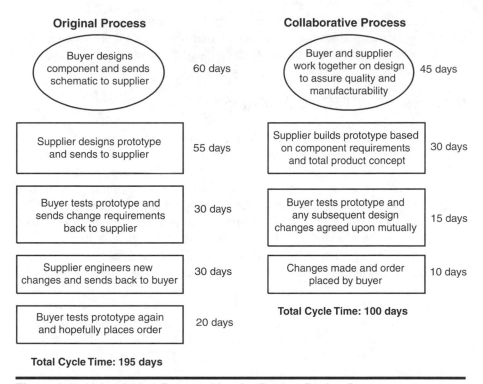

Figure 9.4 Value-Added Process Map for Product Design Process

communication is established from the outset, design of the schematic can be reduced from 60 to 45 days. Because the vendor has a perspective on how its component complements the design and manufacturability of the finished product, the build time for the prototype comes down from 55 to 30 days. As defined in step three, if there are any design changes to be made, they are mutually agreed upon between buyer and seller. Since communication has been open from the outset of the project, the ability to exchange ideas and get answers to questions is improved, reducing design change time from 30 to 15 days.

If the proposed process is implemented, members of the Indian vendor's engineering team feel that they can bring a component to the client's production floor in 100 days, an initial improvement of 95 days over the original process. Continuous tweaking of the vendor/supplier relationship will reap further benefits as time goes by.

This case is a good example of how Six Sigma tools can be applied to the principles of lean manufacturing. As discussed in Chapter 3, the supplier management aspect of the lean methodology plays a pivotal role in global operations.

When the lean mentality is employed in supplier relationships and can be augmented by sigma techniques designed to remove waste from those relationships, the downstream benefits that accrue to the supply chain are appreciable.

CAUSE-AND-EFFECT DIAGRAMS

As one gains an understanding of the application of the techniques found in the sigma toolbox, one will also realize that there is a clear link between the objectives of Six Sigma and the tools that enable a project. In the case of reducing cycle times, both the DPM and VAP map are extremely helpful in pinpointing dead time in a process. COPQ calculations help team members to quantify the expense associated with process variation and begin the task of reducing costs by stabilizing activities. Because Six Sigma is based on the dynamics of causal relationships and recognizes that the quality of an output is contingent upon all of its inputs, use of cause-and-effect diagrams must be part of any project.

The cause-and-effect diagram (also known as a fishbone or Ishikawa diagram) was first developed in Japan and is a carryover from the total quality management and lean manufacturing schools of thought. The diagram itself resembles a fish skeleton, with the problem (effect) placed at the head of the spine on the right-hand side. Each bone of the skeleton represents an input to the process (cause) that may be responsible for the problem. The headers of the bones that connect to the skeleton are categorized by people, process, technology, physical plant and materials. As each category is analyzed in detail, more bones are added to the skeleton, thereby allowing team members to list inputs in an organized fashion.

Figure 9.5 is a cause-and-effect diagram that was prepared by a Taiwanese manufacturer of measuring equipment. Recent shipments received from the company's number one domestic supplier of components and assemblies have shown an inordinate increase in defects. Although never a problem in the past, these supplier shipments have caused lines to go down and work-in-process inventories to grow to unacceptable levels. Fortunately, the manufacturer employs an in-house engineer at the supplier's facility. In conjunction with the supplier and the manufacturer, the engineer organized a series of brainstorming and analysis sessions to eradicate the problem. Part of the analysis was a fishbone diagram that uncovered some interesting facts.

One of the benefits of a fishbone diagram is that it logically organizes inputs and allows for in-depth analysis of each category. In the case of the Taiwanese company, the first "bone" that drew attention was physical plant. The supplier confirmed that it had purchased a new high-end production line in the last three

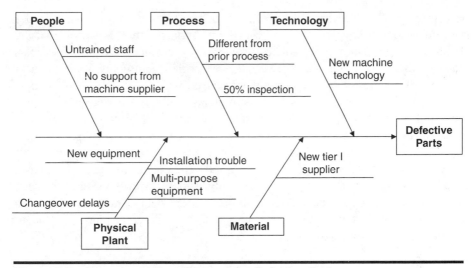

Figure 9.5   Cause-and-Effect Diagram for Defective Parts

months and had experienced certain "problems" with the line. The equipment employed new technology and was intended to be a multi-purpose line. As the team noted, this core change in production spilled over into other areas of the business that contributed to the defective parts problem.

Breakdown of the people section of the diagram revealed that the company that sold the equipment to the supplier had not provided the technical support or training committed to in the contract. Because the equipment utilized a new technology with a different manufacturing process, production personnel could not apply much from their past experience to improve current output. Listed as causes under each header, the combination of the new technology, different production process and untrained personnel caused the line to run out of gauge and produce defective parts.

In addition to the problems caused by the installation of the new equipment, it was also revealed that the supplier had changed a vendor right around the same time that the equipment was brought in. There was a clear breakdown of communication between the purchasing and production departments at the supplier, and all agreed that it was probably not a good idea to change vendors during the same period a new line was being installed. Nevertheless, the diagram exposed that the vendor had its own quality issues that exacerbated the internal problems alluded to above.

As the example of the Taiwanese manufacturer illustrates, preparation of a cause-and-effect diagram has a great deal of value when a team must categorize and analyze process inputs. When used in conjunction with other sigma tools (brainstorming and affinity diagrams, for example), this technique is especially helpful in identifying problem areas. It is important to note, however, that the fishbone diagram not only isolates problems by category but also identifies cause-and-effect relationships between the categories themselves. Without question, the Taiwanese company's problems started with the purchase of the new equipment. However, the impact of the purchase quickly trickled into the process and people categories. Although disconcerting, the ability of the Ishikawa diagram to identify both first- and second-order causal relationships will ultimately help a team to resolve the effect on the entire process, defective parts.

Because of its ability to pinpoint cause-and-effect relationships, the Ishikawa diagram is used frequently during the analyze stage of a Six Sigma project. While the company under analysis still has a great deal of work to do, it can continue through the sigma methodology using other tools that will lead to better process design and performance.

PARETO ANALYSIS

Also known as the 80/20 rule, Pareto analysis bears the name of the Italian economist who first applied its logic. The original application of Dr. Pareto's technique focused on income distribution and his hypothesis that the greatest amount of a population's money was held in very few hands. Basically, Dr. Pareto believed that 80% of all funds were held by roughly 20% of the population. Since that time, Pareto analysis has enjoyed wide application in a variety of commercial scenarios, all of which are based on the cause-and-effect relationships so inherent to operational processes. In a business setting, Pareto analysis states that 80% of all process outcomes are caused by 20% of the potential inputs. Thus, a company may find that 80% of its sales are generated by 20% of its clients or that 80% of all raw materials are purchased from 20% of the total supplier base. Although never 100% accurate, Pareto analysis does allow companies to discriminate between major and minor issues.

In the context of Six Sigma, Pareto analysis is used during the analysis stage to assist in identifying the significant causes of process variation. During a project, the Pareto technique is usually brought in after root causes have been identified via other sigma tools. Once a hypothesis or root cause has been established, Pareto analysis allows team members to identify and begin to tackle the biggest ones first. Once the major offenders have been eliminated, continuous improvement techniques are used to eradicate the problem entirely. Because of the limited time and resources that companies can apply to projects, the Pareto technique allows them to exact the greatest return from their efforts. In that sense, the analysis is indispensable to any sigma undertaking.

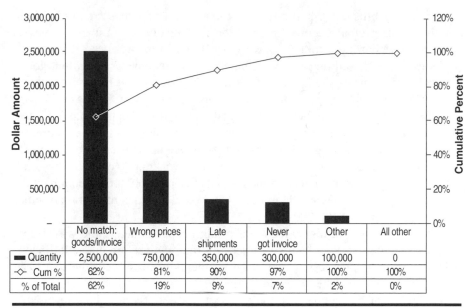

	No match: goods/invoice	Wrong prices	Late shipments	Never got invoice	Other	All other
■ Quantity	2,500,000	750,000	350,000	300,000	100,000	0
◇ Cum %	62%	81%	90%	97%	100%	100%
% of Total	62%	19%	9%	7%	2%	0%

Figure 9.6   Pareto Analysis for Drivers of Late Receivables

Pareto analysis has myriad applications, but for purposes of use in global supply chains, consider the results shown in Figure 9.6. The company in question is Rumba, Inc., a Miami-based exporter of telephone systems to Latin America. In the last six months, accounts receivable have skyrocketed and management is desperate to know why. On the best of days, accounts receivable is a touchy subject in Latin America, and depreciating currencies only make collection that much more tenuous an exercise.

The probability of Rumba, Inc. collecting on old debt decreased with every day that passed, and the company's chief financial officer needed to isolate the problem immediately. A Six Sigma team had advanced sufficiently in the analysis stage of its project to identify several drivers of the growth in accounts receivable. What the team needed to know now, however, was which of the root causes was responsible for the greatest amount of mischief. Using Pareto analysis in concert with other sigma tools, the team was able to uncover telling statistics on the degree of severity of each root cause.

Before breaking down the details of the accounts receivable Pareto analysis, note that the causes are listed cumulatively on the x-axis, and the effects are enumerated on the y-axis. Consistent with the $Y = f(x)$ mentality of sigma thinking, the causes of the company's $4 million over 90 days outstanding are invoice did not match goods received, disputed prices on invoices, late shipments, bill never received and other. For lack of a better explanation, clients were rejecting bills either partially or in their entirety for these reasons. While not the most original excuses in the world, if resolution of these issues is delaying payment, the problems have to be fixed immediately.

Note that $2.5 million can be attributed to the customers' claim that goods shipped did not match the invoices they received. Because it represents almost 63% of the total, the sigma team should focus on this cause first. At $750,000 or 19% of the total is the fact that invoice prices did not match contract rates, the second cause of stalled payments. Cumulatively, these two causes represent almost 82% of the total problem. Moving to the lesser causes, late shipments compelled customers to hold payment to the tune of $350,000 or 9% of the total, while the many customers that claimed they never received a bill accounted for $300,000 or 7.5% of the total $4 million. On the tail end, a combination of other reasons represented $100,000 or 2.5%.

Needless to say, the sigma team has to dig deeper to determine why orders are not matching invoices and why prices on the invoices are allegedly inconsistent with contract prices. Once those problems are resolved, the team can move on to resolving the other problems.

At this point in the analysis, the team knows how the accounts receivable problem is being created. With 15 customers in Latin America, the team's job was now to focus on which represented the greatest amounts. The vector of why and who can easily be created by employing a different Pareto analysis.

Figure 9.7 is a breakdown of the customers that represent the largest percentage of the $4 million over 90 days. Customer #1 represents 31% of the total

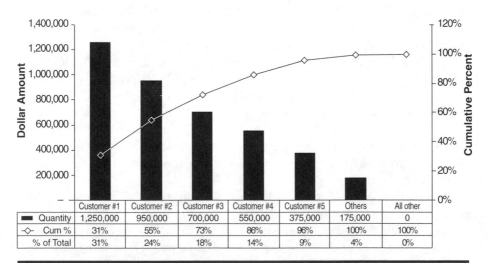

	Customer #1	Customer #2	Customer #3	Customer #4	Customer #5	Others	All other
Quantity	1,250,000	950,000	700,000	550,000	375,000	175,000	0
Cum %	31%	55%	73%	86%	96%	100%	100%
% of Total	31%	24%	18%	14%	9%	4%	0%

Figure 9.7 Pareto Analysis for Customers Over 90 Days

with $1.25 million in debt over 90 days. Together with customer #2 at 24% or $950,000, the cumulative effect of the first two customers is $2.2 million or 55% of the total. Client #3 is at $700,000 or 18% of the total, customer #4 is at $550,000 or 14% and customer #5 is at $375,000 or 9%. A list of other clients rounds out the calculation at $175,000 or 4% of the total.

The combination of the two Pareto analyses has enabled the team to zero in on not only the severity of each cause but also who the clients are that represent the bulk of the past-due amounts. Whereas the team members still have a huge job on their hands, this analysis has allowed them to establish the direction in which they must head and how they need to get there. Because of its emphasis on linking process outputs with their causes, Pareto analysis is yet another tool that must be employed during the course of a Six Sigma project.

SUMMARY

The purpose of this chapter is to demonstrate the possible application of Six Sigma tools in reducing variation across global supply chains. If anything, the analysis should be proof that there is an entire methodology behind the Six Sigma philosophy and that use of the tools has legitimate value in any business environment. It must be pointed out, however, that the techniques discussed here are not a comprehensive depiction of the tool set. Many other tools are available to sigma teams, including trend charts, failure mode and effects analysis, affinity diagrams, histograms, hypothesis testing and correlation analysis. When applied in their entirety to a project, the probability of success is very high.

The goal of the last two chapters has been to present the Six Sigma philosophy within the context of reducing variation in global business models. Consistent with that philosophy, the tools discussed here focus on identifying causal relationships, prioritizing problems, identifying root causes and eliminating variance. If these chapters inspire managers to either adopt the sigma philosophy or continue with ongoing use of the methodology, that goal will have been achieved.

10

THE LENGUA FRANCA OF SUPPLY CHAIN MANAGEMENT

As international trade continues to burgeon, the lexicon of terms, acronyms and buzzwords associated with its myriad activities will grow in kind. Developments in manufacturing planning and control, lean manufacturing and other disciplines have spawned a language unique to each area of expertise, creating an eclectic and oftentimes confusing business jargon. While each school of thought has made valuable contributions to the evolution of supply chain management (SCM), global business requires a mother tongue capable of forging a common theme across industry, geography and culture. On an operational level, it seems that the trait most commonly shared among business models lies in inventory management. Although a true statement, the multi-faceted nature of international business demands a much more vigorous approach to successfully manage global enterprises. Although inventory management is an area of both strategic and tactical interest to managers, the complexities of contemporary SCM are much more robust.

Historically, the greatest operational challenge for management teams has been creating a balance between customer service and inventory investment. Although present-day SCM has grown to encompass activities ranging from product concept to market delivery, the service versus inventory-level dilemma still remains at its core. In pure inventory management terms, the service side of this equilibrium is interpreted as filling a product need in the right place, at the specified time, in the quantities desired and at the price originally quoted. Whether working with raw materials, work in process or finished goods, the goal of the supply side of the equation is to meet customer needs without committing excessive amounts of company funds to inventories.

In addition to the classic customer service challenge, SCM must now contemplate the rationalization of cumulative lead times and the reduction of landed costs. In the case of the former, bloated lead times can result in down production lines, lost sales, damaged customer goodwill or worse. An absence of landed cost controls, on the other hand, can create unstable product costing scenarios, wreak havoc on target pricing models and, ultimately, consume profits.

This three-faceted approach considers not only the importance of inventory management but also the commercial significance of executing on business models in a timely and profitable fashion. Taken from this vantage point, both the goals and trade-offs inherent to SCM can be made clear to most companies. What is less obvious, however, is the functional relationship of these activities with the financial success of an organization.

Without question, quantitative results should be the goal of any supply chain initiative. Regardless of a company's corporate culture, business model or theater of operation, the effectiveness of SCM must be translated into monetary terms and manifested in an organization's financial statements. The inability to trace operational activities to their first- and second-order impact on financial results hobbles an organization, leaving it blindly seeking solutions to the challenges of maneuvering in a global setting. As previously stated, although the tenets of SCM are understood and accepted, the links that must be established between operational execution and financial improvements have been more elusive.

Given this paradox, the next step in the evolution of the SCM philosophy is to identify the implicit ties between operating activities and financial performance. On a tactical level, the effect of initiatives in the areas of inventory management, lead time rationalization and landed cost reductions must be traced through the financial statements of an organization, specifically the balance sheet, income statement and cash flow statement.

The physiology of the relationships between this "supply chain triumvirate" and corresponding financial reports is the true nexus of global SCM and the foundation upon which all supply chain efforts should be built. The remainder of this book is dedicated to identifying the aforementioned links and demonstrating their impact on financial outcomes. Most importantly, the intention is to create a fresh perspective on business model execution that can be used by managers to improve profitability at their companies.

A COMMON LANGUAGE

If the global business mentality is to truly blossom, a common language must be developed that expresses both individual and aggregate performance across supply chains. Because of organizational diversity, different cultures and varying methods of measuring functional effectiveness, companies have fallen short

THE ATTACK OF THE BUZZWORDS

The only aspect of international trade that may be growing faster than commerce itself is the insistence of businesspeople on using buzzwords, acronyms and catchphrases to describe every aspect of their professional lives. Principally designed to bring significance to otherwise mundane ideas, most buzzwords have only served to detract from the few legitimate business concepts that actually have any value. In the jargon of today's businessperson, you don't need a PhD from UCLA to realize that most buzzwords are a bunch of BS.

Two buzzwords that are used throughout this book and that could be accused of the above crimes are "vector" and "velocity." Before passing judgment, however, it would be wise to understand the true mathematical meanings of these terms and their application to business situations.*

As first discussed in the Introduction, a vector is a quantity that has both magnitude and direction. Conceptually, any term that helps businesspeople to understand the scope of their operations and the direction in which they are heading can be considered useful. From a decision-making perspective, the ability to study options from different angles and directions will bring more information to the process and drive down the probability of failure.

Velocity represents the rate of change of position of an object based on its speed and direction. In today's business world, a good strategy (direction) is not enough; a company has to execute before its competition to gain any meaningful advantage. Rapid growth without strategic direction, on the other hand, will ultimately create waste in supply chains that suboptimizes operations. In tactical terms, managers must constantly focus on the speed and direction of their business endeavors, particularly in the areas of manpower, machine and methodology.

Taking the definition of velocity a step further, it is both mathematically and commercially significant to note that the derivative of velocity is acceleration. Thus, from a business perspective, it is important to measure not only the change in position and direction of an organization, but also how quickly that is happening. Even if a business has speed and direction, if it is not continuously accelerating, the competition will eventually catch up.

One may discern from the definitions of vector and velocity that they share a common characteristic: direction. Taken in concert, the intersection of strategic direction (operational scope) with speed and magnitude makes for big medicine. The additional element of acceleration reminds businesspeople that they have to execute their models at continuously increasing speed. From both a mathematical and commercial perspective, it should be clear that the terms vector and velocity have earned their way into the supply chain pantheon.

---

* M.G. Kendall and W.R. Buckland, *A Dictionary of Statistical Terms,* Longman Group, 1971, p. 186.

in the quest to devise metrics that incorporate all components of an international paradigm. The need to create consistency of measurements across fragmented business models regardless of industry, function, geography or language is the cornerstone to the legitimization and advancement of the SCM philosophy.

With the above taken as the genesis of SCM, finance and accounting must be established as the *lengua franca* of the enterprise, serving as the great translator and unifier of multi-lingual commercial activities. Simply stated, finance and accounting must be to other business disciplines what Latin has been to the Romance languages. Finance and accounting is what unites the various business lexicons, creating a single platform from which all functional activities simultaneously are born and into which they feed.

In the case of inventory management, finance and accounting is what bridges the gap between anecdotal support for customer service levels and the exact dollar amounts invested in inventories. With regard to lean or Six Sigma tactics designed to reduce lead time and landed costs, the proper interpretation of period-to-period financial information can clearly measure their effect on balance sheets, income statements and cash flow statements.

Even though countries have different methods of calculating and reporting financial results, there are sufficient similarities in accounting practices to transcend almost all cultural or business differences. At a minimum, most commercially oriented societies utilize the balance sheet and income statement to report activities and changes in financial position. More recently, business entities have also adopted the cash flow statement to augment the traditional measures of organizational performance.[1] An important addition to the accounting arsenal, this allows businesspeople to not only measure profitability or summary changes in general ledger accounts but also identify the sources and uses of cash during measured periods of time.

Used properly, the information found in these reports forms the synapse between operational velocity, asset utilization and profitability. The challenge for today's manager is to truly understand the nature of these relationships while actively managing their well-being to the benefit of the organization. If businesspeople can find the way to blend what financial statements reveal with the principles of lean thinking and application of Six Sigma tools, the result will be much greater than any single component could ever accomplish on its own.

THE BALANCE SHEET, INCOME STATEMENT AND CASH FLOW STATEMENT

Organizations that are committed to the SCM philosophy must also address the challenge of creating a financial orientation in all of their employees. Whether an individual works in purchasing, manufacturing, sales or information technol-

Sales
Sales Returns and Allowances
Net Sales
Cost of Goods Sold
Gross Profit
Operating Expenses
  General, Sales and Administrative
EBITDA
Nonoperating Income
Depreciation
Interest Expense
Income Before Taxes
Income Taxes
Net Income

Figure 10.1   Income Statement

ogy, corporate culture should emphasize finance and accounting as a required component of every employee's portfolio of knowledge.

Today's successful businessperson not only has expertise in his or her particular discipline but also general management skills that are built upon an understanding of how to interpret and act upon what financial statements reveal. An understanding of the cause-and-effect activities that are behind the results found on the income statement, balance sheet and cash flow statement goes a long way in establishing the desired perspective and corporate culture necessary for success in today's international milieu. Returning to a point made earlier, when employees operate out on the margin, margin is a lot easier to understand.

As shown in Figure 10.1, the income statement measures profitability over a specific period of time, itemizing revenues and expenses to arrive at a net profit figure for the time frame under consideration. Given that it gauges sales, returns and allowances, cost of goods sold, as well as general, sales and administrative expenses, the income statement begins to reveal the period-specific impact of supply chain activities from both a sales and cost viewpoint. When properly analyzed, the income statement exposes a great deal about how revenues are generated, what constitutes the real cost of manufacturing and how indirect costs can either bolster or erode operating income.

Portrayed in Figure 10.2 as a snapshot of a company's financial condition at a given moment in time, the balance sheet is critical to understanding supply chain performance for two reasons. First, the balance sheet records changes in assets and liabilities based in part on the activities detailed on the income statement. How a company incurs liabilities as a result of investing in both current and long-term assets can be traced through the balance sheet in the form of cash, inventories, accounts receivable, plant and equipment, accounts payable

Assets
Current Assets
  Cash
  Marketable Securities
  Accounts Receivable
  Inventory
Total Current Assets
Fixed Assets
  Plant and Equipment
Total Assets

Liabilities
Current Liabilities
  Accounts Payable
  Other Current Liabilities
Total Current Liabilities
Long-Term Debt
Total Liabilities

Stockholders' Equity
Common Stock
Retained Earnings
Total Stockholders' Equity

Total Liability and Stockholders' Equity

Figure 10.2   Balance Sheet

and long-term liabilities. Understanding the relationship between these balance sheet items and how they are ultimately transformed into cash is necessary to understand the quantitative component of SCM.

Because the balance sheet itemizes assets and liabilities, it allows for the calculation of vital information related to a company's liquidity, solvency, return on assets and, to a large degree, return on investment and return on equity. The active management of both short- and long-term assets/liabilities is fundamental to comprehensive SCM, as it offers a window into how organizations create value and incur expenses as part of ongoing business activities. In this context, it is essential for organizations to not only focus on reported income but to compare profitability figures with the productivity of assets and the management of debt.

Although both of the aforementioned reports are indispensable to measuring supply chain results, the most telling information relative to understanding the financial effectiveness of global SCM is found in the cash flow statement (CFS). Itemized on the basis of cash flow from operations, investing and financing activities, the CFS in Figure 10.3 details the sources and uses of cash during the same period measured on the income statement. Integral to the structure of

Operating Activities
Net Income
Depreciation
Changes in Accounts Receivable
Changes in Accounts Payable
Changes in Other Payables
Changes in Inventories
Cash from Operating Activities

Investing Activities
Purchase of Fixed Assets
Sale of Marketable Securities
Cash from Investing Activities

Financing Activities
Issuance of Stock
Issuance of Long-Term Notes
Cash from Financing Activities

Net Increase or Decrease in Cash

Figure 10.3 Cash Flow Statement

the CFS is the recognition of net income, changes in working capital, management of long-term assets and sources of financing.

From an operational, financial and investment perspective, the CFS synthesizes the key components of the balance sheet and income statement, focusing not only on profitability but how well a company manages assets as it generates sales. It is the changes in these accounts, as well as the net impact on cash that results from those changes, that is so critical to measuring the real contribution of SCM. Without detailed analysis of the CFS, the results of operating tactics can never really be calculated.

THE CASH FLOW STATEMENT AND SUPPLY CHAIN MEASUREMENT

A closer look at the composition of the CFS in Figure 10.3 reveals its links to strategic and tactical supply chain activities, profitability and asset utilization. The significance of the CFS to supply chains begins with the section on cash flow from operating activities. This section states cash flow generated as a result of net income, with a provision for adding back depreciation on assets.

With net income weighing in as the most important source of cash for an organization, inclusion of income statement results in the CFS emphasizes the significance of all activities related to sales, returns, cost of goods sold, general, sales and administrative expense and depreciation. Although a study of the functional relationships between the income statement and supply chain tactics is necessary, the very appearance of net income on the CFS must be recognized as a positive step toward synthesizing the need for growth and profitability with sources of financing and asset utilization.

Of equal importance, the section on cash flow from operating activities itemizes changes in short-term assets and liabilities, either as a source or use of cash (changes in working capital). This calculation is the ideal counterbalance for the net income figure as it considers not only *reported* profitability but also how well a company manages inventories, collects on receivables and pays it bills.

This concept carries implications for the effective management of global supply chains as net changes in working capital cast a long shadow over the aggregate cash flow figure. For example, if inventories increase from one period to the next, that is considered a use of cash, which in turn has a negative effect on cash flow. From a collections perspective, a decrease in accounts receivable is considered a source of cash and thus has a positive effect on cash flow. Conversely, a decrease in accounts payable between periods is considered a use of cash, again consuming funds.

The overall effect on cash flow from changes in working capital depends on whether the net figure is positive or negative. Basically, if the uses of cash exceed the sources, the effect on cash flow from working capital changes will be negative, having a direct impact on the amount of free cash flow available to the company. If the sources of cash exceed it uses, then, of course, the net figure will have a positive effect on company cash flow.

Without question, the comparison of reported profitability with changes in working capital speaks volumes about the operational effectiveness of an organization's supply chain activities. It must be kept in mind, however, that this section by itself only measures short-term performance and does not consider the importance of managing long-term assets.

Taken again from the viewpoint of sources and uses of cash, the CFS addresses the acquisition and/or sale of assets in the section on cash flow from investing activities. Study of this section should reveal both the strategic and financial consequences from the purchase or sale of big-ticket items like land, production facilities, machines and equipment, warehouses and truck fleets. In global environs, the buying and selling of fixed assets, as well as their overall productivity, are integral to organizational success and should be measured along with the performance of short-term assets.

For purposes of the CFS, sales of long-term assets are a source of cash and as such have a positive impact on overall cash flow. A common example of this is when a company sells a factory or physical plant, the proceeds of which are a substantial (albeit short-term) source of cash. In the opposite scenario, when an organization invests in fixed assets, this type of transaction is considered a use of cash and will have a negative effect on cash flow in the period being measured. Again, a company consumes cash over the period in question by investing in physical plant, equipment or land, with the long-term intent of creating future value for the organization.

While important from a sources and uses of cash flow perspective, a one-dimensional view of managing fixed assets discounts the strategic importance of analyzing this section of the CFS. Specifically, the CFS measures the short-term impact on cash but does not address the long-term effects on productivity and profitability of a company and its global operations. Therefore, an organization must not only look at the short-term net changes in cash as a result of asset management but also consider the strategic rationale behind decisions and their effect on the profitability of future periods.

At first glance, the final portion of the CFS may not appear to be closely associated with tactical SCM. Because the section on cash flow from financing activities deals with sources and uses of cash related to the financing of company activities, it might be reasonable to make this assumption. Some of the line items that appear as a use of cash in this seemingly "supply-chain-neutral" area include payment of dividends, repurchase of company stock (treasury stock) and the retirement of debt. Sources of cash, on the other hand, typically arise from the issuance of stock and bonds or as newly borrowed funds. Closer observation of this section, however, reveals that its relationship with supply chain execution is quite significant.

As noted earlier, the number one source of cash for an organization is net income, a figure that is ultimately driven by supply chain planning and execution. Net income is what perpetuates the viability of a company, allowing for reinvestment in its future, the retirement of debt and the distribution of dividends. Also, net income plays a key quantitative role in the determination of stock price and earnings per share and is the numerator in such calculations as return on investment and return on equity. When a company suffers from weak net income or even losses, the reciprocal nature of its relationship with supply chain operations and financing activities becomes abundantly clear.

What can happen to a company that executes poorly and has anemic net income? First, a paucity of earnings reduces the amount payable in dividends, a fact that may cause downward pressure on stock prices. Also, if a company is even moderately leveraged, the ability to pay down debt is reduced by the absence of net income. Without earnings to back up debt obligations, companies tend to resort to short-term tactics that invariably impact the long-term viability of the organization.

To illustrate this point, consider companies that postpone investments or divert funds earmarked for research and development, product development or employee training in order to cover debt payments. Budgeted investments in new plant or upgrades to existing equipment may be canceled just to meet short-term principal and interest obligations. In more dire circumstances, many companies begin to sell assets that are critical to their current and future business models.

The deep discounting of receivables, the sale of land, plant and equipment or even the wholesale divestiture of entire business units is not beyond the realm of options for companies that are strapped for cash. Needless to say, these tactics are short term in nature and will inevitably serve to create a cycle through which supply chain execution and income statement performance spiral downward.

On a more strategic level, a company can compensate for poor net income figures by issuing additional stock or assuming debt. In the case of the former, diluting of stock to pay debt is never an attractive proposition, particularly for current holders of the issue. With regard to the latter, lenders study two variables when negotiating a loan package: a company's ability and propensity to pay. For a company with limited earnings or losses, the cost of capital would increase due to the additional risk associated with the loan. This situation would worsen if the organization were already leveraged, making the likelihood of repayment lower and, again, the cost of capital higher.

In summary, the subtleties of the relationship between supply chain execution and the CFS components of operating, investing and financing activities can easily be overlooked or discounted as unrelated. The CFS provides a unique look into the activities of a company from contrasting angles and should be used to gauge both the importance of net income and how effective a company is at marshaling finances and productively employing assets. This additional dimension of SCM, along with the traditional analysis of the income statement and balance sheet, is pivotal to a vector approach to business management.

SUMMARY

As we begin to analyze the case study in the following chapters, it is the author's hope that it will be done in the context of the information provided in the first half of this book. When utilized correctly, historical reference can have a powerful effect on future decision-making processes. When applied in kind with the philosophies, methodologies and techniques discussed up to this point, the outlook for future success is very positive. Finally, if one can blend the content presented here with one's own expertise and thus bridge the gap between strategy, tactics and financial outcomes, the primary objective of this book will have been achieved.

NOTE

1. Martin S. Fridson, *Financial Statement Analysis: A Practitioner's Guide,* John Wiley & Sons, 1995, p. 94.

11

MEASURING RESULTS: NIKOTECH, INC.

Given the complex nature of international supply chains, the metrics chosen to measure financial performance must converge on revenue, profitability, productivity, asset utilization and cash flow. Of equal importance, tools that are capable of exposing the cause-and-effect relationships between financial outcomes and areas such as sales, landed costs, lead times and inventory management must also be employed. Because financial performance has the last word on supply chain execution, the methodology for identifying causal relationships should be a diverse exercise that focuses on the elements of time, variance, utilization and profitability. Applying different techniques to period-specific figures puts supply chain execution in the crosshairs of management, allowing managers to make decisions based on a variety of information and angles.

SUPPLY CHAIN EXECUTION, THE BALANCE SHEET AND PROFITABILITY

For better or for worse, many stockholders, institutional investors and creditors base their evaluation of a company on its short-term, period-specific financial results. In fact, judging by how most senior executives are compensated (quarterly or yearly bonuses linked to net income), the same could be said about how those same organizations gauge their own performance.

Because companies are measured in the short term, the natural inclination of most management teams is to focus on results found on the income statement. There is no question that the income statement provides valuable information on sales, cost of goods sold, general, sales and administrative expense and net income. Also, many cause-and-effect relationships can be spotted between individual line items and areas like velocity, productivity and variance. However, it is the same short-term nature of the income statement that may cause managers to lose sight of longer term considerations. Strict profit-and-loss management is more reactionary than strategic, with decisions that impact the future of the organization based on last month's results. The supply-chain-oriented manager realizes that outcomes on the income statement are a function of what is found on the balance sheet. After all, it is investments in plant, equipment and inventories that make sales possible, right?

Depending on one's philosophy of business, a fair rebuttal to the preceding statement would be that market demand and sales are what generate the need to create manufacturing capabilities. While this is a reasonable statement to make, what should be observed is that recognition of the validity of both statements implies a cause-and-effect relationship that cuts both ways. A company cannot generate sales without assets, but there is no need for assets without sales. This is an interesting paradox, yet one can be certain that it is the combination of asset management, profit-and-loss considerations and cash flow that moves businesspeople from reacting to monthly results to managing an enterprise.

It is for the above reasons that the following case study will begin with an analysis of asset velocity and utilization, followed by an in-depth look at the balance sheet itself. Many cause-and-effect relationships will be uncovered, setting the stage for study of the income statement and the additional causal relationships found there. Once the reciprocal links between net income and balance sheet investments are established, a comprehensive breakdown of the cash flow statement will be presented. The financial epicenter of any organization, the cash flow statement unites the short-term concerns of profit and loss with the longer term, strategic issues faced by any company.

Throughout the entire case study, techniques and tools will be introduced that isolate problems, reduce variation, increase productivity and goose supply chain velocity. Completing the circle, all supply chain initiatives are intended to filter up to results on the balance sheet, income statement and, most importantly, the cash flow statement.

CASE STUDY: THE ELECTRONICS MANUFACTURING SERVICES INDUSTRY

The best way to validate the points made thus far in the discussion is by means of a case study. However, if one is to substantiate these ideas while recognizing the difficulties of operating internationally, care must be taken in choosing the industry and business model that best portray reality. In seeking an industry with a scope of operations that spans product concept to final delivery, the electronics manufacturing services (EMS) industry offers the best illustrative characteristics.

EMS companies, or contract manufacturers, assume the manufacturing processes of their customers, taking on such traditional functions as sourcing, purchasing, materials requirements planning and production. Because contract manufacturers operate a production model with sites in multiple countries, they are constantly working to integrate the importation of raw materials with the export of finished goods in a timely and profitable manner. Given that the entire model is founded on the outsourcing philosophy, supplier management also plays an integral role in the success of a company.

This model creates supply chain matrices that are influenced by variables such as labor costs, currency fluctuation and multi-lateral trade agreements. These elements of the business, coupled with the fact that most contract manufacturers operate in the highly volatile technology and telecommunications arena, make EMS the best candidate to use in a supply chain analysis case. To bring the story to life, analysis will center on a fictitious, U.S.-based contract manufacturer, NikoTech, Inc.

NikoTech was founded in 1984 by two high-level executives from the electronics manufacturing sector. With headquarters in San Diego, California and a maquiladora operation just over the border in Tijuana, Mexico, the company started out as an assembly operation catering to the high-tech industry. As outsourcing became more popular and NikoTech evolved into a full-blown manufacturer, the company expanded operations to Hungary, China and Brazil. From its origins in Mexico, NikoTech continues to adhere to a build-to-order production model. The company currently works with 350 raw materials suppliers around the world (65% in Asia) and has six global customers that represent 70% of total sales.

NikoTech rode the wave of growth in the tech sector through the late 1980s and early 1990s, setting up production just in time for the onslaught of demand in telephony and computers. The combination of expanding product families and insatiable demand brought on explosive growth at NikoTech in its early years, with sales reaching the $1 billion plateau well before the turn of the century. To date, NikoTech offers 150 SKUs in four product families: cellular phones, laptops, desktops and routers. Still a small player by industry standards, NikoTech has been able to achieve respectable year-to-year sales growth throughout its history.

When the tide went out on the tech boom, NikoTech saw many of its long-hidden operational challenges exposed. Explosive growth sometimes causes companies to bury problems under a mountain of cash, and NikoTech was not an exception to this phenomenon. By the dawn of the new millennium, management found itself in a position where revenues continued to grow, but profitability was shrinking every quarter. The sales orders were there, but cost of goods sold was outpacing sales growth, and inventories were completely out of control. If current trends continue, the NikoTech founders estimate that the company will be losing money within 18 months.

Recognizing the serious nature of their predicament, management formed a multi-functional team to analyze all facets of the business, beginning with the financial results for the two most recent years (Y1 and Y2). The balance of this book details what was found.

NIKOTECH'S FINANCIAL STATEMENTS

The income statement, balance sheet and cash flow statement in Tables 11.1, 11.2 and 11.3, respectively, are a reflection of the most recent two-year (Y1 and Y2) performance of the organization. To aid the analysis, 17 different ratios and calculations that will assist in evaluating NikoTech's financial health are listed in Table 11.4. Table 11.5 provides the Y1 and Y2 results of those ratios. All figures from the balance sheet, income statement and cash flow statement have been consolidated and simplified for ease of calculation. Based on a calendar year, the most recent year's balance sheet figures are interpreted as being indicative of the average figures for the preceding four quarters. To facilitate the study, it is recommended that the reader make a copy of each report, the formulas and the ratio results prior to beginning the analysis.

NIKOTECH: CURRENT ASSETS, LIABILITIES AND SUPPLY CHAIN VELOCITY

Undoubtedly, the best source of information for measuring short-term financial performance is the income statement. However, in order to take a multi-dimensional view of supply chain execution, one must also focus on the utilization of assets during the same time period measured on the income statement. It is this balance between financial outcomes and asset management that unites the most critical components of a business model, allowing managers to understand the true profitability and productivity of their international operations.

A first step in measuring asset utilization introduces the dimension of time to the analysis. A focus on continuously reducing cumulative lead times, expressed in days, emphasizes the need for velocity in all areas of a company's operations. From this angle, discussion of asset productivity takes on a new dimension, combining traditional ideas on utilization with the need for supply

Table 11.1 NikoTech Year-to-Year Income Statements

Comparative Income Statement ($ in Millions)

	Y2 $	Y2 Margin	Y2 % of Sales	Y1 $	Y1 Margin	Y1 % of Sales	$ Delta Y1–Y2	% Delta Y1–Y2
Sales	1,845			1,500			345	23.0%
Sales Returns and Allowances	147		8.0%	60		4.0%	87	145.0%
Net Sales	1,698			1,440			258	17.9%
Cost of Goods Sold	1,239		73.0%	990		68.8%	249	25.2%
Gross Profit	459	27.0%		450	31.3%		9	2.0%
Operating Expenses								
General, Sales and Administrative	378			360			18	5.0%
EBITDA	81	4.8%		90	6.3%		–9	–10.0%
Nonoperating Income	3			6			–3	–50.0%
Depreciation	36			36			0	0.0%
Interest Expense*	27			18			9	50.0%
Income Before Taxes	21	1.2%		42	2.9%		–21	–50.0%
Income Taxes (40%)	8.4			16.8			–8.4	–50.0%
Net Income	12.6	0.7%		25.2	1.7%		–12.6	–50.0%

* Y1 interest expense of $18 million based on 3.75% of $480 million total. Y2 interest expense of $27 million based on 5% of $540 million total.

Table 11.2   NikoTech Year-to-Year Balance Sheets

Comparative Balance Sheet (in Millions)			
	Y2	Y1	$ Delta
Assets			
Current Assets			
Cash	87	264	−177.0
Marketable Securities	15	30	−15.0
Accounts Receivable	450	285	165.0
Inventory	660	480	180.0
Total Current Assets	1,212	1,059	153.0
Fixed Assets			
Plant and Equipment	564	540	24.0
Total Assets	1,776	1,599	177.0
Liabilities			
Current Liabilities			
Accounts Payable	360	285	75.0
Other Current Liabilities	47.4	18	29.4
Total Current Liabilities	407.4	303	104.4
Long-Term Debt	540	480	60.0
Total Liabilities	947.4	783	164.4
Stockholders' Equity			
Common Stock			
$10 Par Value, 75,300,000 Shares	753	753	
Retained Earnings	75.6	63	
Total Stockholders' Equity	828.6	816	
Total Liability and Stockholders' Equity	$1,776.0	$1,599	

Notes: Depreciation is 15-year period, $36 million per year. The investment in plant and equipment was $60 million, funded by an additional $60 million in long-term debt. Retained earnings in Y0 were $37.8 million, in Y1 were $63 million ($37.8 million + $25.2 million) and in Y2 were $75.6 million ($63 million + $12.6 million).

chain velocity. Using a combination of metrics and tools, both utilization and velocity can be linked to the balance sheet, providing a unique look at the effectiveness of a global operation.

THE OPERATING CYCLE AND CASH-TO-CASH CYCLE

Two concepts that capture the essence of the relationship between time and asset productivity are the operating cycle and the cash-to-cash cycle. The power of both tools lies in their treatment of business activities as time sensitive and the ability to break down integrated processes into the days (or hours) required

Table 11.3   NikoTech Cash Flow Statement

	Y2 (in Millions)
Operating Activities	
Net Income	$12.6
Depreciation	$36
Increase in Accounts Receivable	($165)
Increase in Accounts Payable	$75
Increase in Other Payables	$29.4
Increase in Inventories	($180)
Cash from Operating Activities	($192)
Investing Activities	
Purchase of Fixed Assets	($60)
Sale of Marketable Securities	$15
Cash from Investing Activities	($45)
Financing Activities	
Issuance of Long-Term Notes	$60
Cash from Financing Activities	$60
Net Decrease in Cash	($177)

Table 11.4   Ratios and Formulas for NikoTech Financial Analysis

	Formula
Days of Inventory	Average Inventory/(Cost of Goods Sold/365)
Days of Receivables	Average Receivables/(Net Sales/365)
Operating Cycle	Days of Inventory + Days Receivable Outstanding
Days of Payables	Average Payables/(Cost of Goods Sold/365)
Cash-to-Cash Cycle	(Days of Inventory + Days of Receivables) − Days Payable Outstanding
Inventory Turnover	Cost of Goods Sold/Average Inventory
Receivables Turnover	Net Sales/Average Receivables
Payables Turnover	Cost of Goods Sold/Average Payables
Working Capital	Current Assets − Current Liabilities
Current Ratio	Current Assets/Current Liabilities
Acid Test	Current Assets (Less Inventory) − Current Liabilities
Inventory to Sales	Inventory/Net Sales
Receivables to Sales	Receivables/Net Sales
Working Capital to Sales	Working Capital/Net Sales
Operating Cash Flow to Net Income	Cash from Operating Activities/Net Income
Total Asset Turnover	Net Sales/Total Assets
Return on Investment	Net Income/Total Assets

Table 11.5 NikoTech Calculations for Y1 and Y2 Financial Ratios

		$ in Millions	
	Y2	Y1	Delta
Days of Inventory	$660/($1,239/365) = 194 days	$480/($990/365) = 177 days	17 days
Days of Receivables	$450/($1,698/365) = 97 days	$285/($1,440/365) = 72 days	25 days
Operating Cycle	194 + 97 = 291 days	177 + 72 = 249 days	42 days
Days of Payables	$360/($1,239/365) = 106 days	$285/($990/365) = 105 days	1 day
Cash-to-Cash Cycle	(194 + 97) − 106 = 185 days	(177 + 72) − 105 = 144 days	41 days
Inventory Turnover	$1,239/$660 = 1.9 times	$990/$480 = 2.06 times	(0.15) times
Receivables Turnover	$1,698/$450 = 3.8 times	$1,440/$285 = 5.05 times	(1.25) times
Payables Turnover	$1,239/$360 = 3.44 times	$990/$285 = 3.47 times	(0.03) times
Working Capital	$1,212 − $407.4 = $804.6	$1,059 − $303 = $756	$48.60
Current Ratio	$1,212/$407.4 = 2.97 times	$1,059/$303 = 3.5 times	(0.53) times
Acid Test	$552/$407.4 = $1.35	$579/$303 = $1.91	($0.56)
Inventory to Sales	$660/$1,698 = $0.39	$480/$1,440 = $0.33	$0.06
Receivables to Sales	$450/$1,698 = $0.26	$285/$1,440 = $0.20	$0.06
Working Capital to Sales	$804.6/$1,698 = $0.47	$756/$1,440 = $0.52	($0.05)
Operating Cash Flow to Net Income	($192)/$12.6 = −$15.23		
Total Asset Turnover	$1,698/$1,776 = $0.95	$1,440/$1,599 = $0.90	$0.05
Return on Investment	$12.6/$1,776 = 0.7%	$25.2/$1,599 = 1.6%	0.9%

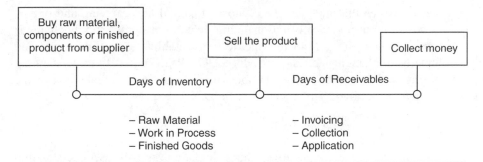

Figure 11.1   Operating Cycle (From Robert S. Kaplan and David P. Norton, *The Balanced Scorecard: Translating Strategy into Action,* Harvard Business School Press, 1996, p. 58. With permission.)

to carry out individual tasks. It is the dissection of these processes that leads managers to identify improvement opportunities within each functional area, as well as to isolate the lags that exist between departmental handoffs. The reduction of time lags in both the operating and cash-to-cash cycle affects the performance of short-term assets, and tactical efforts to improve the cycle ultimately lead to better asset utilization.

As illustrated in Figure 11.1, the operating cycle identifies the length of time it takes to convert inventory and receivables to cash. This metric is important for many reasons, all of which create implications for the balance sheet, income statement and cash flow statement.

The underlying accounting principle that makes the operating cycle so transcendental is "matching," a method through which inventory is drawn down from the balance sheet during the sales process. As transactions are consummated, inventory values are reduced on the balance sheet and appear as cost of goods sold (COGS) on the income statement. The exercise allows accounting managers to "match" sales figures with the original cost of the goods in the appropriate time period, the result of which is the gross profit figure.

This point has implications for revenue and cost recognition on the income statement, but also speaks to the health of the balance sheet due to the inventory values shown in current assets. Based on the fundamentals of accrual accounting and expressed as days of inventory (DOI), the speed with which goods are manufactured and sold is vital to supply chain effectiveness and financial outcomes.

In an effort to understand the importance of the DOI metric, reference is made to Benjamin Franklin's ageless observation that "time is money." Basically, every additional day that an organization has cash tied up in inventory represents a suboptimization of the company's financial resources. When one focuses on issues that include COGS, cost of capital and carrying and opportunity costs, the importance of rationalizing inventories across supply chains is obvious. As such, the goal of this metric is to establish a baseline figure and continue to implement tactics that reduce DOI. With regard to understanding the origins and relevance of the variables in the equation, a breakdown of the calculation is required. The calculation of DOI is expressed as:

$$\text{Average inventory/(COGS/365)}$$

Focusing on the components of this calculation, as well as understanding that the goal of the metric is to reduce the amount of DOI, a series of intuitive points should come to mind. The first recognizes that the variables in the equation come from both the balance sheet and income statement, an arrangement that emphasizes the interdependencies that exist between the two reports. As the NikoTech analysis moves from the balance sheet to the income statement, several cause-and-effect relationships will become apparent. It is the uncovering of these causal relationships that helps management to identify root causes and take measures to improve performance.

Another key issue involves the use of COGS as opposed to net sales in the denominator of the equation. It has been stated throughout the discussion that sales are linked to inventories. So why not use the net sales figure in the denominator? The answer to this question takes the analyst back to the discussion of revenue recognition, the method through which inventory values are drawn from the balance sheet and appear on the income statement as COGS.

COGS is used in this equation because it reflects the actual cost of the goods *before* a sale, a figure that is accurately aligned with inventory values shown on the balance sheet (the balance sheet shows the value of the inventory, not its forecasted sales price). Also, if the net sales figure were used in this formula, it would artificially deflate the result of the calculation and distort its significance (more on that in a moment).

Having stated the above, there are but a few methods available to reduce the quotient of the calculation. Specifically, one can reduce the numerator, increase the denominator or create a situation where both objectives are achieved simultaneously. Simply stated, a company must achieve the same or greater sales with less inventory or achieve higher sales with the same level of inventory. Either way, the goal is to do more with less, generating more sales with minimal inventory in a shorter period of time.

Calculation of the denominator (COGS/365) provides an expression of the COGS incurred on a daily basis. This means that production costs, as a purported function of sales volumes, can be expressed as an average daily amount. The average inventory figure in the numerator divided by this daily number in the denominator provides the analyst with the number of *days* it takes a com-

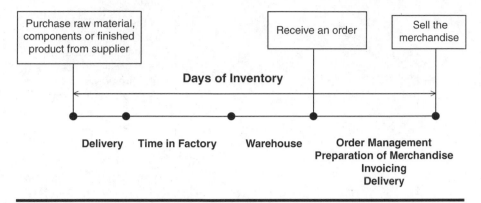

Figure 11.2   Breakdown of Days of Inventory

pany to acquire raw materials, produce finished goods and generate a sale. With suppliers and customers all over creation, this process can become an unwieldy exercise. Figure 11.2 displays the entire process.

A final caveat on the use of the DOI metric involves improving results via increases in its denominator (COGS). From a cause-and-effect perspective, one would assume that sales would have to be growing in order for COGS to increase. While sales growth is always nice, it is a very dangerous assumption to accept that COGS is growing at the same or a slower pace as sales. As illustrated in Figure 11.3, if the slope of the COGS line is steeper than that of the sales line, the two will intersect at some point (and consume margin along the way). This situation implies that COGS is growing faster than sales, a predicament no company wants to find itself in, especially our friends at NikoTech.

If the increase is COGS is in line with sales increases, the DOI metric is much easier to interpret and understand. However, if the COGS number is increasing due to incremental costs that are independent of the sales figure, the number becomes distorted. Emphasis on the origins of COGS and its importance to the income statement will manifest itself further along in the NikoTech analysis. For now, suffice it to say that no figure or calculation should be taken at face value and that supply chain analysis is much more than simple number crunching.

DAYS RECEIVABLE OUTSTANDING

The second and equally important component of the operating cycle is days receivable outstanding (DRO). Graphically defined in Figure 11.4 as the amount

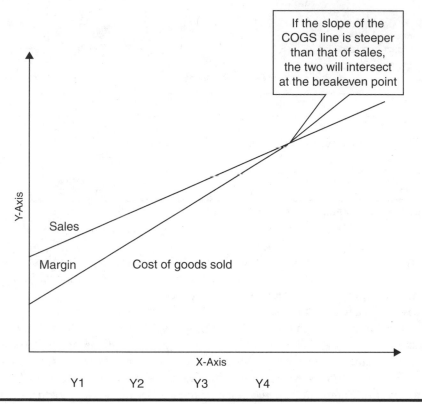

Figure 11.3 Sales Versus Cost of Goods Sold Growth

of time necessary to collect on an outstanding bill, this variable measures the speed with which customers are invoiced and payment is received. The timing of this activity and the haste with which money is then channeled back into the business are vital components of supply chain management. This activity has a major effect on the balance sheet, as swollen receivables reflect poorly on an organization. With regard to the cash flow statement, increases in receivables are recorded as a use of cash and are also a negative indicator of a company's financial health. Calculation of DRO is as follows:

Average receivables/(Net sales/365)

As in the case of DOI, a technical feel for the DRO metric requires an understanding of both its purpose and makeup. Conceptually similar to DOI, DRO measures the amount of time it takes to invoice customers and collect on

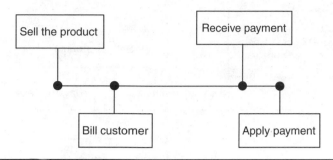

Figure 11.4   Days Receivable Outstanding

debt. Given this fact, the goal of the metric is to once again establish a baseline and use proven tactics to continuously reduce the number.

Mathematically, the exercise focuses on the reduction of the accounts receivable figure in the numerator, increasing the net sales figure in the denominator or a combination of the two. The goal is to generate the same or more sales with fewer dollars tied up in receivables or, at least, to generate more sales with the same amount in receivables. One important difference between DOI and DRO is that the numerator changes in the DRO equation from COGS to net sales. This is due to the fact that receivables are generated based on a sales price, not the value of the goods shown on the balance sheet. Use of any figure other than net sales would not be a true reflection of the days of receivables held by a company.

Using the same mathematical logic behind DOI, calculation of the denominator (net sales/365) gives the daily dollar amount of sales that a company has generated over a 365-day period. When the average accounts receivable figure is divided by this daily sales figure, the result is the amount of DRO held by a company in the period under measurement.

The sum of DOI and DRO measures the entire sales side of the operational process, accounting for the acquisition of assets (inventories), transformation of raw materials to finished goods, revenue generation and collection of receivables. The ability to decrease the number of days needed to complete the cycle, and thus the amount of money tied up in each additional day outstanding, is a primary element of any organization's supply chain mission.

THE CASH-TO-CASH CYCLE

The cash-to-cash cycle is similar to the operating cycle, with one major addition. Whereas the operating cycle measures the number of days necessary to

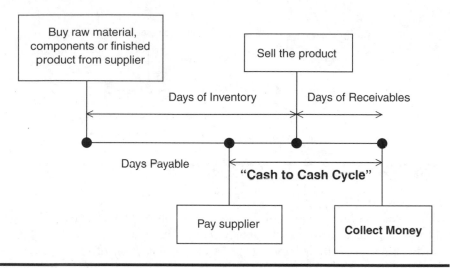

Figure 11.5   Cash-to-Cash Cycle (From Robert S. Kaplan and David P. Norton, *The Balanced Scorecard: Translating Strategy into Action,* Harvard Business School Press, 1996, p. 58. With permission.)

convert inventory to cash, the cash-to-cash cycle determines the number of days that *transpire* between paying suppliers for goods and collecting on sales from customers. Implicit in this model is the use of the two aforementioned components of the operating cycle, as well as an additional tool known as days payable outstanding (DPO).

DPO determines the amount of time in days it takes a company to receive, process and pay its suppliers for goods and services provided. Numerically, the difference in days between when suppliers are paid and money is collected from customers is defined as the sum of DOI and DRO, *minus* DPO. The resulting figure is the cash-to-cash cycle, as shown in Figure 11.5.

Because DOI and DRO have already been discussed, attention is now directed to the additional variable in the cash-to-cash cycle, DPO. As shown graphically in Figure 11.6, the DPO calculation is expressed as:

Average accounts payable/(COGS/365)

The consistency among the conceptual pillars of DOI, DRO and now DPO should be clear. The only difference between the goals of the first two metrics and DPO is a function of corporate culture and company policy. As was mentioned, the goal of DOI and DRO is to reduce the amount of days in each cycle. However, to do that in the case of DPO would imply that suppliers are being paid faster, a practice that conflicts with the payment policies of many

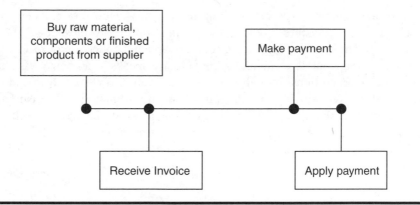

Figure 11.6   Days Payable Outstanding

organizations. In fact, the policy of stretching payables as long as possible has been the foundation of most organizations well into the 1990s.

For reasons to be discussed further along in the analysis, this may not be the best policy for more advanced supply chain thinkers and is certainly not consistent with lean supplier management. NikoTech, for example, was notorious for stretching payments to suppliers and, as the reader will see, suffered dire supply chain consequences as a result.

Notwithstanding these matters, DPO remains an important barometer of organizational performance from both a balance sheet and cash flow statement perspective.

If it is in fact company policy to delay payables, the only way to "improve" DPO is by increasing the numerator or reducing the denominator. The latter would imply a reduction in COGS, which in turn would be driven by the unattractive prospect of reducing sales. Conversely, if COGS were coming down as a result of savings achieved in raw materials or labor and not lost sales, it would be feasible to reduce the denominator. In lieu of that happening, the only way to improve the outcome is to increase the average accounts payable figure.

Accounts payable growth is viable to a certain extent if purchases of raw materials are increasing (again as a function of sales and production growth). However, if purchases are flat, the only way to improve the number is to extend payment to suppliers beyond reason, creating a slew of downstream consequences. If, conversely, the goal of an organization is to rationalize DPO, the exercise becomes a bit easier. Rationalization in this context does not imply a constant quest to reduce DPO but rather to have the amount in line with industry standards, supplier-specific agreements and, most importantly, COGS levels.

The relevance of the cash-to-cash cycle to supply chains lies in its emphasis on the time that transpires between the assumption of payables, acquisition of assets, generation of sales, invoicing of customers and collection of receivables. In a lean world, time is waste and cycle velocity speaks to a company's ability to perpetuate operations through the timely collection of receivables and payment of debt. Recognizing that the journey from raw materials to cash passes through myriad phases, supply chain practitioners would be wise to seek ways to eliminate wasted time in every facet of the transition process.

The analysis continues with a study of NikoTech's asset utilization and supply chain velocity.

12

NIKOTECH: THE OPERATING AND CASH-TO-CASH CYCLE

As explained in the preceding chapter, the operating cycle measures the time that transpires while converting inventories and receivables to cash. For the company in question, this metric is important for a variety of reasons. As a manufacturer, NikoTech must constantly source raw materials and convert them to finished goods. With 350 suppliers feeding plants on four continents, the management of cumulative lead times from the issuance of purchase orders through production and on to finished goods distribution is vital. From a receivables perspective, the days that are consumed during the invoicing and collection process are of equal importance. When taken as an aggregate measure and combined with the aforementioned income statement metrics, the performance of these activities addresses the importance of managing current assets in a productive, timely and profitable fashion. Table 12.1 considers the performance of NikoTech's operating cycle for Y1 and Y2.

The operating cycles for both Y1 and Y2 are graphically represented in Figures 12.1 and 12.2. Beginning with Y1, the first question that comes to mind is whether or not it is necessary to consume the better part of nine months (249 days) to convert inventory and receivables to cash. Because the goal of the metric is to minimize the number of days in the operating cycle, the answer, of course, is no. Using 249 days as a baseline for improvement, a year-to-year

Table 12.1   NikoTech Operating Cycle Y1 and Y2

Formula: Days of Inventory + Days of Receivables		
	Y1 ($ in Millions)	Y2 ($ in Millions)
Days of Inventory	$480/($990/365) = 177 days	$660/($1,239/365) = 194 days
Days of Receivables	$285/($1,440/365) = 72 days	$450/($1,698/365) = 97 days
Operating Cycle	177 + 72 = 249 days	194 + 97 = 291 days

shift to 291 days is even more disconcerting. What this comparison states is that NikoTech is already in trouble in Y1 at 249 days and that the situation has worsened in Y2 by an additional 42 days (a 17% increase).

Once the baseline and trend are established, it is the job of the management team to break down each component part, identifying drivers behind the expan-

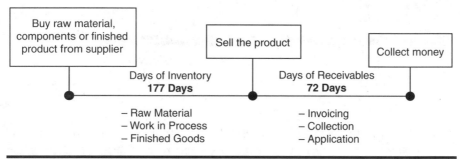

Figure 12.1   Y1 Operating Cycle: 249 Days (Based on Robert S. Kaplan and David P. Norton, *The Balanced Scorecard: Translating Strategy into Action,* Harvard Business School Press, 1996, p. 58. With permission.)

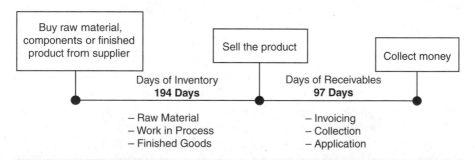

Figure 12.2   Y2 Operating Cycle: 291 Days (Based on Robert S. Kaplan and David P. Norton, *The Balanced Scorecard: Translating Strategy into Action,* Harvard Business School Press, 1996, p. 58. With permission.)

sion of the operating cycle. It is for this reason that supply chain managers must first understand the goal of performance metrics and, more importantly, be able to identify what really moves the numbers at an operating level.

DAYS OF INVENTORY: A CLOSER LOOK

Focusing on days of inventory (DOI) in quantitative terms, the company needs to either reduce the numerator (average inventory) or increase the denominator (cost of goods sold [COGS]) in this equation. The former solution implies generating the same or higher sales with fewer inventories on the balance sheet, which is a valid objective. Increasing the COGS number, however, can be a myopic approach to improving this ratio, depending on the source of the increase.

One hypothesis presented by the NikoTech team is that a percentage of the increase in NikoTech's COGS line is not a function of sales growth, but instead attributed to independent and fast-growing increases in this line item. In this sense, it is imperative that the COGS figure increase as a direct function of sales (at the same or a slower pace); otherwise, DOI becomes a false positive. A detailed analysis of the COGS component of DOI will be undertaken in Chapter 14, at which time major issues related to skyrocketing raw materials costs will indeed be uncovered. Because it suspects that increases in COGS are impacting all areas of the business, NikoTech has also decided to focus on the numerator in the equation, average inventory. This breakdown begins with a horizontal analysis of inventory values relative to sales growth, followed immediately by a vertical analysis of inventory makeup (raw materials, work in process or finished goods) to zero in on the real source of the problem. From there, the team can use other techniques to uncover root causes.

Horizontal analysis of NikoTech's inventory value shows an increase from $480 million in Y1 to $660 million in Y2, a spike of $180 million (37.5%). When inventory investment is compared against Y1 net sales of $1.440 billion, the inventory to net sales ratio reveals that for every dollar of revenue generated, 33 cents in inventory had to be carried to support that sale (inventory/net sales or $480 million/$1.440 billion). Performance was worse in Y2, with 39 cents of inventory for every dollar in sales ($660 million/$1.698 billion). Because inventory values are increasing and not being matched by more sales, the concern is that NikoTech's inventory growth is outpacing its revenue growth, a situation that must be reversed immediately. Table 12.2 validates this concern by showing that inventories are growing twice as fast as net sales (37.5% versus 18%). Based on this information, management decided to look further into the makeup of Y2 inventories with a vertical analysis.

Table 12.2   Year-to-Year Net Sales Versus Inventory Growth

| | in Millions | | | |
	Y1	Y2	Delta	Percentage
Net Sales	$1,440	$1,698	258	18%
Inventory	$480	$660	180	37.5%

The Y2 inventory breakdown in Table 12.3 shows that of the $660 million total, 55% is in raw materials, 25% is in work in process and the remaining 20% is in finished goods. In order to understand the meaning of this breakdown, one must return to the characteristics of the company's business model. Working off of a build-to-order model, the goal of the organization is to hold as little inventory as possible, regardless of its classification. Unfortunately, the reality of working internationally dictates that certain levels of raw materials be maintained to accommodate an unstable production environment. Because of the characteristics of the model, however, the explanation behind the increase in work-in-process and finished goods levels is a bit harder to justify.

At the end of Y2, raw materials inventory represented $363 million (55%) of the total, so the initial focus of the NikoTech management team was centered

Table 12.3   Y2 Inventory Breakdown

	Y2 (in Millions)
Raw Materials (55%)	$363
Work in Process (25%)	$165
Finished Goods (20%)	$132

there. A simple five whys session conducted by the NikoTech team revealed some interesting facts. First, it did not take long to discover that the growth in raw materials inventory was actually a result of the company's sales growth. Because sales grew much faster than any collaborative planning or forecasting exercise could indicate, the demand on raw materials grew proportionately.

The worst nightmare for any buyer is to be the sole person responsible for a line going down due to lack of raw materials (especially if one is responsible for buying them). When demand blew out the forecast, the buyers started to release orders earlier and in greater quantities. Procurement of specific components became disproportionate to actual demand, creating the growth in raw materials inventories. The additional pressure on suppliers destabilized their production plans, creating a ripple effect through the materials side of the supply chain that complicated NikoTech's situation further.

A second and more disconcerting issue revolved around the accuracy of lead times into the plants. The five whys session also revealed that there was major variation in lead times feeding into the plants. While each plant had established lead time commitments from raw materials suppliers into the factories, actual delivery times could vary as much as ten days from the estimated time of arrival. Because buyers had no confidence in lead times and were uncertain of the validity of the forecast, they continued with their practice of ordering earlier and in greater quantities.

Unfortunately, the second-order effects of the lead time issue resonated across the organization and manifested themselves as inventory inaccuracies. Because inbound shipments were moving in such large quantities and at such a furious pace, the receiving entities at each of the four factories began to lose track of what they were taking in. At one point in Brazil, for example, manufacturing was so desperate for parts that as soon as goods arrived, they were delivered directly to the production floor and were never entered into the system.

Without being entered into the system or at least accounted for via a back-flushing mechanism, inventory accuracy related to raw materials reached a low of 60%. Without the ability to know exactly what is in inventory and what is lined up for scheduled receipts, a production facility will eventually go down. Bypassing the receiving process also resulted in skipping over quality checks on incoming merchandise. The second-order effect of not receiving goods into the system created a third situation where defective merchandise got all the way to the production line before problems were discovered. This once again slowed down or stopped lines completely, with a buildup of work in process as a direct result.

Armed with proof as to why raw materials inventories were growing outside of demand, other tools were used to expose what was driving this problem. First, the team established the mean lead time into each plant and compared it with the agreed-to lead times from suppliers in each region (Asia, North and South America and Europe). From there, the standard deviation of lead times into each plant was calculated. Results of these calculations revealed not only that mean lead times were well outside the parameters but that the spread of individual data was all over the map. Subsequent preparation of a value-added process map uncovered several delays in areas that included availability/accuracy of commercial documents from suppliers, cargo routing and customs delays at destination.

At this point, the team should treat lead times into each plant as a separate issue. Because NikoTech works with so many suppliers, it may be wise to carry out a Pareto analysis that shows who the biggest lead time variance offenders are and focus improvement efforts on them. The improvement process can then be facilitated by either a deployment or detailed process map to cut out bottlenecks, delays and unnecessary handoffs across the entire process. While just a beginning, this procedure will bring relief to the increase in raw materials inventories and help to begin the process of reconciling inventory accuracy.

With regard to the inventory accuracy problem, NikoTech must implement a cycle-counting policy that first determines what it has in raw materials inventory and then forces the company to manage accuracy on a daily basis. Only then can NikoTech begin to effectively plan for Y3 and beyond. Inventory accuracy is critical to the gross to net exploding component of the materials requirements planning system, as it allows future net requirements to be based on what is in inventory and what is in the pipeline. Without that initial accuracy, the materials requirements planning system is completely useless and will only cause more confusion in the future.

WORK IN PROCESS

The scenario in raw materials quickly trickled into work in process. In view of the characteristics of the build-to-order model, work in process should be at a minimum at all times. Unfortunately, the quickest way to increase work in process is to begin a production run and half way through it realize that certain necessary components are not available. Inventory accuracy contributes to this situation, but unstable lead times also can create problems for the timing of scheduled receipts. The quick fix is to stop the lot, put it aside and begin production of another order until the necessary parts come in. When parts are coming in from a variety of sources around the world, the wait time can be long, with inventories building at a constant rate.

Work in process is the most dangerous of inventories because as raw materials enter into production, both direct costs and overhead expenses are applied to the goods. As work-in-process inventories lay around gathering dust and taking up space, their dollar value on the balance sheet increases. Again, the solution to this problem speaks directly to inventory accuracy and lead time stabilization. If a production planner cannot rely on the accuracy of raw materials inventory, the buildup in work in process is inevitable. Likewise, if that same planner cannot count on scheduled receipts coming in when planned, the result will be the same, if not worse. This situation, coupled with the inspection-related issue alluded to earlier, created a dangerous situation for NikoTech and its $165 million (25%) in Y2 work-in-process inventories.

Hopefully, the increase in inventory accuracy brought on by the cycle-counting policy will let the plants know exactly what they have in raw materials. From there, and assuming the work-in-process orders are still open, they can get product onto the manufacturing floor that will allow the completion of those orders. For future sales, the combination of stabilized lead times and inventory accuracy will permit planners to not begin a production run unless they are absolutely sure that the goods are in stock or will arrive in time to go into manufacturing.

FINISHED GOODS

Although 80% of NikoTech's inventories were found in raw materials and work in process, another $132 million (20%) remained in finished goods. If the company operated under a build-to-stock model, a $132 million inventory taken as a percentage of sales would be an acceptable number. Unfortunately, NikoTech operates under a build-to-order model that emphasizes a minimum of finished goods inventory. Considering the fundamentals of the model, as well as the dire inventory situation in which management found itself, the NikoTech team was compelled to carry out an ABC analysis on finished goods beginning in late Y2.

ABC analysis is actually based on the tenets of Pareto analysis, a simple yet extremely effective method of uncovering root causes in a variety of situations. First discussed as part of the sigma tool kit in Chapter 9, the Pareto technique allows teams to focus on inputs that are responsible for the greatest amount of variation in a process. For purposes of inventory management, ABC analysis identifies those stockkeeping units (SKUs) that represent the largest percentage of overall inventory value. The rationale behind this practice is if the highest value inventory items can be reduced first, the overall effect of the exercise will be more beneficial to a company. Applying the 80/20 rule, it may be said that 20% of all SKUs represent 80% of the total value of inventories.

An understanding of Pareto analysis makes the ABC breakdown much more intuitive. ABC analysis divides inventories into categories (A, B and C), each

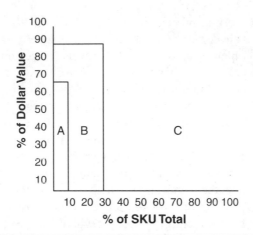

Figure 12.3   ABC Analysis for Inventory Management

of which is based on the dollar value of the SKU. SKUs with the highest value are placed in category A, those with medium value in category B and the remainder in category C. This categorization allows management to focus on the biggest dollar-value items first by taking measures to reduce inventories beginning with the A category.

Cumulative by design, ABC analysis states that 65% of inventory value come from 10% of the SKUs (category A), 25% of the inventory value comes from 20% of the SKUs (category B) and 10% of inventory value comes from the remaining 70% (category C). As displayed in Figure 12.3, ABC analysis states that 90% of the total inventory value (A + B) is driven by 30% of the total number of SKUs.

The results of the NikoTech analysis, implemented across all four plants and shown in Figure 12.4, were revealing. Considering NikoTech's product mix (cellular phones, laptops, desktop computers and routers), it may not be surprising that the majority of the 23 SKUs placed in category A were for laptops and cellular phones. It is also telling to note that the 23 SKUs in question represented 15% of the total SKU count but, more importantly 65% of the total dollar value ($85.8 million). Moving on to category B, 25% of the total SKUs were found in this section (37 out of 150), representing 30% of the total dollar value ($39.6 million). Finally, and not inconsistent with ABC analysis, category C has 60% of the SKUs (90), but only 5% of the value ($6.6 million). While this analysis shows which product families represent the makeup of finished goods inventories, it does not tell management a lot about where the problems were occurring and why they were happening. Based on this information, the team

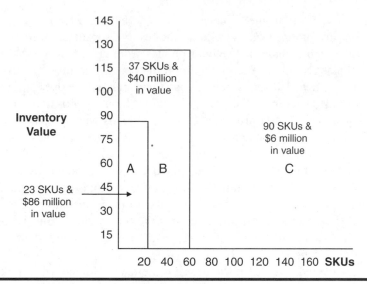

Figure 12.4 ABC Analysis for Finished Goods

was able to dig deeper into the issue and uproot some key drivers of the problem.

The ABC analysis led management to conduct another Pareto exercise on the category A offenders, this time isolating which plants were responsible for the largest amounts of finished goods. Once it was determined that China and Mexico represented the majority of finished goods, all short-term efforts were focused on bringing them in line. The combination of a five why analysis and subsequent deployment process map told an interesting story. First, it was discovered that China had serious problems with laptop returns from major customers in the United States. It seems that the same lead time issue that was plaguing materials management had found its way into finished goods, with customer orders going out the door well after their due dates. Because NikoTech's customers were losing sales due to late deliveries, they exercised delivery time clauses in their contracts with NikoTech and rejected the goods.

A detailed process map of logistics flows out of the China plant revealed that lead times had increased due to the fact that the logistics department had changed ocean carriers. While saving $300 per container in transportation costs, the lead time had increased by 15 days into the port of Long Beach, California. The logistics department never shared this innovation with the sales director, and the problem went unnoticed for months. Once discovered, the logical solution was to revert back to the original carrier so as to be in a position to comply with contractual lead time agreements.

Turning its efforts to the Tijuana plant, the NikoTech team realized there were similar inventory levels of cellular phones, but for different reasons. Due mainly to the high demand for cellular phones from clients in South America, the Tijuana plant could not keep up with production. After a few brainstorming sessions, it was revealed that when the capacity problem cropped up, management had decided to ship partial orders as opposed to no goods at all. However, a process mapping session also showed that as goods were prepared for shipment, the commercial documents (invoice and packing list) did not match the actual quantities of goods. Specifically, the order management personnel did not make adjustments to the orders to reflect the decrease in product shipped. When shipments arrived at destination in South America, customs noticed the discrepancies and either delayed or seized shipments. In many instances, it took over 30 days to fix the problem, again putting NikoTech well beyond its delivery commitment. Predictably, customers rejected orders and sent them back to NikoTech on a freight collect basis.

Once uncovered, the documentation problem was solved via a poka-yoke (foolproofing) mechanism that was built into the process. Basically, copies of the adjusted order information were shared with the shipping area, and a process was put in place whereby all physical cargo had to be reconciled with the paperwork. Consistent with the 3 Cs approach to documentation handling, the Mexico plant was able to be sure that all documents were complete, correct and consistent with the quantity of physical goods. Upon implementation, the process was monitored through the use of trend charts that plotted the delivery time of each shipment. If an individual order was outside of the established parameters, corrective action was taken to make sure the situation did not happen again.

In the case of category A finished goods, the concerted effort of ABC analysis and several Six Sigma tools was able to uncover and eradicate many problems. However, even after taking these measures, NikoTech management felt that there was still too much money tied up in finished goods for a build-to-order model.

ABC analysis can reveal a great many things about the makeup of finished goods inventory. One thing it cannot isolate, however, is the age of the inventory. An inventory aging report requested by the team revealed that of the $132 million in finished goods, $45 million had been on the books for almost two years. The result of poor quality, returns and failed product launches, these products remained on NikoTech's books with little hope of redemption.

It was no secret at NikoTech that the policy on obsolete inventory or no-buyer inventory was to keep values on the balance sheet. As any accountant knows, this practice artificially props up the income statement but has a negative effect on asset utilization. NikoTech deferred losses on the income statement, hiding the obsolete inventory values on its balance sheet. This number inflated the value of the inventory line item, which had an adverse effect on all measures associated with asset utilization and velocity. The solution to this problem is to try and find a buyer, albeit at a discount, for the goods in question. If that does not work, management will eventually have to bite the bullet and take the charge to the income statement. Net income would suffer in the short term, but all asset utilization calculations would improve proportionately.

Based on the breadth and depth of the inventory discussion, few would disagree that the biggest challenge facing supply chain managers today continues to be inventory management. This is particularly true in a production environment, where raw materials, work in process and finished goods can become a runaway train, and a vector approach to measuring performance must be exercised consistently throughout the years. Tools like DOI, cycle counting, Pareto analysis and detailed process mapping are but a few of the methods that have been and continue to be available to businesspeople today. It is the use of these tools, along with an obsession to overturn every operational stone, that will bring companies a step closer to supply chain excellence.

DAYS OF RECEIVABLES: A CLOSER LOOK

As pointed out during the initial discussion on days receivable outstanding (DRO), simple mathematics implies that NikoTech's performance can be enhanced by reducing the numerator in the equation, increasing the denominator or, ideally, through a combination of the two. As first illustrated in the discussion on COGS dynamics, in order for DRO to come down, net sales would have to be growing at a faster pace than receivables. In another possible scenario, NikoTech can improve this figure by increasing sales while maintaining (or reducing) the receivables figure. If revenues do not increase, this ratio can still be improved by reducing the receivables number based on the same amount of sales.

A return to NikoTech's year-to-year DRO shows that the number of days needed to bill and collect on a receivable increased from 72 to 97 in Y2. Stated differently, it took the company an additional 25 days (35% longer) to generate cash from receivables in Y2 than it did in Y1. In other words, utilizing the receivables to sales ratio, the figures portray a situation where for every dollar in net sales in Y1, NikoTech had 20 cents in receivables on the street at any given time. In Y2, the company had 26 cents in receivables for every dollar in sales, a difference of 6 cents.

Similar to NikoTech's original (but untenable) explanation of the growth in COGS being tied to sales, it could be said that the growth in receivables

Table 12.4   Year-to-Year Net Sales Versus Accounts Receivable

	in Millions	
	Y1	Y2
Net Sales Change (18%)	$1,440	$1,698
Accounts Receivable Change (58%)	$285	$450

was a natural result of increasing revenues. Also, it is important to note that NikoTech is a small player in the electronics manufacturing services industry and that six customers account for 70% of its sales. Given this limitation, the payment terms NikoTech offers to customers are a decisive factor in the closing of business. Although both issues may have contributed to a growing accounts receivable figure in Y2, the fact that receivables outgrew net sales at a rate of 58% versus 18% should cause concern. Table 12.4 illustrates the growth trend of both areas.

Continued audits conducted by headquarters on each of the billing entities at the factories brought many issues to light. Using a deployment process map, NikoTech management was able to identify the connection points between all of the departments involved in the accounts receivable process. By then, it was no surprise that many of the downstream problems that the team uncovered actually began farther upstream in the operating areas. In several specific cases, for example, the orders that were rejected in the DOI analysis were proven to be the cause of mischief in accounts receivable. As if the customs delays and returned orders were not enough, clients that actually received partial orders were sent invoices for the entire sale. Predictably, the customers were not paying these invoices, but the problem only surfaced when payment dates arrived. The solution was to reissue invoices and begin the payment process all over again.

Another example of supply chain deficiencies that impacted the company's accounts receivable revolved around the synchronization of shipping lead time with the date that the receivables clock began to run. Although NikoTech shipped to and billed most customers on an ex works basis, a policy change by the senior vice president of sales in Y2 meant that receivables were triggered based on the date of product receipt by the client. This meant that if NikoTech shipped orders via ocean containers from Asia to the United States, for example, a 45-day credit term did not begin until the client received the goods. With an average door-to-door ocean transit time from China to Long Beach, California of 20 to 25 days, a client would really have 65 to 70 days of credit.

This policy was further complicated by the fact that NikoTech never really knew when shipments were received and therefore had to rely on the honesty of its clients in paying their bills on time. The effect was a commensurate swelling of receivables in the over-60-days category. The solution to this problem was to go back to the customers that had enjoyed the fruits of the policy, explain the situation in plain financial terms and negotiate a deal whereby the clock started ticking from the date of invoice or at least from the date of the bill of lading.

The above cases are but a pair of examples of the chaos that pervaded the entire accounts receivable process. Further analysis revealed bills sent out weeks after goods were shipped, customers discounting bills, invoices rife with errors and huge amounts of administrative manpower wasted on fixing problems. Given the severity of the situation, NikoTech management should undertake a full-blown Six Sigma project, starting with an agreement with customers as to what their credit terms will be. Once operational definition is brought to the discussion, NikoTech can begin to quantify its performance.

To achieve this, the team has to establish its sigma level based on a defects per million opportunities calculation. Admittedly a cumbersome task for a global organization, the sigma team has to first identify all of the ways in which an invoice can have an error and design processes to eradicate the offenders. At some point, a Pareto analysis of customers that represent the largest amount in accounts receivable should be conducted, with all subsequent efforts focused on getting some cash out of those clients. Parallel to that activity, an entirely new process should be designed that recognizes the impact of all areas on collections, not just accounts receivable.

NikoTech's management has certainly begun to address some of the problems plaguing accounts receivable, and a comprehensive Six Sigma process redesign will bring further benefits. None of these measures, however, can address the additional $39 million over 180 days that was discovered from an accounts receivable aging report. An axiom of collections is that with the passing of each day, the probability of receiving payment decreases. For this reason, there is absolutely no legitimate reason why a company should have receivables older than 180 days.

The $39 million over 180 days at NikoTech is identical in effect to the obsolete inventories it is carrying on the balance sheet. This money was not just 180 days old — much of it was well over a year old. This residual number was the result of bad billing, rejections and poor collections that now represent zero hope of collection. This is especially true since the bulk of the number is from two top customers and management does not want to antagonize the clients any further and jeopardize future business.

The resolution of this problem requires a write-off of the amount older than 180 days that is determined to be hopelessly uncollectable. In fact, the future policy of NikoTech should be that 50% of the receivable goes straight to the operating entity's income statement as a loss after 6 months and the remaining balance hits the books after 12 months. When people realize that their budget will take a huge hit due to bad collections, their attitude toward the task will take a 180-degree turn.

Bill Hewlett and Dave Packard put it best when they said, "Show me how somebody is measured and I'll show you how they manage." This is definitely the case in accounts receivable management, and NikoTech must tie supply chain performance to the utilization of assets, in this case accounts receivable. To elicit the desired behavior and complete the exercise, any money collected subsequent to a write-off should be included in future income statements as a gain. Regardless of how NikoTech brings about the change, the policy of hiding bad debt on the balance sheet is shortsighted at best, as it shields the income statement from write-offs at the expense of working capital and return on assets.

Up to this point, NikoTech management has focused on reducing the average receivables number in the DRO ratio. It is appropriate to attack the receivables problem at a root cause level, but increasing the denominator of the ratio, net sales, could exact additional improvements as well. Although increased sales is always desirable, another way to augment net sales is by improving returns and allowances (R&A). Cursory analysis of the R&A section of NikoTech's income statement implies that year to year R&A is growing outside the scope of normal increases due to sales activities. The financial impact of decreasing R&A will be covered in detail in Chapter 14 on the income statement. Given the number of problems NikoTech has had with returns and discounted invoices, suffice it to say at this time that R&A is an area rich in potential for bringing improvements to overall performance.

Hopefully, these examples have highlighted not only the need to manage inventories and receivables but that the health of these items depends directly on operating tactics that encompass landed costs, inventory management and lead time rationalization. The relationship between productivity, asset utilization and tactical execution is manifestly clear when employing the operating cycle and, as such, should be included in any portfolio of supply chain measurement tools.

THE CASH-TO-CASH CYCLE

The operating cycle is very helpful in measuring the productivity of short-term assets relative to the time that expires in converting them to cash. What this tool does not recognize, however, is the fact that, at some point in the operation, payment has to be made for the acquisition of goods and services. The cash-to-cash cycle is useful in that it does contemplate the time that expires between paying for raw materials and collecting on the sale of finished goods. By including days payable outstanding (DPO) in the original operating cycle formula, management can focus on the days that transpire between payment and collection, constantly seeking to reduce the cycle to the company's benefit.

Given that an explanation of DOI, DRO and DPO has been provided along with an analytical breakdown of the operating cycle, what requires further discussion is the role of DPO in the cash-to-cash cycle. From there, an in-depth breakdown of the cash-to-cash cycle itself and what it means to a company's balance sheet is required. The opposite of the DRO calculation, DPO measures the time it takes an organization to receive, process and honor accounts payable. The DPO and cash-to-cash calculations for Y1 and Y2 are shown in Tables 12.5 and 12.6.

A year-to-year comparison shows that the cash-to-cash cycle grew by 41 days (185 – 144) from Y1 to Y2. Already in bad shape at 144 days in Y1, NikoTech's slide continued downward in Y2 as the elapsed time between paying suppliers and collecting cash grew to 185 days. As graphically displayed in Figure 12.5, this negative trend speaks volumes about the impact on cash as it surfaces later in the analysis on working capital, return on total assets and return on investment.

By now, breakdown of the cash-to-cash formula should reinforce some foregone conclusions. Because the DPO number only increased by one day in

Table 12.5   NikoTech Days Payable Outstanding

$ in Millions	
Y1	Y2
$285/($990/365) = 105 days	$360/($1,239/365) = 106 days

Table 12.6   NikoTech Cash-to-Cash Cycle

Y1	Y2
(177 + 72) − 105 = **144 days**	(194 + 97) − 106 = **185 days**

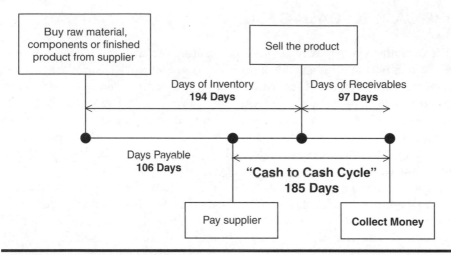

Figure 12.5   Y2 Cash-to-Cash Cycle (Based on Robert S. Kaplan and David P. Norton, *The Balanced Scorecard: Translating Strategy into Action,* Harvard Business School Press, 1996, p. 58. With permission.)

Y2 (105 to 106), all of the swelling in the cash-to-cash cycle can be ascribed to the issues already discussed for inventories and receivables. The tactical remedies suggested for the operating cycle apply equally to the cash-to-cash cycle and should be carried out immediately.

However, a more holistic approach would dictate that management not only focus on a remedy for the asset side of this equation but also take a serious look at what is behind the DPO number. When viewed in the proper context, the inflated DPO actually eclipses the dysfunctional performance of DOI and DRO. While a first glance at the DPO number indicates that it is helping the cash-to-cash cycle, it is really highlighting much more serious issues with which the company must deal.

DAYS PAYABLE OUTSTANDING: A CLOSER LOOK

In this instance, an interpretation based solely on a horizontal comparison of DPO will not reveal much. A one-day increase year to year is not a startling event and may not require further analysis. The real question is why the number is so big to begin with. Whether in Y1 or Y2, DPO is unusually high and when properly interpreted should be a cause for concern. A vertical analysis of the accounts payable breakdown validated the concentration of payables over 90 days, and when a key supplier refused to do business with NikoTech in Y2 due to constant payment problems, another analysis was launched to determine the real impact of DPO on operations.

The reason why NikoTech's DPO is so high can be attributed in part to corporate culture. Since the early days of operations, it had been the practice of management to encourage late payment of bills in order to enhance the cash position of the company. The fact that NikoTech has recently had trouble collecting from its own customers only served to make matters worse, compelling the company to delay payment to suppliers in a corresponding fashion. Although the accounts payable department may have found it good business to stretch payment to suppliers as much as possible, the damage done to supply chains and financial outcomes is actually much greater than any one-dimensional benefit.

Another reason for the high DPO number can be assigned to practices upstream in the operating environment that resurfaced downstream in accounts payable. Reference was made to the plants' practice of receiving goods and rushing them to the production floor without accounting for them in the system. Because there was no record of specific purchase orders or part numbers received, the accounts payable department could not reconcile bills with warehouse receipts. This hole in the process precipitated the rejection or return of invoices, with the effect of extending the payables period until each individual order could be reconciled. Uncovered by the same process mapping exercise conducted during the DOI analysis, the enterprise-wide effect of seemingly isolated practices was becoming more and more clear at NikoTech.

The organizational effect of NikoTech's accounts payable practices begins with a return to the key characteristic of its operations, the low-mix/high-volume model. First mentioned in the discussion on the growth in COGS, a similar comparison can be made between the natural characteristics of a low-mix/high-volume structure and an unusually high DPO.

First, the smaller mix of products translates to fewer parts, which allows for concentration of purchases among select suppliers. Second, the use of common parts further increases the probability of concentrating purchases with key strategic suppliers. The fact that NikoTech has used lean supplier management techniques to rationalize its parts list is admirable. Even with these efforts, however, accounts payable was still out of line with credit terms extended by the suppliers. In addition to these obvious points, a primary characteristic of a "collaborative" relationship between seller and buyer is an open-book approach to costs, as well as conscientious treatment of the payment of bills. Cognizant of all of these points, the first two questions that NikoTech must ask is why it works with 350 suppliers around the world and why it takes an average of 106 days to pay them.

Analysis of these questions uncovers a vicious circle in NikoTech's supply chain, the effect of which infiltrates the balance sheet, income statement and cash flow statement. Since the historic practice of the company had been to sweat its suppliers, commodity managers and buyers over the years found themselves seeking more and more suppliers with which to work. In some cases, vendors got tired of the NikoTech runaround, so the buyers rotated purchases based on how much they owed a given supplier. Although the accounts payable department was delighted with the extended payment plan, the company was oblivious to the shock waves this was causing in product quality, inventory levels, lead times and landed costs.

Because NikoTech was rotating suppliers, the landed cost structure of its products was constantly changing, with different component prices, transportation costs and customs duties acting as the primary drivers of this phenomenon. Again, this point leads the analyst to the study of COGS increases and what the true makeup of that line item was. It may be hard to believe that accounts payable could have an effect on COGS, but that was exactly the case at NikoTech. Also, because suppliers were in different countries and at varying distances, any change would alter delivery dates into the factories and exacerbate the existing lead time problem.

At this point in the discussion, the impact of variations in lead times into a production facility should be well ingrained. Finally, since different suppliers were providing the same parts, quality issues arose in all of the factories, based mainly on the inconsistency among vendors.

A major step toward stabilizing NikoTech's COGS is tied to management changing its accounts payable practices. Basically, management has to change its attitude toward accounts payable by paying down the bills to a reasonable level and rationalizing the list of suppliers with which the company works. The first step in cutting down the number of suppliers revolves around asking the right questions. In this case, the question to ask is why NikoTech deals with so many suppliers, instead of how to staff up in purchasing to handle all of the relationships. Management already knows why there are so many suppliers, so the second question becomes *how* to rationalize the list.

The versatility of Pareto analysis for business applications has been made clear. Supplier rationalization is no exception to this rule, and a quick Pareto analysis of which suppliers represent the bulk of purchases will narrow management's focus considerably. Once identified,. those suppliers need to be paid on an immediate basis. The best gesture that NikoTech could make toward establishing strategic relationships with vendors is to get out of arrears with them. If it is determined that the company wants to continue with those suppliers (and they with NikoTech), a new, open-book approach can be undertaken. If they decide to part ways, NikoTech does not owe them any more money and its reputation in the market will improve.

Pursuant to lean supplier management principles, paring down the supplier list is only the first step in a longer process. Another proven technique that NikoTech might consider is tiering its suppliers. Given the nature of its product families, NikoTech might consider dealing with only tier I suppliers and use them to deliver assemblies. Although this alternative would require additional analysis, it is certainly worth investigating.

Even if NikoTech is successful in reducing its supplier list, thought should also be given to taking waste out of supplier-related processes. As discussed in Chapter 3 on lean manufacturing, seeking ways to eliminate the use of purchase orders may be another project worthy of Six Sigma examination. The management team already knows that the number of purchase orders issued during the last year has increased (for all the wrong reasons). If management is capable of getting its forecast in line with demand or, better yet, working closer with customers to determine actual demand, raw materials purchases can be stabilized. In a stable materials management environment, it is much more feasible to move to a delivery program for components as opposed to issuing purchase orders. This would be a huge undertaking for NikoTech's management but is certainly food for thought. This type of project is enterprise-wide in nature and would require a total redesign of major processes, beginning with forecasting. Considering the direction in which NikoTech is heading, perhaps it is time for a bet-the-business project of this magnitude.

There is one last point to be made about DPO management and the cash-to-cash cycle. It should be clear that if NikoTech reduces its DPO without a corresponding reduction in DOI and DRO, the calculation will worsen. Paying suppliers sooner without completing the operating cycle quicker does not help from a velocity perspective. However, if NikoTech can wring improvements out of the operating cycle via the methods discussed thus far, the effect should be that improvement in inventory and accounts receivable management will eclipse a tighter payables policy.

SUMMARY

The cash-to-cash cycle is a powerful tool for measuring the productivity of assets and the timing of payments with the collection of receivables. However, in order to be truly effective, the components of the formula must be extracted and studied both individually and in the context of their enterprise-wide impact. This financial analysis, taken in conjunction with the application of lean principles and Six Sigma tools, is a solid formula for success.

While calculation of NikoTech's cash-to-cash cycle exposes areas of concern for the company, it cannot reveal the entire supply chain story on its own. This figure must be combined with other ratios and financial measurements in order to accurately portray the situation in which the organization finds itself. Once a comprehensive financial/operational study has been conducted, the trained analyst can move from analyzing data to interpreting and acting upon information. For a broader understanding of the implications of supply chain execution and financial performance, a study of the entire balance sheet is necessary.

13

NIKOTECH AND THE BALANCE SHEET

In addition to providing information on current assets and their role in the business cycle, the balance sheet offers a wealth of data that can be used to measure the relationship between the utilization of total assets, profitability and supply chain execution. Table 13.1 provides a short list of tools that NikoTech management can use to measure the productivity of all assets employed in the supply chain in order to take a comprehensive view of asset performance. Interpretation of NikoTech's performance is as follows.

WORKING CAPITAL

Regardless of company, industry or business model, working capital is one of the first calculations an analyst performs on an organization's financial statements. Oddly enough, although companies place a great deal of emphasis on working capital, few people outside of financial circles understand its real meaning or what supply chain activities are behind its derivation. Working capital is defined as the difference between current assets and current liabilities. That is certainly easy enough to calculate, but what does it mean? Essentially, working capital determines a company's ability to meet short-term obligations with current assets.

As shown in Table 13.2, it seems that working capital has improved (from $756 million in Y1 to $804.6 million in Y2) or that the company had an additional $48.6 million to cover debt in Y2 than it did in Y1. This is a dangerous statement to make even in the most dysfunctional of companies and

Table 13.1 Balance Sheet Ratios

| | $ in Millions | | |
	Y1	Y2	Delta
Working Capital	$1,059 − $303 = $756	$1,212 − $407.4 = $804.6	$48.6
Current Ratio	$1,059/$303 = 3.5 times	$1,212/$407.4 = 2.97 times	(0.53) times
Quick Ratio	$579/$303 = $1.91	$552/$407.4 = $1.35	($0.56)
Inventory Turnover	$990/$480 = 2.06 times	$1,239/$660 = 1.9 times	(0.15) times
Receivables Turnover	$1,440/$285 = 5.05 times	$1,698/$450 = 3.8 times	(1.25) times
Payables Turnover	$990/$285 = 3.47 times	$1,239/$360 = 3.44 times	(0.03) times
Total Asset Turnover	$1,440/$1,599 = $0.90	$1,698/$1,776 = $0.95	$0.05

Table 13.2 Y1 and Y2 Working Capital

| | in Millions | | |
	Y1	Y2	Delta
Working Capital	$756.0	$804.6	$48.6

is especially true in the case of NikoTech. The mechanics of working capital are much more complex than the calculation would indicate, and to really understand what a company should try to accomplish with working capital, the concepts of *utilization* and *liquidity* must be part of any discussion on the subject.

In the realm of working capital, utilization determines how well a company is managing its current assets relative to the amount of current liabilities it has in the period under consideration. An organization wants to have enough in current assets to cover short-term obligations, but too much money tied up there may mean that those assets are not being *utilized* properly. In this light, a company wants to align the amount in current assets with the amount it has in short-term liabilities, constantly working toward a working capital of zero.

The rationale behind this philosophy is that lower working capital translates to a better ratio of assets to liabilities, thus creating the ability to dedicate excess assets to more productive activities. The attitude of a company toward working capital has a lot to do with its aversion to risk, but regardless of company philosophy, the relationship between this figure and supply chain execution is another cornerstone of the overall operating model.

Returning to the NikoTech case with a fresh perspective on working capital management, the analyst can peel back the operational onion to get to the real drivers of this once innocuous calculation. Again, the working capital calculation for Y2 is $1.212 billion − $407.4 million, or $804.6 million. This means that after meeting all of its current obligations, the company still has $804.6 million in assets. A conservative financial policy is always admirable, but even in the staunchest of organizations this figure would be interpreted as out of balance. An understanding of this imbalance and its effect on supply chains requires knowledge of not only utilization but also the importance of liquidity to NikoTech's current assets.

When dealing with assets, liquidity can be defined as the immediacy with which they can be converted to cash. This definition has important implications for supply chain execution and working capital because some assets, by their very nature, are more liquid than others. Cash, for example, is as liquid as an asset can get. Marketable securities are also highly liquid because they can be converted to cash almost immediately. Liquidity becomes a bit more viscous, however, when one considers accounts receivable and inventories.

Accounts receivable are somewhat liquid, depending on how old and, hence, how collectable they are. Inventories, on the other hand, are the least liquid of current assets, because they must be converted into finished goods, sold, billed and collected. Based on the analysis of NikoTech's operating cycle, there is no need to elaborate any further on how long a process that can be. With a view toward utilization and liquidity, a vertical analysis of Y2 current assets will shed additional light on the issue.

Analysis of NikoTech's Y2 current assets in Table 13.3 reveals that cash and marketable securities only account for 8% of the total. This means that accounts receivable and inventory account for 92% of the entire section, with

Table 13.3   Vertical Analysis Y2 Current Assets

	Dollars (in Millions)	Percentage
Cash	87	7.0
Marketable Securities	15	1.0
Accounts Receivable	450	37.0
Inventory	660	55.0
Total	1,212	100.0

■ Cash   □ Marketable Securities   ▩ Accounts Receivable   □ Inventory receivables at 37% and inventory at an alarming 55%. Whereas current assets originally seemed to cover current liabilities, the picture is beginning to take on a darker complexion from a liquidity perspective. As current liabilities come due, NikoTech is much more dependent on converting receivables and inventory to cash to pay bills than on being able to pay bills directly from cash.

Actually, cash on the balance sheet decreased in Y2 by $177 million, which would lead one to believe that overall working capital may decrease as well. However, the growth in inventory and receivables was so great that it netted out the reduction in cash and *still* increased by $48.6 million. Now from a liquidity viewpoint, receivables and inventory surface again as the evil twins plaguing the underlying performance of NikoTech. An important component of working capital analysis is liquidity, and vertical analysis is a quick and valuable tool for putting the figure in the proper context. Two other tools that augment the study and provide another look at working capital are the current ratio and quick ratio.

THE CURRENT RATIO

Designed to work in unison with working capital calculations, the current ratio measures to what extent current assets cover current liabilities (current assets/ current liabilities). Much like working capital figures, the result of this calculation is a relative number, the significance of which is dictated by company philosophy and policy. Whereas a conservative company would want a higher ratio, a more aggressive organization would seek to have a ratio that approximates one (one dollar in assets for every dollar in liabilities). Again, the outcome of this ratio will complement the working capital number insomuch as it uses a different methodology to measure the same variable, namely the ability to meet current liabilities with current assets.

Using Y1 as a base figure, Table 13.4 shows that NikoTech's current ratio was 3.5 ($1.059 billion/$303 million). Quantitatively, this figure states that the company can "cover" its current liabilities 3.5 times. Expressed in less abstract terms, for every dollar that NikoTech had in short-term obligations, it had $3.50 in current assets to cover the payments. In Y2, the ratio moved downward, showing that for every dollar in current liabilities, the company had almost three ($2.97) in current assets ($1.212 billion/$407.4 million). For companies like

Table 13.4   Y1 and Y2 Current Ratio

	Y1	Y2	Delta
Current Ratio	3.5	2.97	0.53

NikoTech that should be seeking a tighter current ratio (or working capital closer to zero), this shift is seen as an improvement. However, it is important to also note that the current ratio decreased even after working capital increased, a phenomenon that puts the current ratio improvement on dubious ground.

The answer to the above paradox lies in the determination of year-to-year line item changes in current assets and liabilities, as well as the ability to interpret the *net* impact of those changes on their respective sections of the balance sheet. Working capital expanded in Y2 due to an increase in receivables and inventories, a figure that still dominated all calculations even after netting out the effect of the $177 million decrease in cash. Add to this the negligible growth in accounts payable, and the growing gap in working capital is easy to explain.

The current ratio, on the other hand, "improved" for all the wrong reasons. Specifically, the combination of the $177 million reduction in cash, coupled with the meager relative increase in current liabilities of $104.4 million, created the illusion of improving the ratio to 2.97. Had the improvements come by way of reducing inventories and/or receivables, NikoTech's current ratio in Y2 would be a much more encouraging number.

The comparison of working capital with the current ratio emphasizes the need for analysts to not only go through the math but to also interpret what they have calculated. In the NikoTech case, a superficial treatment of working capital and the current ratio may lead one to believe that things are moving in the right direction. However, a more visceral feel for the dynamics of accounting and supply chain tactics would dictate otherwise. Armed with a deeper understanding of supply chain and financial dynamics, the analyst is better prepared to reverse negative trends in the present and make intelligent decisions for the future.

THE QUICK RATIO (ACID TEST)

Given that liquidity is a fundamental component of working capital measurement, the quick ratio, or acid test, must be a part of any comprehensive analysis. Designed to eliminate the inherently non-liquid nature of inventories, the ratio recalculates the current ratio, less the value of inventories. This enhanced calculation allows a more realistic view of how well a company can cover current liabilities, removing inventory from the equation entirely.

As displayed in Table 13.5, NikoTech's acid test has taken a turn for the worse. In Y1, the company could cover short-term obligations 1.91 times ($579 million/$303 million), but in Y2 the ratio dropped to 1.35 ($552 million/$407.4 million). When the value of inventories is removed, the Y2 quick ratio shows

Table 13.5   Y1 and Y2 Acid Test

	Y1	Y2	Delta
Acid Test	1.91	1.35	0.56

that the company can cover every dollar in current liabilities with $1.35. This is a rather stark comparison with the original working capital and current ratio results, numbers that now seem to hide an increasingly obvious problem with inventories.

Without question, NikoTech must remedy its inventory and receivables problems by implementing the aforementioned tactics and policies to improve its working capital position. An additional measure that the company may consider involves internal financial policies that promote conscientious asset management. Similar to the penalty levied by companies when they write off bad receivables or obsolete inventory, it may be prudent for NikoTech to institute an internal interest charge on working capital amounts that are outside corporate parameters.

If management dictates a working capital ceiling for each plant, any plant that exceeds its amount would be charged interest on the underutilized assets, much like interest on a loan. This "interest charge" would appear on the income statement as an expense, again detracting from net income. Coupled with the policy on write-offs, this additional mechanism would encourage supply chain managers to actively manage their assets and liabilities on a daily basis.

During the analysis of the cash-to-cash cycle, it was suggested that the days payable outstanding figure should be reduced, with the net impact (upon improving the asset side of the equation) being positive. This statement has important ramifications for the working capital equation because if current liabilities are reduced without a corresponding improvement from current assets, the net outcome for working capital will be worse. Understanding that the goal of organizations is to reduce working capital (better use of assets), a decrease in current liabilities would widen the gap in working capital. The relationship between asset management and improvement of cycle time and its impact, in this case on working capital, is but another example of how supply chain execution tangibly impacts the financial performance of a company.

INVENTORY TURNOVER

One of the most frequently used but least understood measures of asset management is inventory turnover. The confusion around this measure can be attributed to the traditional definition of the term, which is the number of times in a year (or quarter) that a company "turns over" inventory. When an explanation does nothing more than rearrange the composition of the term itself, confusion and misunderstanding will reign.

It is important to understand that inventory turnover is a relative figure, in this instance to cost of goods sold (COGS) (as a function of sales growth). With COGS as the numerator and average inventory the denominator, the ratio states that with a given inventory level, a company is able to produce finished goods, execute sales and repeat the entire process X number of times during the period being measured. In other words, the company completes the days of inventory (DOI) cycle X number of times during the year. Taken from a different angle, NikoTech's Y2 inventory to sales ratio would infer that in order to generate $1.698 billion in net sales, the company needs $660 million in inventory. The question (now rhetorical) for NikoTech's management is to determine whether the veracity of that statement is beyond reproach or if improvements could be sought in both of the equation's variables.

Similar to the question that arose during the DOI calculation, one may be compelled to ask why, if inventory utilization is really a function of net sales, is COGS, and not the sales figure, the numerator in the equation? Bearing in mind that the only way to improve this ratio is to increase the numerator, decrease the denominator or both, it should be obvious that by using the sales figure, the result of the exercise would be unjustifiably inflated.

This point was first elaborated upon in the study of the DOI calculation, and the same implications for the balance sheet are found in the analysis of inventory turnover. Consistent with what was uncovered in the section on DOI, use of the net sales figures would artificially augment the numerator, thus disguising the true utilization of inventories. Recalling that the value of inventories on the balance sheet is the cost of the goods and that inventory values are transferred to the income statement as COGS, an accurate representation of inventory turnover requires use of this number.

If in the case of inventory turnover it is desirable to either increase the numerator or reduce the denominator, NikoTech finds itself in the same dangerous position it did when calculating the operating cycle. If the COGS number is increasing as a function of sales growth, either at the same or a slower pace than sales, then the numerator is a valid number. If, however, the number is growing in part due to issues not related directly to sales, the outcome of the calculation will misrepresent reality and inflate the turnover calculation. With this caveat in mind, one can determine NikoTech's inventory turnover ratio in both Y1 and Y2.

Based on COGS and inventory levels in Y1, Table 13.6 shows that NikoTech was able to produce finished goods, sell them and repeat the process 2.06 times

Table 13.6 Y1 and Y2 Inventory Turnover

	Y1	Y2
Inventory Turnover	2.06	1.9

Table 13.7 Days of Inventory Versus Inventory Turnover

	Y1	Y2
Days of Inventory	177	194
Inventory Turnover	2.06	1.9
Product	365	365

in a 12-month period. All variables remaining equal and untouched, management is saying that in order to generate $1.440 billion in net sales, the company has to carry $480 million in inventory. The situation worsened in Y2, with a turnover figure of less than 2 (1.9). At that level, NikoTech needed to have $660 million in inventories to support $1.698 billion in net sales.

By now, it should be intuitively obvious that the inventory turnover ratio is closely related to the DOI calculation. Actually, they not only are related but are identical. The only distinction between the two is that they use different methodologies to express the exact same concept. To prove this point, consider Table 13.7. In Y1, NikoTech's DOI and inventory turnover were 177 and 2.06, respectively. If one were to multiply 177 by 2.06, the product would be 365, or the number of days in a calendar year. Although a simple calculation, both the DOI and inventory turnover numbers are validated at this time. The same exercise can be completed for Y2, where the product of 194 and 1.9 is 365.

When understood in relative terms, and taken in conjunction with other asset-related measurements, the inventory turnover tool is very valuable. If anything, it is another way to isolate the impact of inventory levels on the financial performance of an organization. Based on similar concepts, equal benefit can be gained from the accounts receivable and accounts payable turnover calculations.

ACCOUNTS RECEIVABLE TURNOVER

Because the accounts receivable turnover calculation is conceptually and quantitatively related to the days receivable outstanding (DRO) cycle, its preparation and comparison to other tools are a fundamental element of the measurement process. Using net sales in the numerator and average accounts receivable in the denominator, the calculation reveals how many times during a period in

Table 13.8   Days Receivable Outstanding Versus Receivables Turnover

	Y1	Y2
Days Receivable Outstanding	72	97
Receivables Turnover	5.05	3.8
Product	365	365

which customers are billed funds are collected and applied to balances. As displayed in Table 13.8, NikoTech's Y1 results show a turnover of a bit more than five times per year and are just below four in Y2.

Akin to the inventory turnover and DOI comparison, accounts receivable turnover and DRO are simply two different ways of expressing the same outcome. As such, it is no surprise that when the Y1 turnover figure of 5.05 is multiplied by 72, the product is 365. Applying the same math to Y2, a turnover of 3.8 times per year times 97 DRO also equals 365 (with allowances for rounding error).

As stand-alone measures, both inventory turnover and accounts receivable turnover provide valuable insight as to how well a company is managing its assets. When combined with other measures, these tools help to validate or disprove what the additional results indicated, creating a vector between utilization and supply chain velocity.

ACCOUNTS PAYABLE TURNOVER

Shifting balance sheet focus for a moment to the section on liabilities, the accounts payable turnover calculation is also an important part of the financial toolbox. With COGS as the numerator and average accounts payable as the denominator, this calculation tells the analyst how many times the payables cycle is completed in a given period. If taken as the opposite of the accounts receivable process, accounts payable is the normal time it takes a company to receive, process and pay its suppliers' bills. When lined up against the days payable outstanding (DPO) calculation, this tool becomes especially helpful in letting management know exactly how many times a year the payment cycle is completed. As such, these measurements not only quantify how well a company is complying with payment terms, but also indicate how efficient the overall process is. Given the open-book nature of lean supplier relationships, accounts payable turnover and DPO support a strategic partnership through constant monitoring of payment compliance.

As suspected, NikoTech's accounts payable turnover is quite low, and the DPO calculations for both years are a leading indicator of that outcome. Again,

Table 13.9   Days Payable Outstanding Versus Payables Turnover

	Y1	Y2
Days Payable Outstanding	105	106
Payables Turnover	3.47	3.44
Product	365	365

whether a company seeks to have a high or low accounts payable turnover is a question of policy and ability to pay. In today's collaborative environment, however, the intentional abuse of supplier goodwill to the short-term benefit of the balance sheet is not advisable.

Because NikoTech's DPO numbers were stable from Y1 to Y2, the accounts payable turnover figure has not shifted much either. Consistent with previous measurement techniques, Table 13.9 shows that NikoTech's accounts payable turnover and DPO for Y1 were 3.47 and 105, respectively. In other words, it took the company 105 days to receive, process and honor payables with its suppliers.

The figure remained relatively stable in Y2, with the company turning over payables 3.44 times per year or about every 106 days. Identical to the conclusion reached during the DPO analysis, the problem with NikoTech's payables does not lie in any year-to-year changes. Rather, the challenge is to drive down payables and improve supplier relationships, an endeavor that will stabilize landed costs and lead times for raw materials into the factories.

One final comment on the importance of accounts payable management in an international environment: The NikoTech case illustrates that stretching payables with suppliers can cause a groundswell that swamps the entire supply chain. Forced to do business on a cash basis with some suppliers and juggle purchases among the rest, NikoTech's entire raw materials program was destabilized. Six Sigma tools helped to uncover the egregious damage done by NikoTech's payment policies. Continued use of sigma tools in the design of new processes, as well as adherence to the principles of lean supplier management, will serve to eradicate most if not all of the pain accounts payable has caused the company. The end result will be a vast improvement in productivity, velocity and, most importantly, net income.

FIXED ASSETS

Up to this point, the NikoTech discussion has focused on the utilization of current assets. Although important, any discussion on current assets should never overshadow the importance of plant and equipment (P&E) in the evaluation of a business model. In light of the fact that the capacity to produce is what eventually creates inventories and accounts receivable, equal weight should be given to the utilization of fixed assets in any model characterized by manufacturing activities.

With four plants and a corporate building in San Diego, California, NikoTech showed a Y1 fixed asset value of $540 million in P&E. Apart from investments the company made in wide area network and videoconferencing equipment, this number consists of physical plant (factories and adjacent warehouses), production lines, materials handling equipment and the corporate building in California. Even with the explosive sales growth at NikoTech, the investment in fixed assets from Y1 to Y2 grew a nominal $60 million, or 11%. As noted on the balance sheet, net investment after depreciation showed an increase of $24 million, or 4.5%. This growth came in the form of additional lines in the plants in Hungary and China, as well as upgrades to existing lines in Brazil and Mexico. Compared with NikoTech's sales growth, this investment appears to be minimal and could cause bottlenecks for future operations should the business continue to grow.

This statement may or may not hold water, depending on how well the company manages its production capacity across plants. Although this requires more study, the overabundance in raw materials and work-in-process inventory might be an indication that production capacity can be better managed. Regardless of how well capacity is currently managed, one point that the company should consider before any further P&E investments is the adoption of lean manufacturing techniques in the factories. It must be pointed out, however, that the feasibility of consolidating warehouses and staging and production areas depends almost exclusively on NikoTech's ability to level its inbound flow of raw materials and production. With so much money tied up in raw materials, work in process and finished goods, it would be pure folly to make space-related decisions or consolidate production lines prior to rectifying the inventory problem.

Once the inventory issue is resolved for good, management can then focus on economies to be found in physical plant. For example, with the inventory problem out of the way, there should be more space in the warehouses. If analysis reveals that NikoTech is in need of additional production capacity, that floor space can be dedicated to more lines instead of warehouse racks. If not, perhaps management can sublease it to strategic suppliers that could then feed production in a true just-in-time fashion. If the supplier idea does not work out, NikoTech can always rent the space to an unrelated third party.

The reality may be that none of the above ideas will come to fruition. However, management will never know until it fixes the inventory debacle once and for all. Only then can brainstorming sessions take place that allow for such creative thinking. Whatever happens, uncovering cause-and-effect relationships in every facet of NikoTech's operation should serve as a reminder of how seemingly discrete decisions find their way into every corner of a company.

DEPRECIATION

No discussion of fixed assets is complete without considering depreciation, its method of calculation and final impact on financial statements. Although somewhat removed from tactical supply chain activities, depreciation does have an effect on the income statement, balance sheet and cash flow statement, a reality that requires analysis of all depreciable items.

Because depreciation is shown as an expense on the income statement, its relationship to net income is palpable. It is for this reason that some companies will slow down the depreciation of assets to boost bottom line figures. This practice always comes back to haunt an organization, however, as a lethargic depreciation policy inevitably creates overvalued assets on the balance sheet. As was the case with obsolete inventories and bad debt, the day of reckoning comes when these values must be written off to the income statement in their entirety. Apart from postponing the inevitable write-offs, inflated values of fixed assets also obscure the interpretation of total asset measurements, including total asset turnover and return on assets.

The above points should be a cause for concern to NikoTech's management. In the incredibly volatile electronics manufacturing services industry, where product life cycles are measured in months or even weeks, retooling, upgrading and/or replacing production lines is a fairly common occurrence. With a view toward fiscal responsibility, in this environment it would be wise to depreciate assets (at least production equipment) at a fairly aggressive pace, so as to avoid financial pain farther down the road. In addition to avoiding income statement hits in future periods, this policy actually improves asset-related measures due to their lower net values on the balance sheet, a desirable scenario for companies with NikoTech's business model.

Historically, NikoTech has employed the straight-line method of depreciation and shows a consistent figure from period to period. Because the net increase in fixed assets was only $24 million in Y2, the figure $36 million was used to depreciate that year's assets. Taken as a percentage of total fixed assets, $36 million represents a Y2 depreciation rate of 6.5%. Considering that NikoTech's depreciable assets are a combination of P&E (land is not depreciated), it seems the company has taken a fairly neutral stance on depreciation. It is neither aggressively depreciating nor being overly generous to its income statement. Based on the fact that NikoTech is in an ever-changing industry, management may consider a more aggressive policy on depreciation of fixed assets.

MEASURING TOTAL ASSETS

After considering the importance of fixed assets as well as the impact of depreciation on financial reporting, how does an organization measure the return not just on current assets but on all of the assets that the company has on its books? In many cases, the value of fixed assets far outweighs current assets on a company's balance sheet. However, in the case of NikoTech, current assets are much higher than fixed in Y2, at $1.212 billion and $564 million, respectively.

Although this may be further indication that NikoTech is a small player in the electronics manufacturing services field, this comparison can be interpreted to mean that compared to its manufacturing capacity, the company has too much money tied up in receivables and inventory. No matter how this fact is interpreted, the inclusion of fixed assets in overall performance is paramount to accurate supply chain measurement.

Two powerful tools that are used to measure the productivity of total assets are total asset turnover and return on total assets. Considered classic measures of asset utilization, their value has not diminished with time. In order to fully understand the significance of each ratio, however, it is first necessary to recognize that both incorporate elements of the balance sheet and income statement. This combination of variables links the productivity of assets with the profitability of operations, the two most basic elements of supply chain measurement. As both ratios are calculated and interpreted, it is also very important to make the distinction between the meaning of turnover and return in measuring supply chain activities.

When referring to *turnover,* it usually involves a comparison between an asset and the sales generated as a result of possessing that asset. This was the case for the inventory/sales and receivables/sales ratios, where sales levels were matched against the levels of inventory and receivables (allegedly) necessary to generate those sales. The total asset turnover ratio is similar to these calculations except that it includes all assets in the denominator and not just the inventory or receivables line item. With net sales in the numerator and total assets in the denominator, this ratio reveals the productivity of all assets the company has employed relative to the sales figure achieved for the period in question.

Return differs from turnover in that it compares the bottom line profitability figure to total assets, a calculation that gauges the performance of the income statement relative to the value of all assets on the balance sheet. This natural link between the balance sheet and income statement goes much deeper than total asset turnover because it uses the raw profit figure after all supply chain and related expenses are accounted for. When both the turnover and return on asset utilization are measured, the supply chain panorama comes into sharper focus.

TOTAL ASSET TURNOVER

A fairly straightforward exercise, total asset turnover gauges the performance of net sales relative to total assets. Again mixing components of the income statement and balance sheet, assets are shown as the denominator and net sales in the numerator. One point that should now be clear with regard to ratio analysis is that most improvements come from increasing the numerator, decreasing the denominator or a combination of the two. Armed with the detailed review of how to improve both figures from previous calculations, the tactics necessary to achieve these goals are abundant at this time. What is not clear is how NikoTech's sales weighed in against its investment in total assets.

Based on the results in Table 13.10, total asset turnover between Y1 and Y2 remained stable (0.9 to 0.95, respectively). Stating NikoTech's numbers relative to sales, the company cycled through, or "turned over," its assets 0.9 times in Y1 and 0.95 times in Y2. Better expressed in the dollar-denominated language of finance, for every dollar invested in assets, NikoTech was able to generate sales of $0.90 and $0.95 in Y1 and Y2, respectively. As was the case in DPO, horizontal analysis does not really tell much of a story, as the shift year to year is noticeable but not huge. To be meaningful, these figures must be viewed from several angles.

If NikoTech compared its total asset turnover with publicly available industry and competitor information, the company would find itself at the low end of the spectrum. Asset turnover is about generating sales as a result of investing in assets, so to have less than a dollar in sales for every dollar in assets is an abomination in most any industry. Even though total asset turnover improved by $0.05 (5.5%) in Y2, in real terms the variables that impact the equations are not healthy and must be attacked immediately. A simple process of elimination

Table 13.10   Y1 and Y2 Total Asset Turnover

	Y1	Y2
Total Asset Turnover	0.9	0.95

will expose the culprits, the determination of which should be of little surprise to NikoTech management.

Focusing on the numerator and denominator of this ratio, the story unfolds rather quickly. Fixed assets only increased by $24 million in Y2, so it is clear that if the growth in the denominator is dragging the ratio down, it did not come from huge investments in P&E. Also, net sales grew by 18% in Y2, so theoretically, if those sales figures could have been achieved while maintaining a relatively stable asset figure, the result would have been favorable for NikoTech. However, it is a well-documented fact that current assets increased dramatically in Y2, consequently offsetting any gains made on the sales side of the equation.

If the sales growth was there and increases in fixed assets were minimal, the study leads NikoTech directly to the perennial troublemakers: inventory and receivables. At the risk of being redundant, NikoTech's management must continue to focus on the methods discussed earlier to rationalize the current asset figures, now to the benefit of ratios that measure the performance of total assets.

It was suggested during a brief discussion on returns and allowances (R&A) that improvements in this line item would have a positive reflection on several financial ratios. In the case of total asset turnover, any reduction in R&A would boost net sales and hence improve the ratio. A hypothetical situation illustrates this point with clarity.

Consider for a moment a scenario in which NikoTech's Y2 R&A is 50% less than the actual number of $147 million, or $73.5 million. Also envision a situation where the R&A improvement is accompanied by a reduction of $210 million in inventory and receivables. Table 13.11 displays the results of improvements in both the numerator and denominator of this ratio.

By working both sides of this supply chain ratio, the total asset turnover calculation improves from 0.95 to 1.13. This positive change of 0.18 signifies a 19% improvement in the ratio; in other words, for every dollar invested in assets, NikoTech would generate $1.13 in sales. Thinking in terms of future tactics, a first-pass enhancement of supply chain execution by NikoTech should harvest similar results, with the benefits cascading through the entire organization.

Table 13.11 Y2 Total Asset Turnover Improvement

	in Millions		
	Net Sales	Total Assets	TAT
Before Improvement	$1,698	$1,776	0.95
After Improvement	$1,771.5	$1,566	1.13

RETURN ON TOTAL ASSETS

Throughout the discussion on asset management, emphasis has been on understanding the makeup of the ratios employed, their relationship to supply chain tactics and, finally, what the effect is on outcomes due to changes in the numerator and denominator. This type of approach is important in any analysis, but it is particularly applicable when dealing with the all-encompassing ratio return on total assets. Even with these points in mind, a true appreciation of the significance of this ratio in terms of execution and performance requires additional knowledge regarding its origin, original purpose and role in today's globalized supply chains. It is for this reason that the discussion now turns to the income statement and the importance of net income to any organization. From that point, return on total assets will be treated in detail in Chapter 15 when the DuPont formula is analyzed.

SUMMARY

Any questions regarding the relationship between the makeup of a company's balance sheet and the outcome of financial ratios should now be answered. Using the NikoTech case as an example, it should also be clear that there are many creative ways to bury operational shortcomings in this report. Several million dollars were found on the balance sheet in the form of bad debt, obsolete inventories and underdepreciated equipment. While mostly legal, this financial sleight of hand only postpones the day of reckoning, when write-offs must be taken. As the NikoTech income statement analysis will soon reveal, propping up short-term results at the expense of the balance sheet is really a zero sum game in which the company (and its shareholders) always comes up on the short end of the stick.

14

NIKOTECH:
THE INCOME
STATEMENT

If one were to focus exclusively on the top-line growth of NikoTech from Y1 to Y2, it would appear that things are going well. In an industry where expansion has slowed over the last few years, 23% year-to-year top-line growth ($1.500 billion to $1.845 billion) is more than an acceptable number. Less impressive, however, is the change in net income from $25.2 million in Y1 to $12.6 million in Y2. Obviously, the challenge for NikoTech's management is to continue the acceleration in sales while reversing the 50% slide in net income. The answer to that challenge is to understand the underlying forces that accelerated sales, isolate the causes of returns and allowances, identify what really constitutes cost of goods sold and, finally, realize that when left unabated, general, sales and administrative expenses can be a voracious consumer of gross profit.

Once it is determined that a product has market appeal, the key factors that drive sales at an operating level are product availability and price. Given NikoTech's build-to-order model, product availability certainly relies on accurate forecasting and collaborative planning, but even more so on the rapid sourcing of raw materials, short cycle times and 100% accurate distribution lead times. Native to the build-to-order model is a minimum of finished goods inventory; therefore, aside from low costs, the key competitive factor for NikoTech is velocity across the entire supply chain. Considering the nature of the industry, as well as the relatively small size of NikoTech, controlling costs and reducing cumulative lead times are two of the most important competitive weapons the company has.

Looking only at the sales numbers, the initial indication is that the company is offering a competitively priced product, is keeping up with customer demand and is compliant with binding lead time agreements. Suffice it to say that customers find NikoTech's products and prices appealing (maybe too appealing); otherwise, sales would not have grown by $345 million in a single year. For this reason, it is important that NikoTech focus on what it is doing well in its supply chain and identify and implement best practices across geographies. However, when one focuses on the drop in net income, it is also clear that there is a big gap between doing the right things and doing things right.

Could it be that the company is pulling out all the stops to comply with the demands of its clients without considering profitability? In a situation where six customers represent 70% of sales, that is a very real possibility.

TOP-LINE SALES VERSUS NET SALES

Although it is important to focus on what a company does well, it is equally important to continuously identify areas of potential improvement. To this end, a leading indicator of supply chain execution can be found on the returns and allowances (R&A) line of the income statement. This line item is ideal for a five why analysis and when properly conducted becomes a gold mine of information that helps to segregate many of the tactical errors that a company can commit. As first peeled back during the NikoTech days of inventory study, customer returns were inflating inventories. While sufficiently detrimental to inventory management, the double whammy of returns is that they are also subtracted from sales on the income statement. Therefore, operational waste not only manifests itself on the balance sheet and in important financial ratios but also appears every month on the income statement.

In both Y1 and Y2, R&A hurt NikoTech's top-line sales ($60 million and $147 million, respectively). Also, the growth in returns as a percentage of sales (4 and 8%, year to year) is a cause for concern and left unchecked could continue to eat away at revenues. Although most businesspeople agree that R&A grows as a function of sales, the dollars at stake dictate that additional analysis be conducted to determine if any external factors are exacerbating the issue.

Many of the root causes associated with NikoTech's returns and swollen inventories were originally uncovered using a combination of Six Sigma tools. However, this study was conducted within the context of inventory management, not the general subject of R&A. It is for this reason that the initial analysis only uncovered instances where returns led to goods being put back in inventory. Note that at no time during the days of inventory analysis was there any mention of allowances. Without any knowledge of the severity of discounted invoices, it would be prudent for management to finish the job it started with returns and focus on allowances as well.

At most companies, policies regarding invoice allowances either were prepared years ago or were never written at all. Either way, a lack of clear and well-communicated policy is eventually supplanted by one-off actions that quickly evolve into at-will unilateral discounts. Losses always seem to find their way into the dark crevices of operational ambiguity, rarely showing their head. It is these "phantom costs" that have to be taken out by the roots and replaced with clear policies and procedures.

Bearing the above in mind, perhaps the first question in the five why analysis should be: "What is the NikoTech policy on accepting allowances?" Based on the answer to that question, management can map the way forward. If there is a policy, it has to be updated with operational definition (what circumstances qualify for an allowance), disseminated to customers and enforced. In the case where there is no policy, one must be established that contains the same quantifiable operational definitions. The key to this exercise, however, is the client. The client is the one taking the allowances, and if a new policy and procedure cannot be mapped with input from the client, the entire exercise will be a waste of time. As such, another early step is to carry out a Pareto analysis that isolates which customers are taking the majority of allowances, with initial efforts focused on them.

At this juncture, it really does not matter if there is an allowances policy in place because nobody is following it anyway. In either case, the same operational definitions (missed ship dates, short shipments, wrong quantities sent, etc.) should be used to establish the defects per million opportunities and Sigma level for the process. From there, a detailed process map should be prepared for the current process and a subsequent version prepared that reflects the new operational definitions. All of this should be done in concert with the client, starting with a mutual understanding of what the operational definitions are and what act(s) qualifies for an allowance. Once designed and enforced consistently, NikoTech will see its percentage of allowances decrease considerably. Taken in conjunction with efforts to reduce returned inventories, the overall impact will be an increase in sales and better performance across the board.

The allowance discussion illustrates how seemingly isolated operational issues create a tremor that extends to the far corners of the supply chain, eventually showing up in a company's financial statements. NikoTech's ability to identify these issues is the first step in correcting its supply chain malaise, a process that requires a relentless questioning of everything the company does.

THE LOW-COST SUPPLY CHAIN

It is clear that NikoTech would not have experienced 23% sales growth in Y2 had it not been getting product out the door. While an admirable accomplishment, NikoTech must also reinforce the elements of a low-cost/high-quality profile in its business model. Beginning with cost of goods sold (COGS) and going through each line item on the income statement, the company needs to constantly seek ways to reduce costs and improve the quality of the customer experience. With many products that are now viewed as quasi-commodities, the company must combine the element of supply chain velocity with low cost structures to profitably grow the business. This point is particularly relevant in the electronics manufacturing services (EMS) industry, where contracts are awarded on the winning combination of quality, lead time reliability and a concept known as "target pricing."

Until fairly recently, most companies arrived at a product's selling price by adding the desired profit margin on top of all costs associated with the manufacture and distribution of that product. The practice of target pricing predetermines what a product can be sold for and works backward to determine if, after accounting for all costs, there is sufficient margin to justify production. In the EMS industry, it is common for potential clients to present contract manufactures with a Request for Proposal that states the price they are willing to pay for specific volumes. In this model, understanding what constitutes COGS, as well as the drivers of this complex line item, speaks to the very survival of a company like NikoTech.

In organizations that emphasize strict COGS practices, it is understood that decisions on issues like product design, bills of material, common parts, geographic sourcing strategies and materials requirements planning will have an effect on net income. For NikoTech, once the target price is agreed upon, any change in the cost structure will create a snowball effect that careens down the income statement, turning profitable contracts into a grandiose waste of time and resources.

When studying COGS figures in a global model, it is important to realize that a large percentage is composed of the landed costs for all raw materials, components and subassemblies used in manufacturing the mix of products detailed in the production plan. These figures make the roll up of the COGS number a complicated exercise, particularly when one considers the number of combinations that exist for the hundreds of suppliers that feed NikoTech's production facilities.

Because of the complexities inherent to international materials management, it is incumbent upon a global organization to make the distinction between unit and landed costs. *Unit costs* are just that — the cost per unit of the product made available to the buyer at the supplier's door. *Landed costs,* on the other hand, include not only unit costs but also all transportation- and customs-related expenses incurred in bringing the raw material to the production floor.

In the case of NikoTech, recall that the organization has 350 suppliers feeding four campuses, each of which has a different customs tariff and logistics cost structure. Driven by the quantity of parts, the countries sourced from and the cost of transporting goods into each facility, the possible number of landed cost matrices per product is difficult to envision. This is a particularly salient point in low-wage countries, where landed costs are the dominant variable in the cost equation. With this in mind, any change in a company's sourcing strategy, be it quality, capacity, price or logistics related, must be carefully considered prior to execution.

The dynamics of landed costs are a very important consideration should NikoTech management truly rationalize its supplier network. Upstream product quality, common parts and tiering all bring benefits, but the strategic decision as to which suppliers to work with should also include a landed cost component. Specifically, the supplier rationalization plan should include matrices that identify inbound transportation costs to each plant from every origin, lead time into the facilities and the customs duties levied on each component. The customs duty aspect of this analysis is perhaps the hardest to ascertain as countries have a variety of duty rates on products, depending on the country of origin. While the information is difficult to compile, NikoTech should be seeking suppliers in countries that have trade agreements with Mexico, Brazil, China and Hungary, so as to enjoy reduced or eliminated duties in every instance possible. Taken in kind with the lean supplier philosophy, good old-fashioned legwork on the cost side of the equation will augment the supplier rationalization initiative.

NIKOTECH AND COST OF GOODS SOLD

For NikoTech, COGS increased 25% from Y1 to Y2 ($990 million to $1.239 billion). When viewed as a direct function of the top-line sales figure, which increased 23% in the same period (from $1.500 billion to $1.845 billion), this may not be a change that requires a great deal of study. COGS did outpace sales growth by 2%, but with downward pressure on pricing, as well as increased costs, this may be interpreted as a trend that the entire industry is experiencing.

Of perhaps more concern is the fact that gross profit only increased $9 million, or 2%, from Y1 to Y2. Expressed in terms of gross margin and shown in Table 14.1, there was actually a decrease of 4.3% in Y2 (from 31.3% to 27%). Given this trend, the insightful analyst will be compelled to inquire as to the

Table 14.1   Y1 Versus Y2 Gross Margin

	Y1	Y2	Delta
Gross Margin	31%	27%	−4%

32%
30%
28%
26%
24%

Gross Margin

■ Y I   ■ Y2

real source of the increase in COGS. As asked throughout earlier discussions, was it simply a function of increased sales and incremental direct costs or were there other forces at play in the model?

The question for managers is not only about the rate at which COGS outpaces sales. The real goal is to determine what drives the growth in COGS and what measures can be taken to level the slope of its growth line. If NikoTech does not attack this issue, at some point in the future growth in COGS will intersect with the sales line (implying a breakeven point). Beyond that moment, losses will begin to accrue and NikoTech will be out of business in short order. Hypothesizing that all of the growth in COGS is not a function of sales leads to several reasons for the real increase. Using several Six Sigma tools, the management team was able to uncover a bevy of unnecessary costs.

For example, the NikoTech plant in China historically sourced almost all of its raw materials from three major domestic suppliers that are located within 30 miles of the NikoTech facility. In the third quarter of Y1, it was announced that two of those suppliers did not renew their contracts with NikoTech for the following year, instead dedicating their capacity to other companies in the EMS field. Management did not foresee this possibility, and NikoTech's commodity managers were forced to reach non-advantageous "hurry-up" agreements with other suppliers in Asia, Eastern Europe and Mexico.

Without considering quality issues or changes in unit costs, transportation expense went up almost 40%, with the total landed cost per component dependent on the countries from which materials were sourced. Also, customs duties had to be figured into the costed bills of material, a situation that did not exist when the China plant was sourcing domestically. This change exacted additional costs that caused the Shanghai plant to be 52% over budget.

Another scenario involved the relationship between NikoTech's materials requirements planning process and the logistics function. Except for parts that cannot be exposed to salt air or humidity, company policy is to ship all internationally sourced raw materials via ocean transportation. For purposes of materials requirements planning execution, the lead times associated with ocean transportation must be considered as part of the lead time offsetting component of the overall process. Because lead time offsetting plots the issuance of raw materials purchase orders against the time needed to deliver goods to the floor, coordination between materials planning and logistics is critical to the successful operation of any plant.

NikoTech was aware of this, but because of sales growth that eclipsed the forecast, the company found itself constantly upgrading ocean shipments to airfreight. This maneuver increased per-unit transportation cost by an average of 40% across the board. Also, because buyers had no confidence in lead times, they were also upgrading shipments to airfreight just to make sure they would have raw materials on the floor. Thus, the uncertainty associated with both forecasts and lead times not only inflated inventories but compelled buyers to bring in goods they did not even need by airfreight. Net sales may have been up but, as illustrated in Figure 14.1, at a cost that caused the slope of the COGS line to be steeper than that of the sales line.

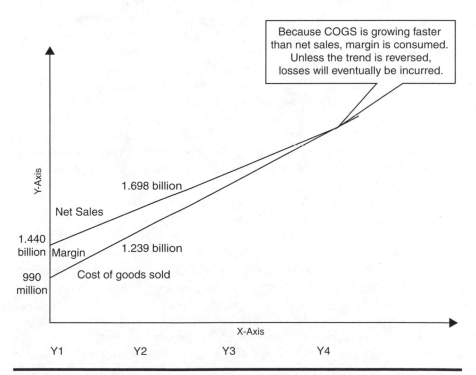

Figure 14.1 NikoTech Sales Versus Cost of Goods Sold Growth

The final example of the challenges that NikoTech faced related to COGS is probably the most disconcerting. Because the problem began upstream in the sales department, it went undetected until the Six Sigma team dug it up during a deployment process mapping exercise. It is precisely these types of phantom costs that chip away at profitability and, most dangerously, without anybody ever being aware of it.

A contract was awarded to the Hungary plant in late Y1 for the production and final distribution of routers to NikoTech's number one customer in Europe and Scandinavia. This was a new program that required drop shipments to end users, with an average gross margin of 30% over the life of the three-year contract. The plant's jubilation was short-lived, however, when it was disclosed that the gross margin was only 22%. Unable to discover why the margin was lower than budgeted, plant management accepted the "extra cost of working internationally" and went about its business. The Six Sigma team saw things a bit differently.

After considerable digging, the cause of the missing margin was traced back to the early sales negotiations that stipulated the Incoterm applicable to the contract. Because Incoterms determine at what point responsibility for logistics and related costs transfer from seller to buyer, inclusion of these costs in a target pricing exercise is fundamental to working up a profitable contract.

Because NikoTech Europe's policy had always been to sell on an ex works basis (with all logistics costs for the account of the buyer), the stipulation in the new contract for a delivered duty paid Incoterm went unnoticed. What nobody questioned was the fact that the delivered duty paid Incoterm stipulates a selling price that includes not only the price of the merchandise but also all transportation- and customs-related costs to the named place(s) listed in the contract. If a company agrees to incur those costs and does not recover them in its invoice price, those unprotected costs remain in COGS without the benefit of being offset by the total sales price. This is precisely what happened to NikoTech at the Hungary plant.

For the better part of Y2, NikoTech delivered finished goods throughout Europe and Scandinavia on a direct-to-user basis without recouping transportation- and customs-related expenses. The company was lucky in the sense that duties from Hungary into Europe and Scandinavia are either reduced or non-existent, so it didn't have to take too big a hit on customs duties. Nevertheless, it was forced to assume all airfreight, trucking and customs clearance charges associated with getting the goods to the final users.

Once uncovered, the pricing had to be renegotiated with the client without the benefit of recovering the months of losses. Senior management was able to get an increase in price, but at a huge cost to the company from both a financial and customer goodwill perspective.

Similar to the examples discussed for R&A, the above cases clearly illustrate the direct functional relationship between COGS figures and lead time management, landed costs analysis and inventory availability. Unfortunately, whether a company is dealing with the revenue or cost side of the supply chain equation, there are many other examples that could be cited. Experience, forward thinking and contingency planning can minimize the probability of problems arising, but the key to supply chain management is the constant quest to uncover even the smallest issue *before* it has an impact on financial performance. To quote Machiavelli's *The Prince*:

> When trouble is sensed well in advance it can easily be remedied; if you wait for it to show itself any medicine will be too late because the disease will have become incurable.[1]

Let's hope it's not to late for the good people at NikoTech.

GENERAL, SALES AND ADMINISTRATIVE EXPENSE: "THE WASTE LINE"

At the beginning of Chapter 11, it was recommended that businesspeople engaged in the analysis of financial statements begin their studies with the balance sheet. It is all too easy to tuck problems away in the balance sheet, and analysts will never know what the income statement should really look like until they clean house.

The above is certainly true, but managers also need to be aware of what is going on with every line item on the income statement. Because each item represents a cost that detracts from net income, an intimate understanding of the activities that drive costs is fundamental to business management. In the long term, managers must create a balance between the short-term realities of how businesses are measured and the long-term strategic well-being of the organization. While NikoTech has temporarily abandoned management of the balance sheet, it has made some progress in keeping costs below the COGS line in order. If management can find the above-mentioned middle ground between the balance sheet and income statement, the company and its shareholders will be much better off.

If sales is considered the top line and net income the bottom line, then it would be appropriate to say that general, sales and administrative (GS&A) expenses form the "waste line." While there are many legitimate expenses found in GS&A expenses, when viewed with an eye toward the often reactionary nature of tactical supply chain management, this characterization is accurate.

It is the journey from gross profit to operating income that writes the final chapter on supply chain performance, and a nonchalant approach to GS&A expenses can turn strong gross margins into non-existent earnings from operations. In this sense, it is once again the responsibility of management to identify the second-order links between unnecessary GS&A expenses that are a product of poor supply chain execution.

A simple but effective method of monitoring GS&A expenses begins with a vertical analysis of each line item in the section. Each line item is taken as a percentage of the total GS&A figure in order to determine which items represent the highest percentage. More often than not, a vertical analysis will reveal that payroll, rent, communications, systems and travel expense are the biggest consumers of gross profit. Focusing on these items, a plant-level root cause analysis of the drivers of increases or decreases can be conducted, with corrective action taken on the former and best practices implemented from the latter.

Even though the NikoTech income statement is consolidated, extra inquiry and analysis can separate each line item and its corresponding contribution to GS&A expense. Actually, NikoTech was able to stabilize its waste line in Y2, only increasing expenses from the previous year by $18 million (5%). In addition to budgeting for these types of expenses, any extra effort to defray the pain suffered at the COGS line will be very well received. Control of GS&A expenses is important at all times, but especially so when COGS is trending upward. Some of the improvements implemented by NikoTech that slowed growth of GS&A expenses are discussed in the following sections.

Outsourcing

In one instance, NikoTech was able to outsource labor that had previously been on the company payroll. Each factory maintains a facility adjacent to the plant from which all shipping, receiving and warehousing activities are conducted. While the company still owns the asset (land and building), management outsourced all labor in the facility to a third-party logistics company. This created a variable cost environment based on throughput, which allowed NikoTech to manage costs as a function of activity. Although the company still had to pay for services rendered, worldwide savings of $2 million per year was attributed to this decision.

Systems

NikoTech had been using the same enterprise management system since its founding. Developed prior to the digital era, the system was not robust enough for use in a global environment and was especially difficult to integrate with the systems of suppliers, customers and strategic partners. A project was undertaken whereby NikoTech decided to employ the services of a Web-based applications service provider to run all of its enterprise-critical applications. The program was finally implemented in late Y1, and productivity gains and savings began to surface immediately, with an estimated savings of $3 million per year. In addition to the savings, the use of an applications service provider precluded the need for excessive expenditures on hardware, which gives the company the benefit of not having to carry more assets on its books or deal with their depreciation.

Telecommunications

Because NikoTech's application software was now Web based, the need for expensive electronic data interchange connections became less of an issue. In early Y2, the company was able to move to Web-based collaborative planning with two key customers, eliminating $1.2 million a year in costs related to electronic data interchange and value-added networks. This cost savings has also had an impact on the quality of demand information coming from the two clients participating in collaborative planning. As more customers come on line and suppliers are brought into the network, it is anticipated that forecasting will improve. The downstream benefit will be the leveling of raw materials purchases with demand and better capacity management in the plants.

Another key area of savings came from the global use of e-mail and local dial-up capabilities. As NikoTech's people traveled to meet with the plants, customers and suppliers, the need for timely access to e-mail grew. In the case of the plants, a wide area network was installed, which allowed all traveling employees speedy and inexpensive access to e-mail via their laptops. Although this savings was important, a big payback came from the solution applied to e-mail access for non-NikoTech sites.

Historically, when NikoTech employees were off-site, they had to dial into remote servers to download their e-mail. The equivalent of a long-distance call, late-night downloads from hotels were costing the company a fortune. Based on the suggestion of a new employee, NikoTech contracted the software services of a global telecommunications outfit to allow access to e-mail servers in almost every major city around the world. Now a local call, the cost of e-mail downloads was reduced considerably. Although difficult to quantify, considering the number of people traveling at any one time and the cost/time associated with at least one download per day by an employee, it was estimated that savings were in the neighborhood of $400,000 per year.

Because the lean philosophy recognizes that the best ideas come from people closest to the work, NikoTech management should build upon this one-off success. Perhaps a formal program for process improvements can be initiated to recognize people for the continuous improvement ideas they implement. The e-mail savings is an excellent example of how ideas come off the front line and should be well publicized throughout the company.

Travel and Entertainment

Although travel and entertainment (T&E) may seem to have the most remote relationship with supply chain execution, the fact is that T&E has everything to do with supply chain management. In a global arena, the natural reaction to a problem or opportunity is to throw bodies at the situation. Best articulated by Frederick P. Brooks, Jr. in *The Mythical Man-Month*,[2] the addition of personnel to a project without prior planning is pure folly and something that NikoTech engaged in with amazing consistency.

Related to many of the supply chain issues alluded to earlier, NikoTech management was dispatching teams of troubleshooters to every corner of the planet to deal with both internal and external problems. This unbridled commitment to supply chain excellence triggered a vertical analysis midway through Y1 that identified T&E as consuming 23% of the total GS&A spend. It was quickly decided that the bleeding had to stop, with immediate measures to be taken.

The first step in reversing this problem involved a change in corporate culture. Whereas in the past any new business opportunity or operating problem precipitated unquestioned travel, NikoTech implemented a travel authorization policy that forced employees to seek travel approval with a written justification for the travel, as well as an estimated cost.

Second, NikoTech invested several hundred thousand dollars in video-conferencing equipment between corporate, the plants, key suppliers and customers. The ability to videoconference, with full graphics capabilities on a second screen, eliminated the need for many trips, which decreased travel time for NikoTech's people, increased their productivity and drove down T&E. The combination of the travel authorization policy and the use of videoconference equipment reduced travel in Y2 by $1.5 million.

In the grand scheme of multi-billion-dollar business operations, the above examples may not appear to represent significant savings or even be related to supply chain execution. As already noted, however, all line items on the income statement are the product of a cause-and-effect relationship, most of which can be associated with supply chain execution. In the case of GS&A expenses, it may not be a first-order cause and effect, but the links can be traced back to either some best practice or malfunction in the model. In a global operation, it is the base hits that win ball games, and the constant pursuit of incremental improvements is what will create savings at the GS&A level of the income statement.

SUMMARY

Whether analyzing the drivers of sales, COGS or GS&A expense, the relationship between income statement performance and the tactical components of lead time, landed costs and inventory availability should now be abundantly clear. The key for today's global manager is to be aware that these links exist, understand their impact at multiple levels of the income statement and, most importantly, be in a position to act on what is uncovered. In conjunction with conscientious, long-term management of the balance sheet, daily attention to the income statement will enhance productivity and, ultimately, profitability. Without this broad-based, financially oriented mentality, organizations will be left to rely on hearsay, guesswork and flawed judgment to run their businesses.

NOTES

1. Niccolo Machiavelli, *The Prince,* Penguin Books, 1961, p. 10.
2. For an excellent explanation of the organizational and communications-related challenges inherent to any organization, see Frederick P. Brooks, Jr., *The Mythical Man-Month,* Addison-Wesley Longman, 1995.

15

GENERAL MOTORS, THE DUPONT FORMULA AND RETURN ON INVESTMENT

Although it may come as little consolation, the issue of balancing asset utilization with profitability has befuddled businesspeople since the beginning of commercial time. Always understood from an anecdotal perspective, the ability to quantitatively address the productivity versus profitability quandary was first presented at the turn of the 20th century by the DuPont Corporation.

In an industry characterized by vertical integration and heavy investment in both physical plant and inventories, the financial geniuses at DuPont developed a formula that allowed for the measurement of productivity and utilization in the same equation. First known as the DuPont formula, and subsequently referred to as return on investment, this calculation was perhaps the first and most significant step in focusing on supply chain execution.

Whereas the DuPont formula was first introduced at the company that bears its name, it did not come into vogue until it resurfaced at the General Motors Corporation in early 1917. With the possible exception of gun manufacturers (like Remington and Smith & Wesson), General Motors and Ford were the forerunners to the "multi-national" enterprise with which we are so familiar today. With manufacturing and sales operations in several countries, the General Motors management team had to deal with the same large-scale issues as contemporary supply chain managers: forecasting, pipeline visibility and inventory management.

The evolution of General Motors as well as the purpose of the DuPont formula are best described in the book *My Years with General Motors* by Alfred P. Sloan, Jr. Published in 1963, the book chronicles the period from 1918 to 1946, during which Mr. Sloan joined GM and eventually became president and CEO of the corporation. Described by Bill Gates as "the best book to read if you only want to read one book on business," *My Years with General Motors* planted the seed for the evolution of business management as both discipline and profession.

Even though the book touches on important topics like competitive analysis, customer financing and risk management, for purposes of the discussion at hand GM's greatest contribution comes in the form of recognizing the importance of synchronizing profitability with asset utilization. In that vein, and perhaps unbeknownst to the author, *My Years with General Motors* remains the best book ever written on the relationship between supply chain execution and financial management.

Operating at a time when access to real-time information was non-existent, the GM team got to the core of the issues it faced with objectivity and resolve, setting the foundation of business principles that are still in use today. Obsessed with the importance of balancing inventory levels with forecast and actual sales, the book is rife with allusions to inventory management. Not unlike most innovations in business, introduction of the DuPont formula at GM was in response to a crisis.

Based on forecasts carried out in 1919, GM had set production schedules 36% higher than the preceding budget period. In anticipation of this growth, GM's finance team set about arranging the sale of $64 million in stock to finance the purchase of raw materials and additional plant capacity. As 1920 unfolded, the minutes of a meeting held in May clearly displayed management's concern with continued expenditures in plant and equipment and inventories rising above a $150 million ceiling that had been set earlier in the year.[1] For reasons unknown to GM management, the situation got worse, with expenditures continuing down the wrong path. The situation had become what Mr. Sloan referred to as "decentralization with a vengeance."

These events depict one of the world's first multi-national corporations as deeply concerned with the relationship between assets and profitability. Equally profound, however, are the overtures in the book regarding the poor reliability of forecasts and how increasing inventories can force a company's financial hand, sending it to the market for additional funds. All these points should sound familiar to today's businessperson, although there is little comfort in knowing that not much has changed in human nature or business over the last 80 years. In fact, if someone were asked to read certain chapters from the book without knowing its name, author or historical context, he or she would be easily convinced that they were fresh off the business press and not from a book about business in the 1920s.

As it turns out, GM's forecast for 1920 was way off and did not anticipate a precipitous drop in purchases that year. Consequently, inventories increased from $137 million in January to $209 million in October. The ripple effect alluded to throughout the NikoTech analysis is by no means a new phenomenon, and GM quickly learned how inventory management affects all areas of a business. With so much money tied up in inventories, by October of 1920 GM managers were hard-pressed to pay suppliers and even their own payroll. In response to this crisis, the record shows that GM was compelled to borrow $83 million in short-term notes to meet its obligations.[2] By that point, not only did the income statement suffer from a lack of sales but the problem had found its way into the balance sheet in both inventories and notes payable.

The combination of profit pressures and a hurting balance sheet left Mr. Sloan and his team with few options. Because the GM team had almost zero visibility into existing and pipeline inventories, the only real option was to stop the presses completely. Under executive order from Mr. Sloan's office, all purchase orders were canceled until such time as exact inventory levels could be determined. While negotiations with suppliers were tough, most understood the severity of the situation and, in the best interest of the supply chain, went along. From there, GM conducted in depth analysis to determine what it had in stock, ascertain what purchase orders had been released with their corresponding receipt dates and compare both with the requirements of a considerably reduced production schedule. Once the floodgates were turned back, execution of the inventory reduction plan continued with a four-month rolling forecast.

.By working much closer with the dealers to estimate demand, GM production planners were able to level the inflow of materials and production and thus begin to drive down historical inventory levels. Although a painful process, the GM team was eventually able to reduce inventories from a September 1920 high of $215 million to $94 million in June 1922. By that time, GM also noted that its inventory turnover ratio had improved to four times per year.[3]

In addition to the drastic measures taken by GM at an operating level, of equal interest were the allusions made to why such measures were taken in the first place. Very similar to what modern-day corporations experience, inflated inventories squeezed cash flow, a situation that prevented divisions from making payroll and accounts payable. Also, GM not only issued stock to finance the purchase of plant and inventories, it then had to take on short-term notes to meet the aforementioned obligations. Taking into consideration the GM inventory overflow and a depressed market because Ford had slashed prices by 30%, it's no wonder that the GM management team placed so much importance on the reconciliation of profit with asset utilization.

Fueled by the economic circumstances in which it found itself, the GM management team decided to implement the DuPont formula across all divisions. The pivotal idea management had to sell to the divisions was that the formula was perfectly suited to measure the organization's goal of balancing net income with asset utilization. The isolation of these variables is achieved by multiplying the quotient of the return on sales ratio with that of the total asset turnover ratio. For purposes of this discussion, note that total asset turnover already has been discussed as a discrete measure and is now being incorporated into the DuPont calculation. First mentioned during the Introduction to this book and detailed in Figure 15.1, the DuPont formula is

$$\text{Net income/Sales} \times \text{Sales/Total assets}$$

The DuPont formula was brought to GM by Donaldson Brown, a former executive of the DuPont Corporation who later became chief financial officer at GM (at that time, DuPont had a large interest in GM stock; hence the relationship). Also known as return on investment (ROI), the formula was found to have immediate strategic and tactical applications in creating the balance between profitability and asset management. Relative to ROI, asset management and the causal relationships inherent to business operations, Mr. Sloan said:

> Rate of Return, of course, is affected by all the factors in the business; hence if one can see how these factors individually bear upon a rate of return, one has a penetrating look into the business.[4]

This excerpt makes it very clear that executives have been aware of the need to align balance sheet and income statement performance for close to a century. Simple math, on the other hand, does the best job of making this point. The most obvious observation one can make about the DuPont formula is that the denominator in the net margin equation and numerator in the asset turnover equation are the same, net sales. Basic algebra dictates that this variable cancels itself out, leaving a new equation that reads:

$$\text{Net income/Total assets}$$

The obvious temptation for any manager or financial analyst is to skip the net margin and asset turnover calculation and move directly to calculation of

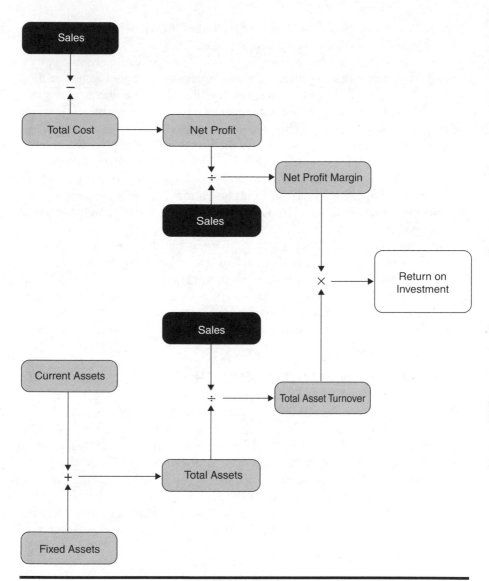

Figure 15.1 Return on Investment Calculation

the ROI figure. However, in the spirit of being thorough, the analyst must realize that he or she should never skip a step in the measurement process because it may eventually leave causes of waste in the supply chain unidentified. Instead, the thorough manager will break down the components of each equation, endeavoring to trace financial results back to operating tactics. This exercise is precisely what Mr. Sloan was alluding to when he stated, "Essentially, it was a matter of making things visible."

If *My Years with General Motors* is the only book to read on business, then the only chapters to read on financial management and supply chain execution are from the excerpts alluded to here. Considering that these events took place in the 1920s in an industry that altered our world forever, the insights of industry's first supply chain pioneers are amazing. In straightforward prose, Mr. Sloan and his team were able to identify the root causes of problems and work systematically to eliminate them. They also understood the financial links that existed between operational challenges and poor financial performance. It was their interpretation of this financial information that led them to confront most of their operational issues and turn GM into the largest corporation in the world at that time.

Of equal relevance in today's global environment, the "aggregating and de-aggregating of figures" speaks precisely to tracing the impact of lead times, landed costs and inventory levels to the individual and overall effect on financial reports. Perhaps in this context a look into the issues of the past is a consolation and, better yet, a guide to today's supply chain executive. One would venture to guess that certainly would be so in the case of NikoTech.

RETURN ON INVESTMENT: NIKOTECH

After a study of the relationship between supply chain tactics, the income statement and the balance sheet, management must come full circle and complete the ROI calculation for NikoTech. Remembering that the DuPont formula is "a function of the profit margin and the rate of turnover of invested capital," the performance of margin versus turnover is immediately set apart. Consider the Y1 and Y2 results detailed in Table 15.1.

Given the amount of discussion dedicated to financial analysis in general, as well as its specific application to NikoTech's business model, management

Table 15.1 Y1 and Y2 Return on Investment

Y1	Y2
$25.2 million/$1.440 billion	$12.6 million/$1.698 billion
× $1.440 billion/$1.599 billion	× $1.698 billion/$1.776 billion
= 0.0175 × 0.9	= 0.0074 × 0.95
= 1.6%	= 0.7%

ROI = net income/sales x sales/total assets. ROI = net income/total assets.

is well prepared to make a critical evaluation of the makeup of ROI. Additionally, Mr. Sloan reminds the analyst to "note only that you can get an increase in ROI by increasing the rate of turnover of capital in relation to sales as well as by increasing profit margins." This point speaks to one of the central themes of ratio analysis throughout the NikoTech discussion, namely that in order for the quotient to grow, the numerator must be increased or the denominator decreased.

The above points hold currency for both margin and turnover. For example, in the case of ROI, the methods of improving net profit margin are to increase net profit or, technically, to decrease sales. Because public companies are measured as much by top-line growth as net income, the option to achieve the same or greater earnings with less sales is really not an option at all. Therefore, the key is to continue to have sales grow, but to have net income grow at a greater pace in order for the quotient to improve. The turnover calculation, on the other hand, is more consistent with ratio improvement theory in that an increase in sales (numerator) and/or decrease in total assets (denominator) would have the desired effect. A combination of both events would have the greatest impact on this calculation.

Beginning with Y1, the net income figure of $25.2 million divided by total assets of $1.599 billion yields a net margin of 1.75%. Even in the electronics manufacturing services industry, where net income can be slim, NikoTech is still below industry standards. When this number is multiplied by the Y1 total asset turnover figure of 0.9, ROI is registered as 1.6%. Now in the ROI calculation, one can clearly see how underutilized assets have a negative effect on all facets of the business. Conversely, Y2 net margin came in low at 0.74%, with a slight improvement in total asset turnover of 0.95. When the two figures are joined to produce the ROI number, the result is 0.7%.

With the drop in net income weighing heavily on the quotient, the ROI for Y2 dropped almost in half from Y1 to 0.7%. The deaggregation of the components of ROI illuminates the situation in a manner consistent with all prior calculations. Specifically, earnings are way off as a function of sales growth and assets have increased at a pace much greater than the growth in net sales. In this sense, ROI writes the last chapter on the malaise that has plagued NikoTech throughout the entire exercise. Just as the results have been consistent from income statement to balance sheet, so are the remedies discussed thus far in the analysis.

In an effort to show one final illustration of the relationship between supply chain execution and financial outcomes, attention is again directed to the hypothetical Y2 improvements in the area of returns and allowances (R&A). In the earlier discussion of R&A and its relation to total asset turnover, it was proven that an increase in the Y2 sales figure of 50% (coming from R&A)

Table 15.2   Y2 Return on Investment Improvement

	in Millions		
	Net Income	Net Sales	Total Assets
Before Improvement	$12.6	$1,698	$1,776
After Improvement	$13.114	$1,771.5	$1,566
ROI Before Improvement	0.7%		
ROI After Improvement	0.84%		

improved total asset turnover from 0.95 to 1.13. Assuming that the net margin in Y2 remained constant at 0.74%, the R&A improvement could also enhance net income performance of NikoTech.

The proposed changes for NikoTech involved an improvement in R&A of 50% (increasing sales by $73.5 million, or up to $1.7715 billion). If the same net margin of 0.7% was assumed for this calculation, net income would improve by $514,500, to $13.114 million. As a complement to the earnings figure, it was also stated that inventories and receivables had been decreased by $210 million, from $660 million to $450 million (bringing total assets in Y2 to $1.566 billion). The change in ROI is summarized in Table 15.2.

This calculation enforces several points. In relation to net margin, the amount of increase in earnings ($514,500) was not enough to keep pace with the increase in net sales in the denominator. For this reason, net margin remained the same. This makes perfect sense, because the same net margin figure (0.74%) was used to calculate the bottom line impact of the increase in net sales of $73.5 million. The reality is that net margin probably would have been higher based on savings associated with reducing R&A (return freight charges, warehouse handling, administrative expense, etc.).

Moving to potential improvements in asset turnover, the impact is more noticeable. By increasing the numerator of net sales and decreasing the denominator of total assets, there is a double positive for NikoTech. First, the improvement in net sales to $1.7715 billion helps the calculation, signifying that more was done with the same or fewer assets. Since inventory and accounts receivable improved by $210 million, total assets came down to $1.566 billion, a tangible improvement. Compared with the real total asset turnover in Y2 of 0.95, the hypothetical improvements enhanced the number to 1.13. This was already illustrated in the total asset turnover calculation, but when multiplied by the net margin number, the ROI figure is improved from 0.7% to 0.83%.

In real terms, one might view the above improvements as not a lot to talk about. However, it is important to point out that all of the actual and suggested financial improvements effected by NikoTech were based on *fixing what was wrong* with the model. Little mention has been made of implementing the best practices at NikoTech that would complement its continuous improvement initiatives. From this vantage point, if NikoTech can continue to do what is right while taking measures to eliminate waste, the overall result will most surely be felt.

Even amongst such luminary measures as return on equity and economic value added, the DuPont formula remains as relevant today as it was in 1920. The reason why ROI has transcended time is because of its ability to dissect financial issues, directing executives to the underlying supply chain activities and processes that created those same results. Or, as Martin S. Fridson so accurately stated in his book *Financial Statement Analysis: A Practitioner's Guide*:

> Like most ratio analysis, the DuPont Formula is valuable not only for the questions it answers but also for the new ones it raises.[5]

For these reasons and many more, the DuPont formula will continue to play a major part in the evaluation of global supply chains.

NOTES

1. Alfred P. Sloan, Jr., *My Years with General Motors,* Doubleday, 1963, p. 30.
2. Ibid., p. 31.
3. Ibid., p. 125.
4. Ibid., p. 141.
5. Martin S. Fridson, *Financial Statement Analysis: A Practitioner's Guide,* John Wiley & Sons, 1995, p. 215.

16

THE CASH FLOW STATEMENT

If one were asked to identify two of the watershed developments in accounting and finance in the 20th century, a strong argument could be made for both the DuPont formula and the introduction of the cash flow statement (CFS) to mandatory Securities and Exchange Commission reporting requirements. Touched upon throughout the first half of this book, the CFS is the ideal counterbalance to the income statement and balance sheet in that it chronicles the *sources* and *uses* of cash throughout the period under consideration.

Of additional benefit is the structure of the CFS itself, with sections on operating, investing and financing activities. This nomenclature, when analyzed by section and as a whole, provides a unique window into the strategic and operational employment of cash. Given the analysis of the CFS in earlier chapters, the reader should now be prepared to examine NikoTech's cash flow performance in Y2 with great dexterity.

NIKOTECH AND THE CASH FLOW STATEMENT

The value of the CFS lies in an understanding of how data are organized and what the original source of information was. First, all of the information on the CFS comes from either the income statement or the balance sheet, the causal nature of which is now well understood by the supply chain analyst. Second, in the case of current assets and current liabilities, the CFS focuses on changes in their respective line items compared with figures from the previous year. For that reason, increases in current assets are considered a use of

233

cash, whereas increases in accounts payable are considered a source of cash. As we shall soon see with NikoTech, those short-term changes, along with net income and depreciation, have a considerable impact on the overall cash position of a company.

CASH FLOW FROM OPERATING ACTIVITIES

Net income, the first item in the operating activities section shown in Table 16.1, summarizes all of NikoTech's revenue- and cost-related initiatives for Y2. At $12.6 million, Y2 performance came in well below expectations and 50% below the previous year's number. Recognizing net income as the only consistent source of cash for a company and that current asset performance was dysfunctional, NikoTech will be challenged to make up for its slow start.

One boost that this section will feel is the "add back" from depreciation. Because depreciation does not represent an additional out-of-pocket expense in the period considered, but rather the matching of costs with revenue in the proper periods, depreciation is always added back as a source of cash in the CFS. With $36 million in depreciation, every little bit helps.

Unfortunately, the remainder of the operating section did not do a lot to enhance NikoTech's cash position. Looking first at accounts receivable, this line item grew from Y1 to Y2 by $165 million (from $285 million to $450 million), a use of cash. Moving on to inventories, the increase was even greater, appearing as a $180 million use of cash (from $480 million to $660 million). Even without considering the consumption of funds related to investing and financing activities, NikoTech already shows a negative cash flow of $296.4 million.

At this juncture, the only hope for the operating section is a compensatory increase from accounts payable and other payables. Although the two items

Table 16.1 NikoTech Cash Flow Statement Operating Activities

	in Millions
Operating Activities	
Net Income	$12.6
Depreciation	$36
Increase in Accounts Receivable	($165)
Increase in Accounts Payable	$75
Increase in Other Payables	$29.4
Increase in Inventories	($180)
Cash from Operating Activities	($192)

combined did show a source of cash of $104.4 million ($75 million plus $29.4 million), it was not nearly enough to net out the impact of accounts receivable and inventories. After accounting for changes in each item, cash flow from operating activities registered a net use of cash of $192 million.

The analyst's wholesale acceptance of this number would leave some potentially instructive insights unchallenged. For example, a large increase in NikoTech's sales may precipitate a commensurate upward tick in both receivables and inventories. As such, in a growth mode, how can a negative number possibly be avoided in the operating section?

Although there may be some truth to this hypothesis, the point can be countered with at least three arguments. First, this rationale assumes that accounts receivable and inventories were at reasonable levels in periods prior to Y2, an enviable scenario that was not the case at NikoTech. The current asset issue did not just surface out of the blue in Y2; it had been building momentum for quite some time. Second, if indeed sales were growing, it would be sound to assume that net income would grow as well, thus augmenting the cash flow figure. As observed, net income dropped by 50% from Y1 to Y2, a trend that does not bode well for the CFS in the future.

Finally, and this point has already been made, if sales are growing, raw materials purchases must be growing too. Logically, this dynamic would precipitate an increase in payables and serve as a source of cash on the CFS. In the NikoTech analysis, total current liabilities did increase by $104.4 million, but the question remains as to whether that number could have been higher. This scenario was analyzed in considerable detail during the discussion on supply chain velocity and asset utilization, with the determination that the entire supplier management program needed revamping.

For purposes of the CFS, if NikoTech rationalized the spread of its payables (i.e., pay old debts), the short-term effects would appear to be harmful, but in future periods the organization would be in a better position to negotiate more reasonable terms and allow for an increase in payables that is more consistent with recent purchase levels. The only difference would be that the growth would be found in the 0- to 60-days sections and not over 60 days. This growth in accounts payable as a function of sales would increase accounts payable in a manner greater than what was observed in Y2, creating a source of cash more consistent with the reality of the operating environment.

If an analyst only studies the period under consideration, results from the section on cash flow from operating activities may distort the future prospects of an organization. With this short-term view in mind, the combination of net income, depreciation and changes in working capital completes the marriage between the income statement and balance sheet. As was the case in NikoTech's balance sheet and fixed assets analysis, however, a longer view of the future of a company must be taken via study of the investing and financing section of the CFS.

CASH FLOW FROM INVESTING ACTIVITIES

As one gets further removed from the operating activities of a company, it may seem that the links between financial considerations and supply chain execution diminish proportionately. Actually, because of the relationship between exccution and outcome, as well as the fact that future investments are partially driven by bottom line results, the need to tie performance to strategic decisions is indeed important. The cash flow from investing activities section of the CFS opens a window into this long-term component of supply chain management while also considering the short-term impact on cash of longer term investments. It is the combination of performance from the operating section with strategic moves in the investing section that creates the proper perspective for businesspeople and allows them to take a view beyond the next quarter.

Analysis of the cash flow from investing activities section should be made within the context of the evolution of the company under analysis. NikoTech has been in business for close to two decades, but, more relevant for the analyst's purposes, the company has undergone a fairly strong growth trend in the last couple of years. For this reason, investments or divestitures by the company should be studied with an eye toward future trends in contract manufacturing, general growth of the industry and, most importantly, growth prospects for NikoTech itself.

Even with the downward spiral in high-tech and telecommunications volumes, all indications are that the traditional original equipment manufacturers and new market entrants will continue to outsource engineering, prototyping and manufacturing services for the foreseeable future. Within that macro-growth trend it appears that NikoTech will continue to enjoy similar if not greater growth to the extent that it can meet the needs of its clients. Although obvious to insiders that management has to get its house in order, from an external perspective NikoTech's prospects for the future are still positive. It is within

Table 16.2 NikoTech Cash Flow Statement Investing Activities

	in Millions
Investing Activities	
Purchase of Fixed Assets	($60)
Sale of Marketable Securities	$15
Cash from Investing Activities	($45)

this context, and against the backdrop of short-term financial realities, that NikoTech's strategic decisions must be made. A summary of NikoTech's investing activities in Y2 is provided in Table 16.2.

As first observed during the balance sheet analysis of fixed assets, there was not an overabundance of activities in this area in Y2. The decision of management to limit investments in plant and equipment has both short- and long-term consequences for the company, but for purposes of the Y2 CFS, it represents a use of cash of $60 million. It is interesting to note the relationship between this expenditure and what actually appears on the balance sheet in plant and equipment. The actual value in plant and equipment only increased by $24 million, from $540 million to $564 million, a figure that may be a source of confusion when compared with the investment of $60 million noted on the CFS.

The net increase on the balance sheet was only $24 million due to the $36 million in depreciation that was deducted from asset values and shown as an expense on the income statement in Y2. This point completes the loop in the depreciation discussion, as its $36 million value was added back as a source of cash in the operating section of the CFS. To repeat, depreciation is a source of cash, and although netted out of asset values, it is always added back as a source of cash in the period it was expensed.

It could be argued that with the sales growth that NikoTech has experienced, a $60 million investment in plant and equipment does not pave the road for future development. In an organization that was operationally well disciplined, this statement would certainly have merit. However, in the case of NikoTech, a company that is off course in the fundamental management of almost all of its operations, perhaps it would be a better idea to get a handle on what it has before setting out on further expansionary expeditions. Starting with its forecasts, which must be conducted in a much more collaborative manner, management must reconcile production planning with capacity planning and ultimately materials requirements planning with the raw materials in-house today.

On the customer side of the equation, management needs to develop client-specific profit-and-loss statements that allow the program managers to operate individual contracts as if they were discrete businesses, which is, after all, what they are. Translated into layman's terms, NikoTech has to focus on making the business it has in-house profitable before it can seriously think about the prospects of future expansion. Growth for the sake of growth can be a dangerous proposition, a situation clearly manifested in the NikoTech analysis.

Given the relentless siren of Wall Street and its demand for compound sales growth, this may be a difficult pill for NikoTech to swallow. The question then becomes whether or not the company was better off in Y1 with net income of $25.2 million on $1.440 billion in sales than it was in Y2 when it achieved sales of $1.698 billion but earnings of only $12.6 million. Given the rudderless ship that was NikoTech in Y2, perhaps the $60 million investment could have been postponed or reduced while management regained control of the operation. Although hindsight is always 20/20, this decision would have helped the CFS in the short term.

To close out the discussion on the investing section of the CFS, note the $15 million in sales of marketable securities. Defined as ownership of stock in other companies, this sale could have been precipitated for a variety of reasons. Because cash on the balance sheet was depleted in Y2, this sale may have been intended to back up future cash outlays. It also could have been that it was simply the right time to unload those stocks. In order to get to the bottom of this particular case, one would have to dig deeper than the information provided on the balance sheet allows. Regardless of the inspiration for the sale, the period-specific impact was to provide NikoTech with a $15 million source of cash, a small offset to the expenditures thus far itemized.

CASH FLOW FROM FINANCING ACTIVITIES

Of the three sections of the CFS, financing activities certainly seems the least related to tactical supply chain execution. To refute this line of thought, however, one can revisit the situation at General Motors in 1920. In order to ramp up for anticipated production, the finance people at GM made an additional stock offering to support the purchase of raw materials. This is not an unusual practice, but when the auto market went south and GM had no revenues, management then had to go to the banks for short-term notes to pay suppliers. Although a difficult situation for any company to find itself in, the scenario has repeated itself dozens if not hundreds of times since the early days of industrialization. Unfortunately, knowledge of the past does not necessarily guarantee that it will not be repeated, and NikoTech falls into the same quagmire in Y2. The company's financing activities are summarized in Table 16.3.

With both earnings and the NikoTech stock price down in Y2, its sources of financing were somewhat limited. Also, the decision to invest $60 million in plant and equipment put pressure on the company's delicate position, com-

Table 16.3   NikoTech Cash Flow Statement Financing Activities

	in Millions
Financing Activities	
Issuance of Long-Term Notes	$60
Cash from Financing Activities	$60

pelling it to issue an equivalent amount in long-term notes. Although shown as a source of cash on the Y2 CFS, the problem with any debt is that it has to be paid back, installments of which (principal and interest) inconveniently find their way to the income statement.

When debt is acquired in less than ideal circumstances, the conditions under which the notes are secured will also be less than optimal. In this case, NikoTech had to offer the notes at a percentage higher than it would have had its net income been healthier.

The three sections analyzed in the CFS combine to form what is known as *free cash flow*. Defined as the amount of cash available to a company after all operational and strategic sources/uses of cash have been accounted for, free cash flow is the oxygen that keeps an organization breathing. As noted on the CFS, NikoTech experienced a net decrease in cash of $177 million, dragging down its cash on the balance sheet from $264 million in Y1 to $87 million in Y2. This event speaks once again to the impact on measures like working capital, return on total assets — virtually any measure that includes current assets in its denominator.

The fact that cash decreased while other current assets increased creates a false sense of improvement in these ratios, a situation that may partially mask more critical issues. Surely a company does not want to have too much tied up in cash, but to deplete this number as a result of poor operating results or bad strategic decisions is even less desirable.

When one considers the number of ratios available to management teams, it should not be difficult to select a handful of tools that put performance in the "supply chain vector" that has been the central theme of this book. Without going overboard, analysts must choose metrics that not only produce reliable figures but also help to reveal the underlying causes of perplexing numbers. Without question, management must include calculations such as return on investment, working capital, the operating cycle and the cash-to-cash cycle. However, much like the way in which the DuPont formula synthesizes net income with asset utilization, other ratios must be found that continue this process of cross-pollination.

Because of its all-encompassing treatment of net income, depreciation, changes in working capital and investing and financing activities in the same report, the CFS is a good place to look for ratios that continue this process of vectorization. Wall Street's obsession with short-term performance and the impact that earnings and changes in working capital have on free cash flow make the search for relevant ratios that much easier.

Of all the sources of financial information, cash flow from operating activities is the most relevant in measuring the *short-term* performance of net income versus investments in current assets. While the return on investment formula measures earnings compared with *total* asset value, the ratio of cash flow from operating activities to net income measures earnings against how well a company manages inventories, collects on debt and pays its bills. This ratio makes a powerful argument: net income is great, but if inventories are not managed, money cannot be collected and there is no cash to pay bills, the entire exercise will be for naught. Calculation of NikoTech's cash from operating activities to net income ratio sheds new and revealing light on an age-old dilemma. The formula reads:

Cash flow from operating activities/Net income

Intuitively speaking, a high quotient is desired for this ratio as it depicts a company whose earnings are backed up by cash. Reporting net income is one thing; getting the funds from customers is another story entirely. Results for NikoTech in Y2 were

($192 million)/$12.6 million = (15.23)

If there is any residual doubt as to the grave state of affairs at NikoTech, the cash flow from operating activities to net income ratio should erase it. True, the ratio is high, but the idea is to have a high ratio that is also *positive*. With a negative ratio of 15.23, this calculation reveals that for every dollar in net income that NikoTech generates, it can expect a negative cash flow of $15.23. Another variation on the same theme is that all the net income in the world is not going to do NikoTech a bit of good until it squares away its current assets.

In fact, even if the company tripled earnings, it would still have an operating activities ratio of ($5). Unless this trend is reversed, NikoTech will continue down the path of cash consumption to the point where it will run out of money and be unable to find a financial institution willing to bail it out.

CONCLUSION

As the discussion on supply chain execution and financial results comes to an end, it should be clear that there are in fact causal relationships between landed cost, lead times and inventory management and what appears on the income statement, balance sheet and, now, the CFS. Hopefully, the general discussion and case study have contributed in a small way to broadening the reader's outlook on business while helping to remove the barriers to success in today's global markets.

The emphasis throughout the study has been on the fundamentals of business discipline, the very same practices that catapulted General Motors to a dominant market position more than 80 years ago. None of the concepts in this analysis has been presented as revolutionary; quite the contrary. The goal has been to uncover the links that exist between execution and results, thereby allowing the analyst to achieve what the Japanese so aptly characterize as the ability "to understand the inner secrets and return to original simplicity."[1] There is nothing simple about executing a global business model, but adherence to basic principles while embracing new ideas and technologies will maximize the probability of success even in the most hostile of environments.

NOTE

1. Thomas Cleary, *Code of the Samurai: A Modern Translation of the Bushido Shoshinsu,* Tuttle Publishing, 1999, p. 32.

BIBLIOGRAPHY

Arnold, J.R. Tony, *Introduction to Materials Management,* Prentice Hall, 1998.

Bandler, James, *How to Use Financial Statements,* McGraw-Hill, 1994.

Christopher, Martin, *Logistics & Supply Chain Management: Strategies for Reducing Costs & Improving Service,* Pitman Publishing, 1992.

Friedlob, George T. and Franklin J. Plewa, *Financial & Business Statements,* Barron's Business Library, 2000.

Harrington, Diane R., *Corporate Financial Analysis in a Global Environment,* South-Western College Publishing, 1998.

Incoterms 2000, International Chamber of Commerce, Paris, 2000.

Kaplan, Robert S. and Robin Cooper, *Cost & Effect,* Harvard Business School Press, 1998.

Kaplan, Robert S. and David P. Norton, *The Balanced Scorecard: Translating Strategy into Action,* Harvard Business School Press, 1996.

Shim, Jae K. and Joel G. Siegel, *Financial Management,* Barron's Business Library, 2000.

Tyran, Michael, *The Vest Pocket Guide to Business Ratios,* Prentice Hall, 1992.

Wild, Tony, *Best Practices in Inventory Management,* John Wiley & Sons, 1997.

INDEX